THE RULE OF
LAWYERS

WALTER K. OLSON

THE RULE OF
LAWYERS

*How the New Litigation Elite
Threatens America's Rule of Law*

T·T

TRUMAN TALLEY BOOKS
ST. MARTIN'S PRESS
NEW YORK

www.stmartins.com

Library of Congress Cataloging-in-Publication Data

Olson, Walter K.
    The rule of lawyers : how the new litigation elite threatens America's rule of law / Walter K. Olson.—1st ed.
        p. cm.
    ISBN 0-312-28085-8
    1. Class actions. (Civil procedure)—United States.   2. Lawyers— United States.   3. Rule of law—United States.   4. Products liability— United States.   I. Title.

    KF8896 .O44   2003
    347.73'53—dc21

                                                           2002514114

First Edition: January 2003

10   9   8   7   6   5   4   3   2   1

To Steve Pippin

CONTENTS

THE RULE OF
LAWYERS

Better Living Through Litigation

A familiar genre in legal writing is the piece proposing that judges create some new right to sue. According to the authors of such pieces, the law has been overly static, inflexible, and preoccupied with precedent, and so has not kept up with the need to provide a remedy for the wrongs of the outside world. Some jurists still believe that it is the legislature's role, not the courts', to push the law into new areas, but the authors of such pieces will argue that only by acting on their own to create broad-ranging new rights to sue can courts ensure real "access to justice."

In the middle 1970s especially, legal writings putting forth this sort of argument were all but ubiquitous. You could no more open a law review without finding them than you could peruse a food magazine without finding recipes. In 1976, there appeared a remarkable essay[1] along these lines published as part of *Verdicts on Lawyers*, a volume edited by Ralph Nader and Mark Green, and still worth revisiting more than a quarter century after its appearance. What makes it remarkable is the way its authors—Beverly C. Moore Jr., a lawyer who worked for Nader for five years after graduating from Harvard Law School and later made a name in legal circles as editor and publisher of *Class Action Reports*, and Fred Harris, former Oklahoma senator and Democratic presidential candidate in 1972 and 1976—sketched out a far-reaching ideological rationale, even a sort of blueprint, for much of the mass litigation that was to follow.

In the article, titled "Class Actions: Let the People In," Moore and Harris argued that courts should act to make it much easier for lawyers to file class-action suits against American business. In and of itself this idea was nothing new, but in this article the authors had a list—a long list of the injuries, ailments, frustrations, and indignities of everyday life over which, in their opinion, the courts should permit class-action lawsuits. The list enumerated some twenty-four varieties of harm, paired in each case with the various businesses that could be sued over them. "Tooth decay . . . Sugar industry (food manufacturers)" was no. 15. "Air, water, noise, other environmental pollution . . . Business enterprises generally" was no. 23. The ill effects of smoking and of liquor consumption, of course, could be laid at the door of the tobacco industry and the producers of alcoholic beverages. Also on the list was lack of durability in consumer goods—that is to say, the tendency of home appliances and similar purchases to break down after the warranty has run out.

And that was just the start. Food manufacturers would face lawsuits over not just tooth decay but a wide range of other maladies, including heart disease, cancers linked to fat intake, and adult-onset diabetes. As befits an essay in a book coedited by Ralph Nader, automakers would come in for a particularly rough time of it. "If the automobile industry were saddled with an annual damage liability of perhaps $100 billion for accidents, air pollution, noise, congestion, and highway- and traffic-control costs, and were forced to raise its prices by that amount, it would have no choice but to redesign its vehicles to minimize these costs and their associated liabilities," the authors wrote. (Litigation opportunities were endless: Next time you get home late because of rush-hour traffic, why not send General Motors or Ford a bill for the value of your lost time? It would serve them right for the sin of having sold all those other drivers their cars.) Automobile prices would be likely to jump severalfold, at least, though Moore and Harris prudently refrained from offering any estimates. Real estate developers would split with automakers the costs of crime and disamenity associated with "urban congestion," while the makers of general consumer products would be saddled, like the automakers, with the cost of accidents of any sort associated with their products—so that bicycle manufacturers would pay the price every time anyone fell off a bicycle.

Wouldn't that leave business enterprises paying for countless injuries that weren't, by any stretch of the word, their fault? Yes, that's just what Moore and Harris had in mind, and they spelled out what they saw as the happy implications of such automatic liability. If drugmakers, for example, were made fully liable for adverse reactions, overdoses, and side effects, regardless of whose fault (if anyone's) they were, "it can be safely predicted that the industry would develop effective mechanisms to ensure that many or most such cases are in fact avoided. In response to similar potential damage liabilities, food corporations would reduce the fat, sugar, salt, and cholesterol content of their products." They would also be forced to find ways to add fiber to their products; Moore and Harris declared that colon trouble, appendicitis, and other ailments should be chargeable to food manufacturers who failed to put enough indigestible matter in their wares. This might lead to puzzling applications in practice, since fiber can be added to more or less any food product, from cotton candy to champagne. Still, even if the assignments of liability did not always track then-current ideas of blameworthiness, consumers would come to see the logic. "The greatest barrier to courtroom justice," the authors observed, "is the marketplace reality that most victims are not even aware that they have been injured."

By even a conservative reckoning, the items on the list would have led to the redistribution of well over $1 trillion a year back in 1976, at a time when the gross national product (GNP) of the United States stood at $1.8 trillion; the figure would be considerably higher in today's depreciated dollars. More than half the nation's GNP, in other words, would be routed through lawyers' offices. A lot of it would stay there: Moore and Harris enthusiastically endorsed the arrangements by which courts let class-action lawyers collect fees for their efforts, amounting to a share of the class's claimed recovery—sometimes as high as a third. "Of course," they conceded in a footnote, "it might be advisable to phase in these new liabilities over a reasonable period of time." Which is basically what we've been doing ever since.

The United States has long had a higher rate of litigation than other advanced democracies, and many of the reasons are not particularly mysterious. Unlike nearly all other countries' legal systems, ours does not observe the sort of "loser pays" or "costs follow the event" principle that, in other countries, gives litigants an incentive to fold their hands on weak positions and consider taking a reasonable settlement.[2] Our system, unlike most others, permits lawyers who file suits to accept a proportionate share of their clients' damages as a contingency fee. Other countries think that tying lawyers' own fortunes so closely to their courtroom success gives them too tempting an incentive to overplay their clients' hands. We have also historically awarded a higher (and less predictable) level of damages for a typical injury—a broken bone in an accident, say—than other countries, in part because we ask sympathetic juries to assign a price tag for injuries rather than leave such price-tag setting to judges, whose concern is more likely to be to maintain a uniform level of compensation from one case to the next. Unlike other countries, we also allow juries to levy punitive damages, which have a pick-a-number quality that depends greatly on jurors' subjective anger, sympathy, lawyers' eloquence, and random factors. Punitive damages are handed down in the absence of a range of due-process protections enjoyed by defendants in criminal cases and can be levied repeatedly by juries around the country against the same defendant for the same conduct.

All these local peculiarities—the occasionally enormous sums to be had by suing, the lack of a downside in the form of loser pays, and the entrepreneurial role that lawyers were encouraged to take—mean that even fifty years ago America was known as the land of the speculative or "long-shot" legal case, in which an injury could come to seem a lottery ticket collectible from the nearest deep-pocket defendant. And while other countries tend to assess some sort of penalty, in fees or otherwise, on the claimant who exaggerates the amount owed him in an otherwise rightful claim, we do no such thing, which means it practically counts as malpractice for an American lawyer not to ask for a sum far in excess of what the court is expected to grant.

Even so, until sometime around 1970, it had long been taken more or less as a given in the U.S. legal system, as in others, that litigation was something to be discouraged, a destructive and costly last resort, certainly not as the first line of response to ordinary social problems. It was recognized, after all, that litigation is acrimonious, delay-ridden, and enormously expensive. Lawsuits tend to paralyze the getting on with life; their outcomes have a high unavoidable random factor; they are favored by the bullies of the world for use as a tactical weapon; they feed a sense of ego and entitlement; they tend to corrupt even reasonably honest participants, tempting them to shade or hide evidence and stoking appetites for revenge and cost infliction. While no one imagined that lawsuits could somehow be done away with entirely, our legal tradition still joined with that of every great nation's in trying to discourage their use in doubtful cases and certainly discouraging lawyers from promoting them or puffing them up for their own profit. A whole set of ethical rules curbed lawyers from "stirring up" litigation by advertising, direct solicitation of clients, or other means. Once a case was in hand, lawyers were not supposed to avail themselves of any and all lawful means to win, but were to think of themselves as quasipublic "officers of the court." Procedural rules assigned some of the inevitable costs of litigation to those who initiated it and not to its targets alone. Selection of forums in which to file suit was limited by various geographical rules, which had the effect of impeding the chances for "forum shopping," the practice of selecting a venue at which defendants would find themselves at some form of disadvantage.

Starting in the early to mid–twentieth century and accelerating markedly around 1970, American law began to knock down many of these old barriers to litigation. Rules of procedure were drastically liberalized to make it easier to sue and harder to get a suit dismissed. "Notice pleading" invited lawyers to sue first and then begin rummaging around to see whether they had a case. Liberalization of pretrial discovery in the 1970s made it easier for lawyers to go on so-called fishing expeditions, hoping that the contents of their opponents' filing cabinets would contain something, anything, justifying their suit. "Long-arm" jurisdiction made it easier for litigants to shop around for a court and juries convenient to them or hostile to their opponent. And, symbolically, old ideas of legal ethics were fast being overturned. In 1977, by a five-to-four majority, the U.S. Supreme Court decided that lawyers have a constitutional right to advertise and chase business in other ways. The majority of justices agreed that this change would have the effect of encouraging more litigation, but they had come to view this as one of the advantages of the change.

There had begun, in fact, among the American legal establishment a love affair with the lawsuit. The more lawsuits that were permitted, the more justice courts could do, reasoned a generation of law professors and commentators. And who could be against providing more "access to justice"? Furthermore, the prospect of being more actively sued would make doctors, public officials, and businesspeople more careful and responsible in their work. Aside from this function of *deterrence*, lawsuits could achieve *compensation* for the needy, putting cash in the hands of persons victimized by accidents, job loss, or other of life's reversals. By the late 1970s, the mood and attitude in law schools had turned around, with litigation now widely seen as an engine of social progress. Lawyers who made suing a first resort could now be admired as productive and entrepreneurial. In 1975, one of the most widely quoted of the new legal ethicists could write of a "professional responsibility to chase ambulances."[3]

Meanwhile the substantive law of liability—determining who could be made to pay for what—was being rapidly liberalized, and in few areas more rapidly than in *product liability*, a body of law most of which courts invented from scratch after 1955 or so. Starting from the premise that manufacturers should be made to pay more often for accidents resulting from the use of their products, courts created new duties to warn, struck down freely consented to waivers of liability as invalid, did away with accident victims' own contributory negligence as a bar to suit, and narrowed or abolished defenses based on the concept of "assumption of risk"—the idea that people knowingly expose themselves to many hazards in life, from the scalding nature of hot coffee that might spill in your lap to the risk of being hit by a flying pebble from a lawn mower. They began to find "defectiveness," not just when a product was manufactured in a way that departed from its intended design (with loose bolt screws, say, or an adulterating ingredient), but also when a product's design itself was considered to fall short of what a court decided would be socially beneficial.[4]

By midcentury some thinkers in the law schools and elsewhere had come to see lawsuits as a kind of surrogate social insurance, identifying deep pockets from whom accident victims might obtain compensation. Justice Roger Traynor of the California Supreme Court, in an influential concurring opinion in a 1944 case called *Escola v. Coca-Coca Bottling Co.*,[5] led the way by proposing that courts should not have to find that manufacturers had behaved negligently to hold them liable for injuries resulting from defects in their products: "Even if there is no negligence . . . public policy demands that responsibility be fixed wherever it will most effectively reduce the hazards to life and health inherent in defective products that reach the market."

Among the other procedural innovations of the 1960s and 1970s were new rules making it much easier for lawyers to file class-action lawsuits,[6] another specialty of the American legal system. It had long been recognized that there were some circumstances in which it might be efficient and economical for many litigants to press the same sort of claim at once; these might include situations where claims were too small to be worth vindicating individually but added up to a substantial aggregate. Concerned about the possible abuses in letting claimants' rights be adjudicated without their presence or consent, however, the courts maintained numerous rules that carefully regulated the prosecution of class actions. For example, they often required that at an early stage class members be notified individually, if possible, of what was going on in their name, and the process of notifying class members was bound to be expensive, as was the process of mailing small checks to them at the end of a successful case. In federal courts, many class actions could go forward only if a judge certified on a preliminary basis that they were likely to have merit.

Now a new ideology, one with far fewer misgivings about the class-action format, was coming to the fore. What, it was asked, was so wrong with lawyer-driven litigation anyway? These lawyers obtained money for clients, after all. They enabled courts to right wrongs, and they deterred business misconduct in a really emphatic way. Maybe, the idea continued, we should envision the class-action lawyer as a sort of *private attorney general*, who advanced the public interest just as elected officials did.

Beverly C. Moore Jr. and Fred Harris were far from the first or only advocates eagerly talking up the merits of the class-action device and urging that its use be liberalized. As a variety of Ralph Nader acolytes, forward-minded law professors, and others pressed the issue, many of the old hurdles began falling. Notification of class members? Maybe it was enough to put an ad in the paper at the *end* of the case. Reaching them all with checks? Perhaps it should be up to them to have to apply for any refunds to which they might be entitled, or it might make sense to give out money to an organization representing their interests, such as a consumer group. The U.S. Supreme Court did away with the federal rule requiring early certification of likely merit. "Opt-in" models of the class action, in which class members had to make a conscious decision to join, gave way to more expansive "opt-out" models, under which class members could automatically be counted as litigants unless they specifically asked *not* to be. In larger classes, where only a small sum was at stake per member, it was typical for most class members to take no action one way or the other, which meant that the lucky lawyer designated to manage the action might acquire a huge book of nominal "clients" who were in no position to oversee the manner in which he handled their interests.

Even with the liberalization of rules, many important restrictions on class actions remained. Before courts would approve, or "certify," a claim to go forward as a class action, they were supposed to satisfy themselves as to its *typicality*: The claims had to be close enough to identical that once one class member's case was decided, it would be a virtual logical certainty that other members' cases would have to come out the same way. Cases also had to be *manageable* in size and scope: The archetypal fact pattern was the financial dispute over some standardized marketing, investment, or accounting practice from which consumers or investors had passively suffered small, identical losses, so that a formula could be devised that would allow for calculation of how large a settlement check or rebate should be made available to each member of the plaintiff class.

Among the most important restrictions on class actions was that they weren't used in handling personal-injury cases. To begin with, the damages in such cases are often substantial enough to interest lawyers in pursuing the case individually. Then, too, the effects of bodily injuries are not easily standardized from one person to the next. Unlike the cases of passive financial injury that are most often asserted as class actions, personal-injury cases are routinely countered with defenses, such as a plaintiff's contributory negligence or assumption of the risk, which may be asserted successfully against one plaintiff but fail against another, throwing into doubt the requisite "typicality." And to collectivize the handling of such cases would be to deprive individuals of control of a type of action often of peculiarly intimate significance to them or to their family members. A 1966 panel on class-action procedure made clear that even as it was being made easier to fit other types of litigation into a class-action format, courts were still expected to give personal-injury cases individual treatment.

The model of a personal-injury suit had always been a highly individualized dispute: After a localized and one-time incident, such as a highway crash, grocery store slip-and-fall, or medical operation gone wrong, a particular victim files a legal action against a particular defendant. But the economics of litigation were beginning to shift in a big way. At least since the 1970s, the fastest growing share of the docket has come to consist of *mass torts* in which lawyers bring thousands, even tens of thousands of claims from all parts of the country alleging injury from a product design or a business practice. Today such cases are usually pursued by means of "pattern" or "cookie-cutter" techniques, and are often disposed of through settlement in large batches. Sometimes the product or practice being sued over is standard among businesses in a field, and the mass tort then takes the form of *industrywide litigation*, in which all the companies in a field are taken to court. And while individual suits against doctors or drivers may suffice to build up the practice of the garden-variety millionaire trial lawyer, it is through mass production of claims that an ambitious attorney is more likely to vault into the more exalted ranks of the multimillionaires.

As mass torts began to proliferate in the 1970s, courts trying to cope with huge dockets of individually filed cases came under intense pressure to rethink the procedural logic that required them to handle personal injury suits individually. More judges decided that it was consistent with the spirit of the rules to assemble dozens, hundreds, or even thousands of individual suits over such substances as asbestos, diethylstilbestrol (DES), or the notorious Dalkon Shield contraceptive into "consolidated" actions. Sometimes this was done by consent of the parties, but on other occasions judges forced it through against the will of one or even both sides. Such consolidations also began to be seen in cases of localized disasters where victims had been injured in a uniform way, such as plane crashes and building fires.

Until tobacco came along, by far the biggest mass tort was asbestos litigation. For decades the fibrous mineral had been used almost ubiquitously in industry for its safety and insulating properties, until the 1960s when alarms were sounded about its potential for causing respiratory problems and cancer in workers who handled it. In 1965, coincidentally, new developments in product-liability law provided that companies could (retroactively) be sued for failing to warn about harmful characteristics of the products they sold, even when those characteristics were generic to the product and inherent in its nature. This little-heralded change in the law was to provide the impetus for the asbestos litigation, which still stands as the largest body of injury litigation in history, redistributing tens of billions of dollars from defendants to claimants, bankrupting a long list of prominent industrial companies, and nearly capsizing the venerable Lloyd's of London, whose underwriters had written insurance policies decades before and now found themselves facing tens of billions of dollars in liabilities for which they had not set aside correspondingly immense reserves. Most of the early asbestos cases were filed by workers who were seriously or even fatally ill, but the caseload soon shifted toward the worried-but-well, and continued to do so to the point that by the end of the century the great majority of cases, hundreds of thousands of them, were being filed by workers who were comparatively unimpaired but were presented by their lawyers as greatly fearful of contracting future illness. And the rules of asbestos litigation were formulated in such a way that defendants wound up paying very large sums of money collectively to these uninjured claimants.

The course of asbestos litigation traced an arc that would become familiar later on, from early courtroom defeats to an eventual opening of floodgates. Juries rejected most of the early claims, nor were they at first willing to assign liability to so-called peripheral defendants who had not been players in the asbestos industry as such but had merely incorporated some quantity of the mineral into their product. But eventually there would come a breakthrough victory or two that would tend to establish these defendants' guilt in many minds, and before long the companies would be settling thousands more cases. If defendants held out for trial, they risked a "bet the company" defeat. If they offered a settlement to avert that prospect, they ensured that lawyers would name them in more suits, and the defense of many suits could in itself be overwhelming as a sheer logistical matter. Significantly, trial lawyers began to discover or develop certain favorable jurisdictions whose judges, juries, or procedures were amenable to the cases they were bringing. Wide-open venue laws often provided that cases from other cities and states could then be imported to the favorable jurisdiction, so that before long thousands or tens of thousands of cases might be pending in one of their favored courts in some remote part of the country, though only a handful of the cases might have arisen locally.

Asbestos and the mass torts that came later also brought a new model of injury law practice to the fore. For lawyers pressing these cases, the economies-of-scale factor was overwhelming: It cost a substantial investment of time and resources to get up to speed on one such controversy, but once you'd done it, the marginal cost of adding more clients to your roster dropped steeply. Moreover, lawyers enjoyed much more leverage in settlement bargaining with defendants if they brought a big inventory of cases to the table since they could offer to settle a large batch at once (or threaten to proceed with all of them). The mass tort business emerged as a relatively concentrated one, with particular law firms emerging as powerful national players coming to control thousands of clients' cases, which they moved around like tokens on a game board. The occasional sensational jury award was important for its role as a settlement "hammer," but the real money, as always, lay in settling cases out of court. The cumulative sums could be quite impressive: Peter Angelos[7] of Baltimore, for example, pocketed an estimated $250–350 million in contingency fees settling asbestos cases referred to him by the steelworkers' union, while Walter Umphrey of Texas became one of the nation's wealthiest lawyers, in part because of a long friendship with the oil and chemical workers union.

Despite its extremely high overhead and the injustice of many of its outcomes, mass asbestos litigation went on for years without arousing much real outcry, in large part because it was widely agreed that the product being sued over had indeed caused an appalling degree of grave and genuine injury. But with the silicone breast-implant affair of the early 1990s, it became apparent that billions of dollars could also be extracted on a theory of product-related injury that was spurious from start to finish. Lawyers and their allies skillfully stimulated and kept going a baseless public panic to the effect that silicone breast implants were causing an epidemic of autoimmune disease in American women. In due time, studies by leading medical institutions proceeded to set the concerns to rest. By that point, however, lawyers had succeeded in recruiting hundreds of thousands of claimants, soon driving the leading producer of silicone compounds, Midland, Michigan–based Dow Corning, into bankruptcy, and even after the scientific basis of the claims was refuted, obtaining an overall settlement package valued at $7 billion, including a couple of billion in legal fees.

The implant affair drove home an important lesson: Publicity skillfully managed by trial lawyers and their allies, especially where juries and the public can be kept sufficiently confused about the state of the science, can fuel a mass tort despite weakness on the facts, the law, or both. And in many mass torts, the publicity campaign outside the courtroom was to prove at least as important in shaping the outcome as any ruling handed down by a judge. In crusades against Detroit carmakers over allegedly defective automotive designs, for example, the most valuable asset for lawyers on the attack was the willingness of producers at major TV newsmagazine shows—*60 Minutes, 20/20, Dateline NBC*, or their lesser counterparts—to recast the allegations in their suits in the form of breathtaking safety exposés of supposedly exploding or overturning vehicles. Misleading though such journalism could be—or even, as in a famous *Dateline NBC* case, out-and-out faked—it proved invaluable to trial lawyers in planting negative impressions among likely jurors and raising the cost to the defendant of resisting, as well as in recruiting more clients.

Most instances of mass tort and industrywide litigation thus proceed as parallel campaigns inside and outside the courtroom, with the outside part—directed by trial lawyers and their allies at the press and public opinion—often the more important. Each campaign against a product can build on those that have gone before, contributing new legal precedents, new public suspicion of target industries, new political allies, and, not least, new cash for the trial lawyers' war chest. Even campaigns that wind up failing, as many do, can serve a valuable test-marketing or research-and-development function for the lawyers, probing weaknesses in the opposition or shedding light on what audiences in the media and the jury box will accept. And as mass tort campaigns proceeded, trial lawyers learned to overcome old rivalries and to coordinate their activities with each other; to bring down larger prey, they began running in packs. It was because asbestos plaintiffs' lawyers had already been working with each other for years—accumulating priceless experience and courthouse/political connections along the way—that they could pull off the tobacco campaign as successfully as they did.

For years, but without success, individual trial lawyers had been trying to sue the tobacco industry over smokers' illnesses. Their key breakthrough came after trial lawyer Dickie Scruggs had the idea of teaming up with an ambitious government official—his old law school acquaintance, Mississippi attorney general Michael Moore—in an alliance to make the state itself, rather than any particular sick smoker, the complainant in the suit. Their premise was simple, if audacious: Tobacco sellers should compensate Mississippi for the sums the state had expended caring for sick smokers in publicly funded programs like Medicaid. The effect was baldly retroactive: It was to demand that tobacco companies pay for all the cigarettes they had sold in past years when no one dreamed they were under any legal obligation to set aside such funds. The affair would be handled on a contingency fee, giving Scruggs (and the many lawyers who followed his lead) a personal stake in the action. This was an almost unheard of way of handling the government's legal work.

To enlist support from other states, Moore and Scruggs

proceeded to fly around the country in Scruggs's private plane persuading other attorneys general to join the action by hiring Scruggs and other private lawyers on a contingency basis. Who got picked for these lucrative deals? In most big states, attorneys general selected the outside counsel with a minimum of competitive bidding, publicity, or other formalities. Again and again they picked lawyers who were among their own biggest campaign donors or were strongly tied in other ways to the state's political establishment. Billions upon billions of dollars in public assets were transferred to the effective ownership of private trial lawyers by means of deals that might have raised eyebrows had they been used to put out highway-resurfacing contracts in the Louisiana of Huey Long.

The theories of liability raised in the state tobacco suits were remarkably ambitious, and full of implications for other industries that might get sued in the future. For example, courts considering claims of liability had historically insisted on "individualized" proofs that particular defendants had harmed particular plaintiffs. Back in the 1970s, Moore and Harris had recognized this insistence as a serious obstacle to the pressing of suits on behalf of large groups of plaintiffs against multiple defendants. Their proposed solution? "Statistical projections" of harm done based on companies' past sales and market shares, along with a similarly statistical approach to the compensation of the victim class: "Damages . . . could be computed on an aggregate injury basis and could be awarded in a lump sum to the class as a whole." In the intervening years, courts had shown considerable reluctance to venture far down the path of "market-share" liability or statistically projected damages to amorphous classes. By interposing the state itself as a plaintiff, however, Moore and Scruggs were able to conveniently sidestep any chance for defendants to start wrangling about whether this or that individual case of illness had been caused by one particular company's products. And the idea of statistically matching industries to illnesses was indispensable in most of the rounds that were to follow, including the municipal gun litigation and proposed rounds over lead paint, fast food, liquor, and so forth.

By 1998, the plaintiff's coalition had the tobacco companies cornered: Not only had it recruited most attorneys general to join the action, but some of its suits had landed (in part thanks to shrewd judge shopping) in the courtrooms of judges whose rulings were consistently favorable to the plaintiffs. Both in Mississippi, where the judge had denied the tobacco company defendants the right to a jury trial, and in Florida, defendants faced potentially ruinous "appeals bond" requirements that could prohibit them from filing appeals unless they posted what might be billions of dollars in security to reflect the size of an initial verdict.

But the trial lawyers and their attorney general allies were taking no chances. In an act of remarkable audacity, and in defiance of centuries-old ideas about the rule of law, they pushed through the legislatures of Florida and Maryland new enactments that simply retroactively declared null and void the tobacco industry's historic defenses to liability against the state—rewriting the game's rules long after the relevant innings had been played. "We changed centuries of precedent[8] to assure a win in this case," said a Maryland lawmaker. With little outcry arising in the press against such legalized expropriation, the tobacco companies could see the handwriting on the wall well enough, and they came to the settlement table, agreeing in the end to pay the states an extraordinary $246 billion. The private lawyers for the states, for their part, were slated to receive billions.

The prize having been gulped down, the great tobacco agitation subsided even more abruptly than it had arisen. In a remarkably short period, the tobacco industry had emerged as what the *New York Times Magazine* called "the great common foe. . . . [9] The industry practically took the place of the Soviet Union." Tobacco selling, long seen as one of the more humdrum of the industries based on human vice and weakness, had now come to be compared with (according to *New York Times* reporter Philip Hilts) the activities of "guards and doctors in the Nazi death camps."[10] "History will record the modern-day tobacco industry alongside the worst of civilization's evil empires,"[11] said Texas attorney general Dan Morales. "It's the only issue I know of where there aren't two sides—two intelligent sides," another antismoking activist told the *New York Times*. "I have a comic book mentality—I grew up with comic books—and I see this as good versus evil."[12] Such views dominated the newspapers for a season or two, and then suddenly the story-a-day flow of bad press for the tobacco companies in the papers ceased almost as if a faucet had been turned off.

For other industries, however, it was just getting underway. Now that the idea of statistical liability no longer seemed so novel, sellers of cheeseburgers and ice cream could be seen as having inflicted heart attacks and colon cancer just as surely as R. J. Reynolds peddled emphysema and lung cancer. During the tobacco campaign, trial lawyers had been at particular pains to deny that there was any merit to the frequently offered comparison between to-bacco and fattening foods or alcoholic beverages. "I know of no instance where any of my colleagues across the coun-try believes a liability action lies against liquor,"[13] a past president of the New York State Trial Lawyers Association assured one reporter. But once tobacco was safely in hand, it became clear that the logic of "social cost" was not easily contained. "Certainly I think it's worth pursuing [liquor company liability] once these tobacco matters are settled," said George Hacker, director of the Alcohol Policies Proj-ect at the Center for Science in the Public Interest (CSPI). "There's no question that alcohol imposes enormous harms on society and on public expenditures." By the summer of 2000, *Time* reported that some lawyers were interested in adapting tobacco theories to liquor, and the Nader-founded Public Citizen was putting out literature bracketing liquor and gambling companies with tobacco and gun makers as supposed "killer industries."

By 2001, social reformers and public health visionaries were beginning to talk seriously about turning loose the nation's lawyers to wage tobacco-style warfare on the makers of fast foods and fattening snacks, and perhaps also on the man-ufacturers of violent videogames. Moore and Harris's orig-inal loopy vision of universal enterprise liability—in which Schick and Gillette would pay for your razor nicks, Toyota

for your bad driving skills, and Baskin-Robbins for the extra pounds you owed to its Jamoca Almond Fudge—was now the stuff of respectable discourse. Turn the management of the country over to class-action lawyers? In twenty-five years the idea had gone from something nutty to something that had begun to sound almost mainstream.

Every expansion of private lawyers' power to claim to represent the interests of large groups of clients—through class actions, aggregative methods, and fictions of government representation—was sold as a way to "let the people in" (to borrow the subtitle of Moore and Harris's essay) so that a suitably competent counterforce could be fielded against the defendant Goliaths of the legal world and the little guy at last be afforded access to justice. The much more unambiguous function of class-action suits was to further empower lawyers themselves, who could now demand a great deal more money, menace opponents with far more effective weaponry than before, and presume to speak on behalf of vast groups within the American population, secure in the knowledge that their supposed constituents would not be in a position to fire them.

The Joy of Tobacco Fees

It is generally acknowledged that American politics offers few power bases more attractive than that of a state attorney general. Running on a separate statewide ballot line of their own, most attorneys general cannot be fired by their state's governor, a contrast with the subservience of the U.S. attorney general to the president at the federal level. Since their work is considered to be akin to that of prosecutors, however, they operate with a fair degree of independence from legislators as well. Attorneys general are seldom defeated for reelection—few politically active people are eager to pick fights with their state's chief law-enforcement officer—and many go on to higher office, the National Association of Attorneys General (NAAG) often nicknamed the National Association of Aspiring Governors. "Among former attorneys general who have made their mark in Washington," notes Martha Derthick of the University of Virginia, "are John Ashcroft, Bruce Babbitt, Jeff Bingaman, Bill Clinton, John Danforth, Dennis DeConcini, Thomas Eagleton, Slade Gorton, Jacob Javits, Jim Jeffords, Joseph Lieberman, Walter Mondale, Elliot Richardson, Warren

Rudman, William Saxbe, David Souter, and Robert Stafford."[1] The most famous of these, Clinton, liked to tell people the best government job he'd ever held had been his elected post as attorney general of Arkansas.

While most of the really dark side of law enforcement—the murder cases and bombings and kidnappings—falls to the responsibility of other levels of government, attorneys general have an inbox of a more broadly discretionary nature. They can and do launch investigations and crusades on whatever issues captivate the press at any given moment, be it child neglect, utility rates, elderly persons' access to the Internet, you name it. This broad enforcement discretion seems to lead naturally to such episodes as 1999's "Santa settlement." In Kansas, for example—to pick a state more or less at random—news editors were sent a May 25, 1999, press release from the state capital of Topeka headlined: "Attorney General Reaches Settlement with Toy Companies." "AG Carla J. Stovall announced today that her Consumer Protection Division has reached settlements with Toys-R-Us, Mattel Inc. and Little Tikes Co. totaling $473,098 in cash and toys." The settlement, which resolved charges made under the antitrust laws that toy companies had withheld inventory from discount warehouse stores, "will provide thousands of less fortunate Kansas children with toys for the next three holiday seasons." Santa had come early.

Around the country that very same day, press releases were going out to newsrooms crediting other states' attorneys general with the same vaguely Lone Rangerish accomplishment of having successfully challenged several well-known national businesses. "Thousands of needy

Tennessee children" would benefit, said a press release from that state's attorney general. Attorneys general from Ohio, California, Oregon, and many other states used almost identical language. As a reader would learn if diligent enough to make it down to paragraph five of Stovall's release, the toy affair was, in fact, a joint action of forty-four states' attorneys general, coordinated through NAAG. In the national settlement, the defendants agreed to provide $12.8 million to the state governments (earmarked for children's programs, which seemed much fairer than if it had just been used to reduce Mom and Dad's taxes or something); $1.8 million to the various state offices of attorneys general to compensate them for their enforcement efforts; $335,000 for NAAG itself; and, best of all, the big toy giveaway, a face value of tens of millions of dollars' worth of toys from the companies' inventory to be distributed to poor kids at Christmas.

As an exercise in the transmutation of the raw material of legal muscle into the end product of favorable publicity for the wielder of the muscle, the "Santa settlement" was pretty much perfect. The merits of the suit were at best murky: The toy companies' sin had been to let warehouse discounters carry only "multipack" toy sets of the sort that might appeal to thrifty larger families, while declining to supply the stores with their full line of individual toys. No one knew which, if any, toy-buying families might have suffered because of this practice or whether a judge would, in the end, have found it illegal under antitrust laws. But no toy company executive in his right mind wanted to face the cost of being taken to court in such a suit, the resulting bad press, or the risk of going to trial against forty-four states.

For the attorneys general, the resulting settlement offered not only the chance for an initial flurry of favorable publicity—complete with generic press releases they could make look local for their state—but photo opportunities for many holiday seasons to come of their beaming presence amid needy kids being handed toys. At the same time, their office would get a welcome slug of cash to assist with its staffing and budgeting needs—deliciously, the defendants could actually be made to pay for the privilege of having been investigated and sued, which actually turned the offices of attorneys general into a sort of profit center within state government, meaning that they wouldn't be so much at the mercy of some cranky appropriations chairman in their state legislature. To be sure, toy companies might raise prices on buyers in general to cover the cost of such a giveaway, but that was hardly the fault of the attorneys general.

And so it went in the happy life of an attorney general: the large book of ongoing enforcement business that they could acquire just by signing up with the NAAG group actions; the stream of self-congratulatory press releases that would result; the occasional well-chosen intervention into a local controversy by threatening to sue, for example, the owners of a sports franchise or notable business that was making noises about moving out of state; the chance to function as a sort of freestanding law firm within state government's ever-needy bureaucracy. Best of all was the self-satisfaction about the way they were improving the moral tone of government. Other officials engaged in grubby wheeler-dealing with interest groups, but attorneys general were "watchdogs," whose role was to keep everyone else honest.

Even amid the iridescent moral luster of an NAAG convention—attorneys general, like peacocks, achieve their greatest splendor when massed—ambitious young Mike Moore of Mississippi, who led the crusade against tobacco companies, stood out for his star quality. In 1994, *People* magazine had picked him as one of its "25 most intriguing people of the year"; later he was to play himself in the 1999 Warner Bros. production, *The Insider.* To begin with, Mike Moore had mastered the Jimmy-Stewart-meets-Cotton-Mather blend of down-home ordinariness and fierce indignation that characterizes attorney general–speak. Moore compared tobacco companies to heroin dealers and said going after them was "just the right thing to do, pure and simple."[2] The papers often remarked on what they called his choirboy image; according to Michael Orey's admiring 1999 book, *Assuming the Risk: The Mavericks, the Lawyers, and the Whistle-Blowers Who Beat Big Tobacco,* Moore had originally enrolled in law school "to help people" and "to make a difference."[3]

Viewed in hindsight, the milestones of Moore's early career are not free from irony. As a young DA, he made his name in his hometown of Pascagoula by nailing the county's political boss in a public contracting scandal.[4] Although Moore was never able to prove classic hard-core corruption—suitcases full of money, or that sort of thing—he did show that vendors doing business with the county felt expected to perform favors for local officials. Since officials weren't keeping contractors at proper arms' length, it stood to reason that they weren't negotiating the contracts in the hard-nosed way that would secure full benefits from such contracts for the city and its taxpayers. A jury agreed, gave

Moore the convictions he was seeking, and his political career was off with a bang. Soon he was elected to the statewide position of attorney general, with more than a little help from his fellow Pascagoulan and law school acquaintance Dickie Scruggs, the successful injury lawyer. Scruggs had not only given generously to Moore's campaign but had flown him to campaign appearances around the state in his four-seater plane.

There was nothing especially uncommon, as it happened, about an attorney general like Moore having close relations with an ambitious plaintiff's lawyer like Scruggs. Attorneys general served, within state government, as leading voices on matters of law and litigation, making them important persons for a powerful lawyer to cultivate. Many attorneys general had practiced as plaintiff's lawyers themselves before taking office or gone to bat for those lawyers' interests in state legislatures; California's Bill Lockyer, for example, fit both descriptions before winning his state's attorney generalship, having been the longtime head of the state senate's judiciary panel and himself a practicing attorney. Beyond that, it often happened that both AGs and private trial lawyers sued the same defendants over the same alleged sins, which might give them occasion to piggyback on each others' efforts by sharing information, coordinating publicity efforts, or even jointly negotiating an eventual settlement of public and private claims at once. In the toy antitrust affair, for instance, the attorneys general pursued the "Santa settlement" in coordination with private class-action lawyers suing the same toy companies, who got $3.25 million in fees for their participation.

There was in particular one little project that Scruggs

had in mind for Moore to pursue when he took office. Building owners around the country had lately been spending substantial amounts of money to remove old insulation and other asbestos-laden products from existing buildings, and lawyers had been helping them file suit against makers of the original asbestos-containing materials, asking the courts to order them to help reimburse the removal costs. The state of Mississippi was spending money to remove asbestos from old buildings and might recover substantial sums if it filed a suit like this. And such litigation would be so big and complicated that it really should be entrusted to an expert rather than to the lawyers in Moore's own office, shouldn't it? What was needed was a law firm with acknowledged expertise in asbestos litigation, one like, well, his own (Dickie Scruggs's) firm.

For many legal ethicists, alarm bells would have begun to go off at this point. The American Bar Association (ABA) had joined with many other professional groups in deploring the practice known as "pay-to-play," in which elected officials farm out public legal work to law firms that have donated to their campaigns. In fact, pay-to-play was not so different from the I'll-scratch-your-back-you-scratch-mine public contracting abuses Moore had made his crusading reputation helping to root out back in Pascagoula. And there was a further, vital angle to Scruggs's asbestos proposal. Pay-to-play abuses usually came up in the hiring of lawyers who worked on such matters as bond issues, and who charged hourly fees for their work. But Scruggs wanted to handle the rip-out claims on contingency—the state would pay nothing unless he won, and in return he would take a share of its eventual recovery. Most countries flatly ban lawyers from accepting share-of-recovery contingency fees even from private clients; they believe lawyers will be over-tempted to play hardball to win their cases if doing so will make them personally rich, nor do they want to let clients develop a sense of having nothing directly at risk if they press a questionable case. The United States had long justified its departure from other countries' practices on this issue on the grounds that otherwise some poorer clients might be unable to obtain a lawyer at all. But no one was seriously claiming that no lawyer could be found to handle the asbestos case for the state of Mississippi on an hourly fee basis.

Until quite recently the notion of letting lawyers represent government on a contingency-fee basis would have been seen as pernicious, absurd, or both. But as Scruggs was no doubt aware, times were changing fast. Many of America's legal authorities had begun to regard contingency fees—and the encouragement they gave to speculative litigation—not as a lesser evil that should be limited to the cases where it was necessary, but as something wholesome and beneficial in itself. The first experiments had already been noted by the end of the 1980s, with the state of Massachusetts hiring private lawyers on contingency for asbestos rip-out cases.[5] If contingency fees for public lawyering could pass the smell test in the state that was home to Harvard Law School, why shouldn't they do so in Mississippi, too?

So it came to pass that one of the very first things the newly elected Moore did on taking office was to venture into a little public contracting of his own, hiring Scruggs to pursue the asbestos rip-out suits. The arrangement worked out to both sides' satisfaction—Scruggs took home a tidy $2.4 million share of the state's winnings—and proved to be just a demonstration project of sorts for an idea that Moore and Scruggs had been contemplating for a while, which would be almost unthinkably bigger and more audacious. It was aimed at the tobacco industry, and would demand that tobacco companies reimburse the state of Mississippi for money the state had spent treating the smoking-related illnesses of Medicaid patients. Moore described his brainchild as the "most important public health litigation ever in history": "It has the potential to save more lives than anything that's ever been done."[6]

It had been known for centuries that the use of tobacco formed a habit difficult to break and hazardous to health, in fact often lethal to its users. In the 1950s and 1960s, a series of medical findings began to quantify these risks and confirm that they were, if anything, more serious than they had been assumed to be. Agitation by the U.S. Surgeon General's Office helped focus press and public attention on these findings and raised the question whether the government itself should do more to get people to quit smoking.

Any such effort would represent a decided turnabout in government policy, which had long made its peace with tobacco given the product's extreme usefulness as a source of tax revenue.[7] Many advanced countries reserved cigarette manufacturing to the government itself as a state monopoly and revenue source, and in virtually all the rest of the world it was heavily taxed and its distribution closely supervised by public authorities. In the United States it was common for government at all levels to collectively pocket several times more revenue from cigarette sales than the tobacco companies themselves kept in bottom-line profits. In a sense, the state had installed itself as a senior partner in a tobacco-selling enterprise of which Brown & Williamson, R. J. Reynolds, and the rest were merely the publicly visible face. Like the governments of other countries, the federal government had also gone to considerable lengths to promote smoking within its military, the nicotine habit being useful in holding at bay the fear and monotony to which soldiers are subject. In World War I, General Pershing famously said that tobacco was as critical an item of materiel to be rushed to the front as food and ammunition, and never did per-capita cigarette production in America rise as fast as it did during World War II.

Why not just raise cigarette taxes, which would promise to discourage the smoking habit while (at least temporarily) bringing the government more revenue than ever? The conventional explanation was that tobacco companies were too powerful a lobby to let that happen, but this was almost surely too simple an explanation. To begin with, as legislators knew well, few taxes are more "regressive" than the tax on tobacco, the burdens of which fall disproportionately on the poorest consumers. Large tax hikes on a state-by-state basis would also tend to worsen the already thriving market in cigarette smuggling. The alternative best suited to curbing smuggling would be a uniform nationwide tax hike, but legislators from poorer and more rural states stoutly resisted such a hike, and no wonder: The sort of ten-or-twenty-dollar-a-carton price hike that big-city smokers might brush off as an annoyance could force a real reduction in the standard of living of residents of a state like Mississippi, where per-capita personal income stood at just $19,000.

Economists had long been fascinated by the question of where the right level would be to set the cigarette tax assuming that the object was to make smoking pay for itself, that is to say, to ensure that neither smokers nor nonsmokers were in some sense subsidizing the other. Depending on what assumptions you wanted to plug into the model, you could make the exercise come out in any of a wide variety of places; but studies premised on middle-of-the-road assumptions had repeatedly found that existing tobacco taxes were already more than enough to cover the external costs imposed by the smoking habit, defined as the costs imposed on persons outside the smoker's own household.[8] A 1989 RAND corporation study estimated the external costs of smoking at about fifteen cents per pack, compared with an average tax per pack of thirty-eight cents; five years later a Congressional Research Service report came up with a higher estimate of external per-pack costs at thirty-three cents, but by that time the average per-pack tax burden had risen to fifty-seven cents.

Those figures might well amaze the casual observer of the tobacco litigation controversy, since it was taken as an article of faith in innumerable press accounts that smokers incur vast health-care expenses that nonsmokers wind up paying for. But experts have long disputed that notion. The more accurate statement is that smokers pose a burden to the health-care system *earlier* in their lives. Every non-smoker also winds up dying of something in the end, and nonsmokers' health expenses during their final year or two of life tend to be high, just as do those of smokers. A 1997 study published in *The New England Journal of Medicine*, for example, did not find that smokers had higher lifetime health-care costs. Nonsmokers also spend more time in nursing homes, a significant source of expense. And when it comes to Social Security and pension annuities, it is generally nonsmokers, with their longer lifespans, who wind up getting subsidized by smokers.

Scruggs, Moore, and their allies enjoyed much success in the press portraying their suit as the first real effort to make the tobacco trade pay for the costs it imposed on outsiders. Yet their demands in fact reflected no coherent theory of subsidy correction, but were merely designed to extract as much cash from their opponents as possible.[9] They proffered numbers for the "excess" Medicaid expenditures due to smoking, for example, which seemed to imply that the state would not have to spend money treating the patients had they gone on to die of anything else. They argued that none of the vast tax revenue the state had taken in from tobacco over the years should be regarded as an offset.

And, of course, there was the whole business of applying the new rules retroactively. Neither Mississippi nor any other state had passed a law putting tobacco companies on notice that they would be obliged to serve as a backup health insurer. Even if the state did pass such a law, it would logically attach such an obligation to sales of cigarettes after the effective date of the law, not to cigarettes sold in years and even decades before. Moreover, this was not the first time the question had arisen of whether the government had the right to recoup money it had laid out on account of some business's negligent conduct, and the precedents stood squarely in what, for Moore and Scruggs, was the wrong direction. For example, federal courts had specifically rejected attempts by city governments to recoup emergency response costs from a railroad and an airline following crashes,[10] and the U.S. Supreme Court, in a 1947 case, had followed similar logic in rejecting a claim by the U.S. government itself over having had to cover some of the costs of an accident it said was caused by a private company. It was true that insurance law had developed a concept known as "subrogation," under which a private insurer (but not a government social-insurance fund) who pays a claim for an injury can sometimes sue and recoup money from the one who caused the mishap. But in such a case the insurer obtains that right by contract from its insured. Moreover, it was a basic principle of subrogation that the insurer must "step into the shoes of" its insured, so that if the defendant it sues could have asserted any defense against the original victim (such as comparative negligence or assumption of risk), it must also be allowed to assert that defense against the insurer seeking reimbursement.

And as a long string of courtroom victories by tobacco companies had made clear, the industry's defenses carried a lot of weight both with juries and as a matter of law. The Restatement (Second) of Torts,[11] put out in 1966 and still cited by courts around the country as a definitive statement of the law, names tobacco, along with whiskey and artery-clogging butter, as products that may harm the user but do not on that account expose the maker to liability, since their injuriousness is a matter of public knowledge: "Good tobacco is not unreasonably dangerous merely because the effects of smoking may be harmful." Courts had frequently thrown out lawsuits against tobacco companies citing the restatement language or another nearby passage that had ruled out manufacturer liability for product defectiveness "unless a product is dangerous to an extent beyond which would be contemplated by the ordinary consumer with knowledge in the community." Moreover, juries had historically placed considerable weight on the principle of assumption of risk: smokers had had plenty of chances to learn about the health dangers of the habit in the thirty or forty years since they had begun to be widely publicized.[12] In fact, so well had the word about smoking's dangerousness gotten out that Harvard economist W. Kip Viscusi has found that both smokers and nonsmokers actually overrate the number of years the habit subtracts from the average smoker's life (most estimates range between four to seven years) and also overrate the likelihood that smoking-related ailments, as opposed to other diseases, will carry off a typical smoker.

Although there was no getting around the fact that the dangers of smoking had been blared from the rooftops for thirty years or more, antitobacco forces played heavily on the theme that the industry's slick and expensive ad campaigns worked to overcome new smokers' better judgment, perhaps even planting in novices a desire to smoke that would otherwise never have occurred to them. Yet experience around the globe cast doubt on the idea that the intensity of marketing efforts by tobacco companies could account for people's decisions to pursue the habit. Countries where the capitalist profit motive had long been excluded from the tobacco trade, such as Russia and China, had some of the world's highest male smoking rates, while other countries with very high smoking rates, such as Japan and South Korea, had long maintained government tobacco monopolies (ended by Japan as recently as 1985). Nor is the presence of tobacco advertising a good predictor of whether or not a nation will smoke heavily.[13] Norway, for example, banned print cigarette ads entirely by 1975, yet continues to have a smoking rate markedly higher than that of the United States. "There is no consistent relationship" between the two, observes Jacob Sullum, author of *For Your Own Good*, a history of the antitobacco crusade. "Sometimes smoking drops after advertising is banned; sometimes it doesn't."

While antitobacco activists were indignant that it continued to be lawful to promote cigarette smoking in this country, there was only a limited amount they had been able to do about it without running into the First Amendment. The U.S. Supreme Court, in a series of modern rulings, had bestowed a certain degree of constitutional free-speech protection on the advertising of lawful products and services ("commercial speech"), although no one was quite sure how far the Court would take this principle, it might well strike down a broad ban on all truthful cigarette advertising as unconstitutional. (Broadcast media was a different case: There is a legal fiction that the government owns the airwaves, but hardly anyone thinks the government in any sense owns the nation's printing presses.) But litigation campaigns opened an alternative method of assault on tobacco company advertising: They could be sued for damages on the grounds that the advertising had caused people to smoke.

Recognizing that the recoupment theory would look a lot less lame if many states besides Mississippi could be persuaded to join in, Scruggs and Moore set off on a campaign to convince other attorneys general to join the action. Toward this end, they began flying around the country in Scruggs's plane (by this point upgraded to a Learjet) to pitch their case. When a new attorney general agreed to bring his state into the action, he of course had the choice of relying on his own existing legal staff (and those in a few states, including California and Colorado, did just that). But most attorneys general hired outside private lawyers, signing up for contingency contracts with them. And the preexisting relationship between attorneys general and powerful trial lawyers—who were often among their most important campaign donors—was a pay-to-play scandal waiting to happen.

Most of the states hired both one or more "national" counsel who could participate in the overall effort and "local counsel" from their own backyard. The national counsel collectively constituted much of the brain trust of the operation and consisted of prominent firms each of which typically came to represent a whole string of states; among them the successful Charleston, South Carolina–based asbestos firm Ness Motley, the San Francisco class-action powerhouse Lieff Cabraser, and Steve Berman's Hagens and Berman out of Seattle. Scruggs, Millette was one of the most successful firms at signing up states, and Moore specifically recommended Scruggs[14] for this purpose in communication with fellow attorneys general. Many of the national firms either were already or soon became contributors to the attorneys general campaigns.

It was in the hiring of local counsel, however, that the attorneys general could really cut loose. In state after state they selected local law firms that had donated generously to their campaigns or with whom they had long-standing political connections of other sorts; in more than one case they picked firms with whom they had themselves practiced law before ascending to the attorney generalship. Thus in Illinois, AG Jim Ryan picked as in-state counsel the firm of Freeborn & Peters, with which he had what the *Chicago Sun-Times* called "close ties."[15] Iowa's Tom Miller picked a "former senior assistant and confidante," as sympathetic arbitrators later put it, "who Miller testified was a person he could trust to stay the course in this most difficult litigation."[16] Pennsylvania attorney general Mike Fisher selected two prominent law firms, both of which numbered among his major campaign contributors, saying "there was a familiarity factor"[17] and "that was how the decision was made." Florida governor Lawton Chiles got deeply involved in the process: "Tobacco trial lawyers say they had to hire [Gov. Lawton] Chiles' friends" was the resulting headline in the *St. Petersburg Times*.[18] Among firms hired to represent New York was Manhattan's Schneider, Kleinick, Weitz, Damashek & Shoot, perhaps best known for its later association with litigator Johnnie Cochran; it rented office space to New York assembly speaker Sheldon Silver for his private law practice. In Missouri, the five law firms picked had made campaign contributions of $561,000 to state politicians, including $139,000 to AG Jay Nixon and $113,000 to the late governor Mel Carnahan; also cut in on the deal were a prominent Republican former judge and a Democratic former mayor of St. Louis.[19]

Carla Stovall of Kansas—who helped Attorney General Moore of Mississippi and his allies clear a key psychological hurdle by becoming the first Republican attorney general to join the action—hired as local counsel her own former law firm, Topeka's Entz & Chanay, claiming she couldn't find another firm to take the work on the terms offered.[20] When Stovall ran for reelection, Sheila Cherry reports in *Insight* magazine, the Entz firm "provided her with an office and campaign contributions."[21] In Connecticut, the three in-state firms AG Richard Blumenthal picked to do the work included his own former firm, Silver Golub & Teitell. Of the other two firms, one was Carmody & Torrance of Waterbury, whose managing partner was the personal counselor to Republican governor John Rowland; while the other was Stamford's Emmett & Glander, whose name partner, Kathryn Emmett, is married to partner David Golub of Silver Golub & Teitell. "I know how it [looks]," conceded Golub. As for other law firms that might have wanted to be considered for the work, Robert Reardon of New London, a former president of the Connecticut Trial Lawyers Association, said he couldn't even get in the door for a meeting. Later, Attorney General Blumenthal affected a studious inattention to the whole issue of who had profited by his contracting decisions and to what extent. As the *Connecticut Law Tribune* noted, Blumenthal "was extraordinarily active in the litigation and settlement—more so than any other attorney general"—but blandly replied, "I have no idea," when asked how high a fee his own former law firm and its cohorts might be in line to collect.[22]

In New Jersey, the ultimately successful six-lawyer consortium was hatched in a "brainstorm sitting around the convention center having a couple of drinks";[23] it included five former presidents of the Association of Trial Lawyers, of America–NJ (ATLA-NJ), though most of its members were very light on experience in tobacco or any other kind of mass tort litigation. The team's original proposal for representation was billed as a "public interest" proposal made through a nonprofit foundation, "but the foundation's role was later quietly eliminated, if it ever existed," the *New Jersey Law Journal* reported. Meanwhile, nearly $100,000 in campaign contributions was flowing in a six-month period from ATLA-NJ's Political Action Committee (PAC) to Republican lawmakers, including $4,350 in checks written the day after the lawyers got the contract.

Were states negotiating the toughest possible deals with their outside lawyers, confining their fees to the minimum practicable? One reason to doubt that they did is that the terms of the various representation deals varied widely. The contingency percentages kept by the lawyers, for example, ranged from 25 percent down to a mere 3 percent. It is common in contingency-fee contracts for percentages to apply on a sliding scale, so that if the case settles before trial or appeal, the lawyer takes a lower percentage in recognition of having done much less work; some of the contracts incorporated this feature, some did not.

Even if lawyers are being paid on contingency, it is much easier to monitor and audit their work if they keep time sheets or logs indicating how much time they spent on various matters. But in state after state, attorneys general adopted an extremely relaxed approach about requiring any such documentation. The lack of a resulting paper trail greatly complicated later efforts to gauge how hard the lawyers had worked, making it more likely that the lawyers' own (baldly self-serving) retrospective guesses on that matter would have to be accepted. The lawyers representing Louisiana, for example, eventually saw fit to claim that they had put in an impressive 85,000 hours working for the state, but now that you mention it, by golly, it was true that they hadn't kept time sheets. The state's attorney general, Richard Ieyoub, hadn't bothered to ask for backup of that sort: "I had a good sense of how hard they were working." According to the New Orleans *Times-Picayune*, Ieyoub had "close political connections" with the firm of Badon & Ranier, which hailed from his hometown of Lake Charles.[24] Texas at first required that its outside law firms check in with a running tally of the expenses they were incurring, but AG Dan Morales dropped that requirement after the first year. Morales had bypassed the competitive-bid procurement process and installed a consortium of five bigtime trial lawyers, each a major Democratic donor, four of the five also major contributors to his own campaign.

As the number of states joining the action climbed toward fifty, it became clear that on a practical level the companies would have no choice but to settle. Following piecemeal settlements with four states, negotiators accordingly announced to the public in November 1998 that both sides had agreed to a so-called Master Settlement Agreement (MSA), which would end the litigation in exchange for the tobacco companies' agreement to a long series of concessions. The centerpiece of the agreement was the largest lawsuit-driven redistribution of wealth in history: an estimated $246 billion to be paid by tobacco companies to the states over a period of decades.

This was by any measure a remarkable sum, and from the way people in the offices of attorneys general talked about it, you might almost have thought it had fallen from the sky as a free windfall. "It could mean hundreds of millions of dollars to the people of Mississippi," Asst. AG Trey Bobinger of that state exulted.[25] That would be "tremendous." It would mean "better schools, better roads, better hospitals, better health care." Some naysayers murmured that smokers were going to wind up shouldering the cost of the deal, but attorneys general were emphatic in denying that any sort of tax on cigarettes was going to be involved. The settlement "does not tax anything or anybody," declared Ohio attorney general Betty Montgomery.[26] And yet shortly after the settlement was announced, cigarette prices jumped by forty-five cents a pack, and further substantial increases followed. If there hadn't been a new tax, what exactly had happened?

It's no wonder the attorneys general would insist that the new money flows from tobacco companies' transfers to state coffers should be regarded as a damage settlement for past misconduct, rather than as a new tax. The job descriptions of attorneys general aren't supposed to include the levying of new taxes on their own citizens, a function that in our constitutional scheme is assigned to legislatures. Nor are new tax levies supposed to be accompanied by percentage rake-offs for private parties who had helped arrange them.

So which was it, a damages settlement or a new tax? One

obvious difference between the two is that a damage settlement will normally be proportionate to the defendants' past
misconduct, whereas a tax is normally imposed on their current activity. The settlement's payment formula, however,
makes tobacco companies pay up proportionally to their
new, not their old, sales. A company that had a low market
share before 1998 but had sold more cigarettes recently
would pay more steeply than one for whom the reverse was
true. "There'll be adjustments each year based on inflation,"
said an Idaho official.[27] "If cigarette volume goes down, our
payments will go down. If volume goes up, our payments
will go up even more." These provisions are very unlike
those you would expect from a damage settlement, but exactly what you would expect of a tax.

A damage settlement, furthermore, could hardly be made
to apply to a company that was not in business at the time
of the purported misconduct. A start-up tobacco company,
or a foreign maker tackling the U.S. market for the first
time, would certainly not owe money based on old-line
American companies' actions in 1965 or 1980. Yet under
the settlement, new companies that wanted to begin selling
cigarettes are obliged to set aside substantial payments into
a state-run fund, supposedly as an escrow against future
liability payouts—though older companies, equally exposed
to such risk of future payouts, need make no such contributions. The point of these elaborate provisions has been
admitted by many of the participants: It is to make sure
new entrants, accused of no past wrongdoing and thus free
from the cost of supporting the settlement, cannot undercut
the older companies and thus undermine their ability to
keep forking over money to the states.

Economists have a word for what's going on here: *cartelization*. The incumbent companies (whose stock prices did well after the settlement) get protected from the rigors of competition, while the states safeguard their immense revenue stream against the menace posed by heretofore guiltless newcomers. Had tobacco executives plotted privately among themselves to raise prices, freeze market shares, confine small competitors to minor allocations on the fringe of the market, and penalize defectors and new entrants, they could have been packed off to prison as antitrust violators. This way it was all allegedly legal—in fact, signed-off-on, blessed, and stamped by the very same attorneys general who have long posed as our country's most incorruptible enforcers of antitrust law.

Among all the things the settlement accomplished, one notable thing it did *not* accomplish was to revolutionize the marketing practices of tobacco companies. Despite the huge fuss that had been made about youth marketing, the settlement imposed only some relatively minor marketing restrictions, which an unsympathetic eye might dismiss as window dressing. They included a ban on tobacco promotional use of animated characters, logo-bearing clothing and other merchandise, as well as billboard and transit advertising. Minnesota attorney general Skip Humphrey, a major force in the suit, called the new restrictions "minor."[28]

There remained the question of how the lawyers were going to get paid. Vague references had been made to arbitration panels and little was said at first about this question. Then on December 11, 1998, it was announced that private lawyers representing three states were going to be given by far the largest haul of legal fees in the history of the planet: $3.3 billion for the lawyers representing Texas (who had devoted less than two years to the matter), $1.4 billion for those representing Mississippi, and $3.4 billion for those representing Florida, totaling more than $8 billion in all. These were only three of fifty states, which meant many more billions in tobacco-fee awards were sure to follow. The announcement was met with gasps. The *Washington Post* reported that legal experts "were flabbergasted by the size of the fees. . . . [29] Washington trial lawyer John Coale, who also has sued the industry, said that while all the lawyers 'did a great job . . . these figures are beyond human comprehension and the work does not justify them.'" Of course the beneficiaries took a different view: "It sounds fair to me," said Florida lawyer Robert Kerrigan, whose little sliver's worth of his state's action was slated to bring him $200 million.[30]

It turned out that the MSA, in its generous way, allowed lawyers to select whatever method of payment they preferred: They could (as the Texas-Florida-Mississippi group had done) accept direct payments from the tobacco company defendants by way of closed arbitrations, or, alternatively, they could still try to collect on their contingency-fee contracts from the states if that course appeared more lucrative. It would be up to them. Most chose arbitration, especially after it became clear that the initial mega-awards were not going to be flukes. Lawyers for Louisiana asked for $1.3 billion from the arbitration panel and got $575 million, with the law firm linked to Attorney General Ieyoub slated to get $115 million of that total. Massachusetts lawyers asked for $2 billion and got $775 million. In New York, $625 million went to six firms that represented the state, with locally influential Schneider, Kleinick bagging $98 million of that. Lawyers for Oklahoma got $250 million; lawyers for Ohio got $265 million.

The biggest winners were the national firms that had strung together portfolios of many states as clients. Thus, of New York's $625 million fee award, $343.8 million was designated for three of the national firms, Ness Motley, Scruggs's, and Berman's. With many different states on the string, the fee entitlements of some national firms would plausibly mount into the billions of dollars. Ten law firms, including class-action powerhouses Milberg Weiss and Lieff Cabraser, were to share $637.5 million *not* for representing California—they hadn't done that—but rather for representing cities and counties within California who successfully agitated for half the state's $25 billion winnings to be turned over to them.

It was true that the tobacco industry had won one important concession in the negotiations: Its fee-paying obligation would be stretched out, with no more than $500 million having to be paid in any one year. On the other hand, since lawyers' claims were quickly mounting past the $10 billion mark, it was not unlikely that the payments would stretch on for decades, with revenues from cigarette sales henceforth furnishing a near-permanent annuity to the plaintiffs' lawyers of America.

By this point the interest of many in the press had been piqued. Yet, astoundingly, many of the lawyers proceeded to take the position that the details of their fees were none of the press's or public's affair, even though the fees had supposedly been earned by representing the public on official business. The *Fort Worth Star-Telegram*, *Baltimore Sun*, and *Milwaukee Journal Sentinel* all had to resort to legal action under open-records laws before they could get copies of the billing records for the suits in their states. The Wisconsin law firms, trying to keep the records secret, poignantly cited "ethical issues." Many lawyers asserted that since their fees were officially being paid directly by tobacco companies rather than deducted from states' settlements, no one had the right to object. "The attorneys' fees issue is really a non-issue," as Scruggs put it later.[31]

When the Milwaukee paper's open-records-law battle revealed the billing records for the state's lawyers, it became even more apparent why the lawyers had fought so hard to keep them private. The three private law firms representing the state had demanded $847 million plus expenses, based on a promised 20 percent of the $4 billion the state was slated to receive over twenty-five years. Although the Wisconsin lawyers had done very little of the heavy lifting in the national suit, they claimed to have spent a staggering 26,284 hours on the case. Even taking that claim at face value, their initial fee demand had worked out to an average rate exceeding $32,000 an hour—which was more, as the Ashland *Daily Press* in northern Wisconsin pointed out, than the typical family in that part of the state earned in well over a year. All three of the firms had political associations, two Republican and one Democratic, a partner in one of them being GOP governor Tommy Thompson's personal attorney (Democratic attorney general James Doyle had pushed the suit, with Governor Thompson coming on board after some initial reluctance). The governor had chosen to follow what his spokesman described as a less formal process of selection; and, in fact, an inquiry under the open-records law revealed that the state had spurned a law firm that had been interested in taking on the work for a lower fee.

Of the claimed hours, how many were reasonable and necessary? They included time spent purportedly by lawyers on matters more often handled by office administrators, such as setting up bank accounts and securing office space, furniture, and parking. By the lawyers' own accounting, their bill also included ample amounts of time spent on fee negotiations themselves, on working the press and scoping out the governor and other political players, and in preparing a constitutional challenge to proposed legislation in the state capital that would have curbed their fees (yes, they were getting paid for that, too). And expenses? Those turned out to include $7,800 for a chartered plane to fly attorney Robert Habush, former president of the Association of Trial Lawyers of America (ATLA), round-trip from Florida to Washington (coach fare: $906) and a stack of limo bills typified by an $851 entry to whisk Habush from Milwaukee to Madison and back on May 5, 1997.

As public outcry mounted, the Wisconsin lawyers agreed to accept a mere $75 million instead of the originally demanded $847 million—a remarkable 90-percent-plus stand-down, rather as if a used-car dealer had initially tagged a vehicle at $8,470 and then preemptively offered to slice its asking price to $750. Even at the lower figure, they were still set to make $2,853 an hour based on their own report of hours worked. Meanwhile, the state had asked $209 an hour as compensation for its own lawyers, the ones who worked full time for the government.[32] In Texas, an official estimated that the fee award in his state exceeded $105,000 an hour.[33]

The Wisconsin lawyers were not alone in demanding a fortune in fees even though their state had basically just hitched a ride in the national tobacco litigation parade. Of the fifty states' cases, only two had reached trial (both settled before a verdict), which meant that in the other forty-eight states the lawyers generally did not face the biggest source of costs in an ordinary lawsuit. On the matter of legal research and pretrial paperwork, Minnesota and a few other lead states had put intense efforts into developing the case. By contrast, Illinois was a classic tag-along state: It hadn't taken any depositions and had done "relatively little" to advance its claims toward trial. That didn't stop arbitrators from awarding Illinois' lawyers $121 million. Lawyers for New Jersey got $350 million, though the *New Jersey Law Journal* found that they hadn't been involved in national settlement talks and had relied on a national law firm representing the state for "most of the substantive legal work, including court arguments" on their behalf.[34] In Missouri, another tag-along state, lawyers demanded $480 million, then said they would settle for $100 million. Attorneys for Michigan were given $450 million, although arbitrators conceded: "Private Counsel's work in the Michigan state-specific litigation was modest" and that "there was not substantial discovery taking place in the Michigan case at the time the National settlement occurred."

Even lawyers for states that joined the action at a late stage—well after a critical mass had formed, making it clear that some deal to resolve the case was likely to be forthcoming—claimed that their legal representation had been unusually risky, thus supposedly justifying a fee enhancement. And while many lawyers also claimed that their contributions had been supercreative—the analogy of top Hollywood stars or rock singers at the peaks of their careers was often put forth—the reality was that much of the effort had been the same sort of crashingly routine scutwork that goes on in other litigation. The *Baltimore Sun*'s successful open-records demand, for example, revealed that of the legal work Peter Angelos wanted Maryland taxpayers to reimburse at $30,000 an hour, nearly a quarter had actually been performed by lawyers he'd hired from a temp agency at $21 an hour.[35] It was like reselling tap water at the price of French perfume.

The fee demands were even closer to pure profit because lawyers could write off so many of the costs of prosecuting the suit as separately reimburseable expenses. These could be made to include not only meals and travel, hired experts, and jury consultants but also simple office overhead, given that a separate office with phones and staff could be established to handle the tobacco work. The Texas lawyers billed more than $30 million in expense claims that included charter aircraft, a $952 lunch and $300 coffee service, and more than $100,000 for the services of a PR firm.[36] They had also quietly hired many of the nation's best-known law professors, including Lawrence Tribe and Arthur Miller of Harvard and Robert Blakey of Notre Dame, at $50,000 a pop, plus living expenses and bonuses.[37] In Pennsylvania, as one newspaper account put it: "One lawyer spent 12 minutes reading the *Wall Street Journal* and billed $62. Another charged $290 for the hour he took identifying and ordering books."[38]

After the settlement, a remarkable number of lawyers, academics, and others emerged from the woodwork to say they'd been promised a share in the booty. In one of the most curious episodes, a Houston lawyer named Marc Murr, an old friend of Texas attorney general Dan Morales, who'd worked with him earlier at the same law firm, stepped forward after the settlement to claim a $520 million share of the proceeds, later scaled back to $260 million. It was a mystifying claim in many ways, since participants could not remember Murr doing work on the case or being considered part of the state's team. Murr claimed his role had been to give strategic advice behind the scenes, and he pointed to a hitherto unsuspected contract with Morales entitling him to a piece of the action. Morales supported his claim, and the matter proceeded to an arbitration panel selected by the two sides in the not-all-that-disputatious dispute, Morales and Murr, which proceeded to award Murr $260 million. Before leaving office, Morales even signed an extremely unusual agreement abandoning, on the state's behalf, the right to contest Murr's fees. His successor, incoming attorney general John Cornyn, hired forensic experts who concluded that the contract had been doctored and backdated. Rather than be put under oath about the matter, Murr withdrew his claim to the fees.[39]

Morales was the one who'd selected the Big Five consortium of prominent injury lawyers, all major Democratic Party donors, to handle the state's case. (The five were Walter Umphrey of Beaumont's Provost & Umphrey; John Eddie Williams Jr. of Houston's Williams Bailey; Harold Nix of Daingerfield; Wayne Reaud of Beaumont's Reaud, Morgan & Quinn; and John O'Quinn of Houston.) When then-Texas governor George W. Bush and several state legislators stepped forward to challenge the $3.3 billion fee award, Morales accused them of "meddling" and unsuccessfully asked a court to impose $25 million in sanctions on them personally. On taking office as Morales's successor, Republican Cornyn was eager to investigate what the *Houston Chronicle* had described as "longtime allegations that [Morales] solicited large sums of money from lawyers he considered hiring" for the suit. In 1998, famed Houston attorney Joe Jamail—who wasn't among those representing the state—said "Morales solicited $1 million from each of several lawyers he considered hiring," in addition to the $2 million that each of the five agreed to furnish up front to finance the case, purportedly "for a fund to help Morales defend himself against political or public relations attacks from cigarette companies during the litigation." In a sworn 1999 testimony, Dawn Nelson, ex-wife of Big Five lawyer John Eddie Williams Jr. said, "Williams had told her that Morales wanted $1 million from one or more of the lawyers that were hired for the tobacco case," the *Houston Chronicle* reported. (The five filed statements in court saying they had not paid any consideration for the chance to participate in the litigation.) But Cornyn ran into a stonewall of nonco-operation in attempting to investigate the matter further. The five refused to go under oath to answer his questions, and skillful lawyering on their behalf by famed attorney Michael Tigar kept that alarming prospect at bay. The five also sought a court order to prevent the press, or anyone else, from getting a look at documents generated by the investigation.[40]

In other states, too, there was a surprising degree of un-certainty as it came time to divide fees on the central ques-tion of exactly who had been representing a state. Two well-known academics, Alan Dershowitz of Harvard and Richard Daynard of Northeastern, both claimed to have been promised portions of the settlement, but in neither case did the relevant lawyers agree that a promise had been made.[41] According to the *Winston-Salem Journal*, reporters got the distinct impression from North Carolina attorney general Mike Easley that the state had not hired any outside lawyers in the tobacco case; later it developed that Easley had hired one of his own departing aides to take on that extraordinarily lucrative assignment. (Easley said his former statements might have been mischaracterized.)[42]

Amazingly, the pact between Moore and Scruggs—cen-tral to the whole operation, and the model for everything that came after—was itself shrouded in almost complete obscurity. Various Mississippians had been trying for some time to lay their hands on the agreement between the two of them, which it was thought would have set out Scruggs's duties, expected compensation, what would happen if the arrangement broke up, and so forth. Finally Scruggs explained why they were finding it so hard to obtain a copy of that agreement—it didn't exist! Instead, he claimed that he and Moore had undertaken the whole vast project on the strength of an unwritten "understanding."[43]

That was a highly unusual arrangement, to say the least. In our many-lawyered society, even relatively minor and informal undertakings get committed to paper to protect both sides (and third parties) from a clash of recollections, misinterpretations, or unexpected circumstances that might dash the original plan. (If the lightning bolt of an angry Providence had knocked the Scruggs-Moore Learjet out of the sky, how would their heirs and assigns have known who owed what to whom?) Public agreements affecting the tax-payers' welfare are naturally among those that most need to be set on paper. And Scruggs was taking no chances with the various other law firms with whom he divvied up his tobacco work when it came to the allocation of risks and rewards due *them;* he and they spelled things out very spe-cifically in joint-venture agreements.[44]

If you were of charitable mind, you might conclude that Moore simply trusted Scruggs so much, and vice versa, that neither felt any written agreement was necessary to protect the interests of either side or those of the people of Mis-sissippi. If you were less charitable, you might observe how convenient it was for the two to have an understanding that could be altered or reinterpreted later without anyone's be-ing able to prove what had happened and which provided no paper trail for curious auditors or anyone else who might come around to snoop. In the end, Scruggs proceeded to declare that the intent of the agreement all along had been to ask a court to award an attorneys' fee from the cigarette-company defendants, and there was nothing in the written record to contradict that (or any other) account.

The three-member arbitration panels set up to award fees wielded a fantastic amount of power with essentially zero accountability. Their rulings were not subject to appeal of any kind. Although they issued short statements with their decisions, the arguments they heard from the lawyers and on which they based their decisions took place in closed-door sessions from which the public and press were rigorously excluded. As for the panels' membership, that was to consist of one seat nominated by the plaintiffs' lawyers, to which they usually named a veteran Washington lawyer named Harry Huge; another seat nominated by the tobacco companies, to which they named former federal judge Charles Renfrew of San Francisco; and a "permanent" chairman of the panel, a former federal mediator named John Calhoun Wells, who was supposed to be acceptable to both. Chairman Wells and Huge, the lawyers' representative, most often were observed forming a majority bloc of two, both supporting high fees. Judge Renfrew, for his part, sometimes joined the opinions—making them unanimous— and sometimes dissented.[45]

The word "arbitration" conjures up an image of neutrality, objectivity, and impartiality, so it might come as a bit of a shock that arbitrator Harry Huge, nominated by the trial lawyers to a seat on most of the panels, is the father of attorney Theodore Huge, who practices with South Carolina's Ness Motley—none other than the national firm that had the largest portfolio of states as clients and was expected to emerge as the biggest single recipient of tobacco fees. Huge did not fill the lawyer's seat on all the panels, however. *Texas Lawyer* reported that "raising eyebrows"[46] in Lone Star State legal circles was the situation of Texas Tech University law school dean Frank Newton, who first solicited a $12.5 million donation for his university from tobacco lawyer Wayne Reaud and then agreed to serve on the arbitration panel that awarded $3.3 billion in fees to Reaud and the other Big Five Texas tobacco lawyers. "Newton saw no conflict since everyone, including the tobacco firms, knew where his loyalties lay. 'There's no question about who I am or what my role was,' he said. 'The tobacco companies knew that I was going to try and get the most money for Texas [and its attorneys].' "

The arbitration panels' terse opinions, as well as scattered reports from lawyers who made presentations to them, give us some idea of their manner of proceeding. Lawyers for each state would come forward to argue that they deserved stupendous sums because their efforts had been so utterly crucial to the overall crusade against the tobacco companies. Massachusetts lawyers, one party recalled, hired a PR firm[47] that spent three months quizzing participants to "extract the hottest and most memorable details" and pitch them to the panel. In any event, the panels proved a soft touch indeed: The terse rationales they gave for their decisions to grant huge fees in each successive case typically praised the lawyers for virtually every state, even the most humdrum of the tag-alongs, as having been really distinctive, unusually productive, and well deserving of high fees. Louisiana's lawyers got an enhancement for having pursued a legal theory that went nowhere—after all, it still increased the pressure on the defendants, right? Ohio's lawyers got an enhancement for pursuing a theory that lost outright.

Nor was it by inadvertence that, after the few obviously industrious legal teams like Minnesota's had been accounted for, it was so hard to sort out which other states' lawyers had made which contributions. In fact, the lawyers who ran the case had pursued artful techniques of work sharing, resembling that of an experienced mom whose children want to help bake a cake: Everyone gets something to do that lets them say their efforts were indispensable to the final result, which means everyone gets to lick the frosting bowl.

Some of the grounds for enhancement cited by the majority arbitrators, however, raised disturbing questions as to what exactly was being rewarded. Thus, the arbitators found grounds for enhancement of lawyers' fees in the fact that joining the suit had roused strong political opposition in some states; the presence of vocal opposition, it reasoned, meant that lawyers had accomplished more by getting their states to sue. (Result: The less the extent to which a decision to sue really reflected the opinions of a state's residents, the richer their lawyers could make themselves.)[48] In Ohio's case, the arbitrators found it noteworthy—and reason for generosity—that the mostly tag-along state had been number twenty-six to file, thus tipping beyond the halfway point the number of states that had joined the action. In the case of four protobacco states that had been among the last of the fifty to join the action—North Carolina, Kentucky, South Carolina, and Tennessee—it might have seemed almost impossible to justify high fees, but lawyers had an answer for that one too: they'd played a crucial role, they said, in protecting the interests of tobacco farmers. Thus the arbitrators awarded an $82.5 million fee to the South Carolina lawyers despite a futile dissent from Renfrew, who called the sum "grossly excessive." It certainly will go down as one of the most richly compensated instances in the history of farmer "representation"—with no need, of course, for any showing that actual farmers in the states had been able to exercise control over the attorneys supposedly looking out for their interests.

The arbitration proceedings themselves provided an opportunity for millions more dollars to be spread widely around among the same sorts of academics and out-of-work politicians who had been put on the lawyers' retainers during the litigation proper, plus some new ones. Even former California attorney general Dan Lungren, a straight-arrow Republican who'd mostly fought the plaintiffs' lawyers while in office, saw the light after leaving office, accepting more than $200,000 over eleven months as an expert witness and consultant to the Castano group of sixty law firms.[49]

Munificent though the arbitration process promised to be, some lawyers rejected it and instead insisted on the payment of the originally agreed-on contingency percentages. States that put up resistance to these demands might find that the same attorneys who'd seemed so nice and public-spirited just a little while before were quick to slap on liens, holding up the disbursement of the state's full tobacco windfall, in order to obtain leverage while their claims went forward; this happened, or was used as a threat, in states like Illinois, Massachusetts, and New Jersey. Giauque, Crockett, Bendinger & Peterson, one of the law firms representing Utah, filed a lien to claim 25 percent of the state's settlement, or about $250 million. A contract was a contract, wasn't it? And Maryland's Peter Angelos tied up the state in court for a couple of years trying to enforce a fee agreement giving him $1 billion before eventually settling for $150 million.

In one of their fanciest bits of footwork, lawyers had so arranged the arbitration process that (in their view, at least) the results would be insulated from challenge or scrutiny by concerned members of the public or even lawmakers. The device they used was a relatively novel one called "the separately negotiated fee."

Until the early 1990s, it had been taken as a matter of course that legal fees in class and mass litigation would be deducted from the "common fund" that had been obtained for the clients' benefit. Then some clever lawyers came up with a new wrinkle: They would cut a deal with the opponent to pay them a fee directly at the end of the litigation. The negotiations as to the magnitude and conditions of this direct-from-defendant fee, the judge would be assured, were completely adversarial and arms' length and also entirely separate from the negotiations over the terms of the main settlement itself. As an innovation "unknown to previous fee jurisprudence," noted class-action critic Lawrence Schonbrun in 1996, the separately negotiated fee "offered several immediate advantages. The amount could depend on the discretion of both sides. And the greatest advantage of all—or so class counsel regularly argue with a straight face—is that this method of attorney compensation, unlike the common fund method, doesn't reduce the class's recovery." Which meant, if you accepted its backers' logic, that members of the originally represented client class had no right to show up in court objecting to their lawyers' fees as excessive: After all, the fees weren't coming out of their hide, and any court-ordered reduction in them would benefit only the defendant, not the client class. The defendant, for its part, has already agreed not to object. So the almost magical result was that no one at all had standing to object to the lawyers' cashing in richly. Writes Schonbrun:

> This argument simply cannot be taken seriously. Suppose lawyers for accident victims were discovered to be striking side deals by which they recovered handsome fees from the insurance company after agreement on their clients' recovery. Would they really get away with assuring ethical inquisitors that, after all, the nice fees were no skin off their clients' backs; the clients' settlement would have been the same regardless of the amount of the attorneys' fee which they had negotiated for themselves? Wouldn't clients and bystanders be justified in questioning the implicit trade-off going on in such negotiations: lower settlement sums for higher attorneys' fees? It is quite clear that in normal litigation the law would view such arrangements as constituting an impermissible conflict of interest.[50]

The incentives of defendants, for their part, were clear enough: They wanted to "negotiate to a bottom line" and had no reason to care how much of the overall payout went to the lawyers and how much to the clients. Still, enough judges were willing to rubber stamp the new separately negotiated fee that it soon became highly popular in class-action litigation, where it was to serve as a model for the tobacco deal. Since the tobacco lawyers' payday was formally coming at the expense of tobacco companies, the lawyers enjoyed success getting legal challenges against the fees thrown out on grounds of lack of standing. (Even state legislatures, they argued, had no right to intervene.) The rationale was good enough for New York attorney general Eliot Spitzer, who later said that one of the "misconceptions about the tobacco settlement is that the attorneys' fees are coming out of the public's pocket. . . . these fees are not state property."[51] But Yale law professor John Langbein, an authority on civil procedure, disagreed. Money obtained by the assertion of public claims, Langbein said, whether earmarked for a settlement fund or for attorneys' fees, was public money and cannot escape public accountability and control simply by arranging it to emerge from a settlement room with a label of private pasted on it. "This money is every bit as much public property as the Washington Monument or any other public asset."[52] And in this case it vanished into the lawyers' pockets in a way studiously engineered to bypass public accountability—a bold and piratical hijacking of public assets.

———

Around the country, many newspapers—both conservative and liberal—expressed editorial dismay at the fee episode. The *St. Petersburg Times* called the Florida award "breathtakingly excessive ... utterly unconscionable. ... [the lawyers have put] a face on greed," while *USA Today* called the "mega-paydays" a "sorry legacy" of the tobacco deal. The *St. Louis Post-Dispatch* said the $100 million that five law firms were expected to split for representing Missouri "grossly overpays the lawyers involved" and is "a political gravy train ... private money in the public trough." Madison's *Capital Times*, a leading liberal voice in Wisconsin, called the tobacco fee affair "the latest in a long line of official missteps that have cost taxpayers millions and virtually destroyed Wisconsin's reputation for patronage-free governance."[53]

Yet the abuses of the legal system that characterized the tobacco affair from start to finish, and the fee issue in particular, never quite made it onto the national news agenda. One important reason on a national level was the stance taken by the influential *New York Times*, which ran only perfunctory news coverage of the gargantuan fee awards and whose editorials sided generally with the attorneys general, and then mostly fell silent as the fee issue played itself out.[54] There was, however, a wider reason why outrage never crystallized into a news moment, and that was the success of the attorneys general and their lawyers in protecting their work from sustained public scrutiny.

Why, for example, were the settlement's anticompetitive provisions, the ones allocating market share and discouraging new firms from entering the tobacco market, not widely reported in the press until months after the monumental deal was struck? A major reason was that the Master Settlement Agreement (MSA) not only was exceptionally long and opaque even by the standards of legal documents but was never widely circulated in published form, and was only sporadically available even on the Internet.[55] Even more striking, it lacked the kind of overview documents— a table of contents, an outline, an executive summary, an index—that would have helped reporters or concerned citizens make sense of it. Recall that the attorneys general and their private lawyers had on retainer a teeming roster of articulate lawyers, public relations specialists, law professors, and sundry others who could readily have drafted clear summaries of how the settlement worked and what its various sections accomplished. But that would merely have invited public discussion of the settlement's provisions, which—to put it mildly—does not seem to have been a high priority of the attorneys general and their lawyers. The tobacco company defendants, for their part, had agreed not to resist; and we may doubt, in any case, that they had much interest in calling public attention to the cartelization provisions. No sophisticated interest groups had a stake in directing the press's attention to the anticompetitive provisions. So reporters were left dependent on what attorneys general and their lawyers chose to tell them. It is hard to avoid the conclusion that there was virtually no public debate about the settlement's many questionable provisions because its drafters wanted it that way.

Another issue that would have been well worth debating is the propriety of the MSA's having achieved its restrictions on tobacco company advertising by way of an end run around constitutional scrutiny, specifically the Supreme Court precedents that suggested the First Amendment might accord some protection to the advertising of otherwise lawful products. If the states had tried to enact such bans by direct legislation, the tobacco companies would quickly have challenged their actions in court, and the courts would have had a chance to rule on their constitutionality. Instead, the MSA was based on the fiction that the defendants had "voluntarily" waived any First Amendment rights they might have. It was a disturbing precedent: By exerting its overwhelming power as a litigant, the government could strong-arm an unpopular interest group into giving up rights to communicate with the public, even though a court might have found direct infringement of those rights to be unconstitutional. What other unpopular interest groups could be treated that way in the future?

Equally troubling, and even less remarked in the press at the time, were provisions aimed at curtailing the companies' ability to influence public and legislative opinion. For openers, as one summary puts it, the settlement "prohibited the cigarette companies from lobbying against any of the terms of the MSA or challenging their constitutionality. . . . It also barred them from lobbying against various state and local legislative proposals." In a drastic step, the agreement ordered the disbanding of the tobacco industry's former voices in public debate, the Tobacco Institute and the Council for Tobacco Research (CTR), with the groups' files to be turned over to antitobacco forces to pick over the once-confidential memos contained therein; furthermore, the agreement attached stringent controls to any newly formed entity that the industry might form intended to influence public discussion of tobacco. In her book on tobacco politics, *Up in Smoke*, University of Virginia political scientist Martha Derthick writes that these provisions were the first aspect in news reports of the settlement to catch her attention.[56] "When did the governments in the United States get the right to abolish lobbies?" she recalls wondering. "What country am I living in?" Even widely hated interest groups had routinely been allowed to maintain vigorous lobbies and air their views freely in public debate. This was now to change; from now on, if an interest group could be made unpopular enough, it could be coerced into "voluntarily" giving up its right to offer public dissent from future government policies or test them in court. And yet there seemed to be no outcry over settlement provisions that Derthick calls "deeply problematic from the point of view of American political traditions."

Another noteworthy feature of the MSA was the way it allowed attorneys general to dictate terms to their supposed masters and employers, the governments of the fifty states. The MSA required states (on pain of losing some of the big new money flow) to pass legislation ("Qualifying Statutes") in a form exactly as prescribed. State judges, too, were put on notice that they had better go along with the new scheme unless they wanted their state to suffer serious financial shortfalls: Payouts to a state would be reduced by up to 65 percent if its courts found their legislature's Qualifying Statute in violation of their state constitution.[57] Effectively, this arm-twisted courts into gliding as rapidly as possible over any misgivings. (Nor could a state's voters themselves depart from the pattern without losing benefits.) Such throwing around of weight on pain of funding cutoffs might have been considered objectionably high-handed if done by the federal government in Washington, but the consortium of attorneys general seemed to have no qualms about putting it over.

At the same time the MSA did as little as possible to rein in the future options of the attorneys general. Not only did it lack, as one commentator observed, "mechanisms by which the public or legislatures can hold the attorneys general accountable for their performance," but it gave no indications of how the agreement might be changed in the light of any altered future circumstances. This left the clear impression that the attorneys general intended to handle any such future changes through more back-room negotiations, whose results would once again be announced to the public as a done deal (unless they ended in an impasse, also a danger given the lack of prescribed methods of amendment). As a governing mechanism for future tobacco industry practices, this fell far short of predictability, transparency, or accountability.

Before long reports began appearing in the press that state governments were actually spending very little of their new windfalls on what had not long before been described as the supremely urgent, life-or-death task of discouraging smoking. Instead, they were racing to fund new spending projects, ranging from highway improvements to the hiring of new layers of administrators for existing bureaucracies. "This is going to be pretty much a feeding frenzy," said one legislator. "I mean, it's free money." Few states applied any of the new revenue to lowering taxes, despite the frequent talk about how the purpose of the suits had been to recoup Medicaid outlays for taxpayers.

And what of the issue flogged so hard during the litigation campaign—teenage smoking? Adult smoking, it is true, did continue to drop after 1998, and there is little doubt that the new and higher cigarette prices contributed to that drop, just as tax increases had long been known to do. Since the standard position of the attorneys general was that the settlement had not in any way raised taxes on smokers, it was hard for them to take credit for this development. Contrary to all assumptions, however, the rate of smoking among teens appeared to have gone up rather than down during the litigation campaign and even afterward.[58] A late-2000 analysis for the National Bureau of Economic Research (NBER) by Jonathan Gruber and Jonathan Zinman found the proportion of teens who smoke bottomed out around 1991 or so after a fifteen-year decline and had since risen by one-third.

It's hard to know exactly why this might happen; teenagers often rebel against what is expected of them, and the "forbidden fruit" thesis has many supporters. We do know that conventional wisdom on the relationship between youth smoking patterns and advertising has often proved deceptive in the past. According to a 1997 analysis by Washington University's Center for the Study of American Business, "tobacco advertising bans in Finland, Sweden, Norway and Australia [were] followed by increases in youth smoking instead of decreases."[59] Youth smoking in this country actually declined significantly during the notorious "Joe Camel" campaign, considered Exhibit A in the moral indictment of the tobacco industry for marketing to youth.[60]

Only months before, large sections of the political class of the United States had been comparing tobacco companies to premeditated murderers, to drug dealers, to sadistic death camp guards. But now that the financial health of the tobacco trade was a bulwark of state revenue projections, their tune began to shift. When the progress of the massive *Engle v. R. J. Reynolds Tobacco Company* class action in Florida raised the possibility of judgments that might force the industry to declare bankruptcy, bringing to an end the states' entitlement to the continuing money flow, the legislature of Florida—Florida, of all states, which had considered no tactic too underhanded to use in winning its own tobacco case—promptly scrambled to enact a bill heading off the immediate threat by ensuring that tobacco company defendants would not have to put up a prohibitive bond before appealing. And the same state soon quietly decided to resume investing its pension fund money in the stock of tobacco companies. It was one thing to call someone a mass murderer, but why should that stand in the way of going into the coffin-nail business with them? The same old deal by which the government tolerated smoking because it served as a handy source of official revenue had suddenly reappeared in full force. When it came to "tobacco control," the attorneys general may have struck a pose as Savonarola, but their real role was as sellers of indulgences.

Serial Litigation

Every magazine photo editor dreads the need to illustrate an article about lawyers, given their reputation for insisting on being pictured against the same familiar backdrop of a stuffy law library. So the staff at *George* must have marveled at its good fortune in June 1999 when the now-defunct magazine profiled six attorneys who were cutting a wide swath on the political scene after having collectively "raked in more than $5 billion for their firms from tobacco litigation." In the lavish photo spread (entitled "Puff Daddies") the attorneys were pleased to pose amid emblems of luxury consumption more often seen in the likes of *Town & Country* than in *The National Law Journal*. Among the scenery was the racing boat, conspicuously labeled *Gunsmoke*, of Pascagoula, Mississippi's Dickie Scruggs, whose law firm was expected to pocket more than $1 billion in fees for its role in the tobacco litigation; the twenty-horse equestrian estate of Charleston, South Carolina's Joseph Rice (whose firm of Ness Motley was in for probably upwards of $2 billion); the private putting green on the estate of Pensacola, Florida's Fred Levin ($325 million); and the opulent bathtub where South Florida's Robert Montgomery ($678 million) reclined fully clothed under a painting of a naked lady.[1]

Not all the profiled lawyers struck materialistic themes. Thus politically ambitious Michael Ciresi of Minnesota ($440 million) cheerfully agreed, "Some of the fees *are* excessive," while gearing up for a race for the U.S. Senate (it was to prove unsuccessful) and showing off the facilities of a new foundation he had endowed. Seattle's Steve Berman (hundreds of millions, at least), who had made a fortune filing shareholder class-action suits, spoke of the ideological satisfactions of making a big score: "I got the notion in the '60s that you can protest by growing your hair long or you can get trained in the methods of the establishment and use their own tools to beat them. There's nothing better than beating them at their own game."

One striking thing about the six lawyers pictured in the magazine spread was that they were just a small sampling of the new class of tobacco-fee tycoons. There were plenty more where they came from who would have scored almost as high in wealth, flamboyance, or both. A colorful feature might have been written about the five legal gladiators (Walter Umphrey, Wayne Reaud, John Eddie Williams Jr., John O'Quinn, and Robert Nix), all politically active, whose firms split a $3.3 billion fee for their work in pursuing and then settling out of court the tobacco case filed by the state of Texas. Even before the tobacco fees, the presence of über-lawyers Umphrey and Reaud had been felt everywhere in their hometown of Beaumont, Texas. "It's like out of a movie," a lawyer who practices against them told *Texas Lawyer*.[2] "They own the banks, the buildings, a newspaper.

What they don't own, they've donated heavily to." Umphrey's fleet of airplanes is said to compare favorably with the one serving the general public at the Beaumont airport, which does not keep him from affecting a modest stance: "Other than airplanes and helicopters, I don't have a flamboyant lifestyle at all," said the veteran asbestos lawyer, one of whose co-owned ranches in Australia comprised 3.4 million acres.

Nor did the Texas lawyers even set the record among paydays for representing a single state in the tobacco litigation: $3.4 billion went to the consortium of lawyers representing Florida, which included Fredric Levin, Robert Montgomery, and others. (Levin has conceded that his firm's $300 million take was "totally obscene.")[3] Baltimore's Peter Angelos—famous for having bought the hometown baseball Orioles with the fees from asbestos lawsuits—was demanding an even $1 billion for handling the state of Maryland's tobacco case, though he was eventually to settle for less. And so forth around the country. All told, the private law firms hired by the state attorneys general were, as of 2002, expected to wind up bagging somewhere around $14 billion, the figures uncertain in part because so many of the lawyers—though ostensibly earning the fees on public business—had kept the details of their fees and retainer agreements from public view.

It was not these lawyers' expenditures on Learjets, Old Masters, or island villas, however, that made them a continuing news story. It was the way they were going about reinvesting their windfalls in the same political and legal processes that had brought them wealth to begin with. Never before in history had there arisen a class of individuals more munificent in their political campaign donations than American plaintiffs' lawyers, and now the tobacco lawyers were raising the bar for generosity to new and unheard-of heights. Aside from bestowing millions on favored candidates, they also ranked high among givers of "soft money" to political parties. Ness Motley and the Angelos firm, for example, each gave $1.2 million to the national Democrats, placing them among the top donors, while John Eddie Williams Jr.'s Houston firm of Williams Bailey topped that at $1.4 million; others on the Texas tobacco team were making donations in the $400,000–$800,000 range. (By way of comparison, heavy-hitting labor unions like the electrical workers and the American Federation of Teachers (AFT) were giving $1.7 million each to the Democrats over the same cycle, while the 3-million-member National Rifle Association (NRA) gave $1.5 million to the Republicans.) As for the state level, the five Texas tobacco law firms were giving more to the state Democratic Party than all its other donors combined. Many leading trial lawyers served as key party fund-raisers; thus, during the 2000 campaign, Al Gore and Bill Clinton hopscotched around the country to attend a seemingly endless series of fund-raisers thrown by such figures as Robert Montgomery ($10,000/plate), Fred Baron ($25,000/couple), and Willie Gary and Stanley Chesley ($500,000 events each).

The political influence of the trial bar, of course, predated the tobacco round. Dallas's Frederick Baron "plays golf with [then-president Clinton] and dines several times a year at the White House," a *New York Times* profile observed.[4] Peter Angelos is "viewed by many political insiders as the most powerful private citizen in Maryland," the

Washington Post notes.[5] Scruggs is a bipartisan threat, do-
nating heavily to Democrats, though he also happens to be
the brother-in-law of GOP Senate majority leader Trent
Lott. Especially noteworthy is the extent to which the tort
bar underwrites the campaigns of state judges, who unlike
federal judges mostly run for election. Thus when the city
of Detroit sued gun makers, the defendants were alarmed
to learn that the the private lawyer representing the city
had been one of the biggest campaign donors to the judge
assigned to hear the case. The donor-lawyer, however,
shrugged off the connection as no big deal, since his law
firm donated to "about 90 percent of the judges in Wayne
County." The chief judge's boss agreed that the criticism
was misplaced. "This happens all the time," he said. "Who
do you think donates to judicial campaigns? It isn't Aunt
Susie—it's lawyers."[6]

And giant donations have served as rocket propellants
to a higher status in the larger society, specifically within
the legal profession, of which the personal-injury bar was
once a relatively marginal component. A symbolic mile-
stone has come with the renaming of a number of large law
schools—or in some cases, their libraries, buildings, or clinical programs—after a plaintiff's lawyer following massive
donations. Thus a $10 million donation transformed the
University of Florida's law school into the Levin College of
Law, while Temple University in Philadelphia renamed its
law school after James Beasley. Baylor Law School moved
out of its old digs into the spiffy Sheila and Walter Umphrey Law Center. The University of Houston now sports
a John M. O'Quinn Law Library, after the lawyer who
dominated breast-implant litigation, with a full-length oil

portrait of the master himself to loom as an inspirational presence over the students. Texas Tech thought it had a deal to rename its law school after Wayne Reaud in exchange for $12.5 million, but the deal fell through when trustees wanted to hold out for twice that sum. Fred Baron agreed to pony up $1 million to endow a chair at the University of Texas School of Law, which already has a number of trophy properties named after Jamail, including a Jamail Center for Legal Research.[7]

Many lawyers and attorneys general who participated in the tobacco litigation had vehemently denied that it would set a precedent for similar attacks on other industries. Attorneys "insist there's no list of industries they are targeting," reported *Lawyers Weekly USA* in 1999.[8] "Trial lawyers say big industry is trying to scare the public into thinking that a kind of serial litigation is underway. In fact, they say, there is no cohesive group of lawyers moving from one target to the next."

These assurances were false. Before the tobacco litigation had even settled, one group of lawyers—working closely with gun-control groups—had begun signing up mayors of big cities to file suits against gun makers, demanding reimbursement for the costs of responding to gun-related crime, modeling their cases on the successful tobacco action.

Shortly before the state tobacco settlement was signed in November 1998, the curtain was pulled back and the mayor of New Orleans announced the first of the resulting suits. A powwow of trial lawyers met in Chicago shortly thereafter to get their stories straight before fanning out around the country to "pitch their services to mayors and city attorneys" on the new project, according to *The American Lawyer*.[9] "[We] have the resources to start a war instead of taking little potshots," said attorney John Coale, who—like most of the big-name lawyers active in the gun campaign—had also worked on tobacco. "Well, we've started a war."

With "the ink barely dry" on the tobacco settlement, the *Baltimore Sun* reported, tobacco-veteran lawyers such as Ness Motley and the Angelos firm began signing up governments to join as litigants in a campaign demanding that DuPont, Imperial Chemical Industries (ICI), and other large companies that made lead paint for interior use more than fifty years ago fork over billions to cities, counties, and states to help abate hazardous residues of the substance lingering in public buildings and private tenements.[10] "If I don't bring the entire lead paint industry to its knees within three years," vowed senior partner Ron Motley, "I will give them my [120-foot] boat."[11] The antilead-paint lawyers went on to sign up a roster of government clients that included the state of Rhode Island, the city of Milwaukee, and school districts in Texas and California. Angelos, for his part, also filed a fusillade of lawsuits against the cellphone industry, alleging that it had covered up evidence of a link between its product and cancer—though most scientists seemed to be of the view that any such link was an imaginary one.[12]

Government officials gladly embraced the idea of hiring private lawyers on a contingency basis to sue for the reimbursement of public expenditures occasioned by one or another human vice or controversial business practice. The attorney general of Rhode Island proposed that his colleagues join him in an action against latex glove makers to recover the cost of health-care workers' latex allergies.[13] Delaware attorney general Jane Brady told a newspaper about one of the occupational hazards of attending meetings of the National Association of Attorneys General (NAAG). She had "been approached on a number of occasions by trial lawyers and asked to consider joining litigation and hiring them to represent us."[14] The state of Alabama hired a law firm whose attorneys had been among Gov. Don Siegelman's biggest campaign contributors to sue ExxonMobil in a royalty dispute, which led to a $1 billion jury verdict estimated to yield nearly $500 million in contingency fees to the lawyers, if upheld.[15] Charles Condon, the conservative Republican attorney general of South Carolina, urged his fellow attorneys general to develop lawsuits to make Hollywood youth marketing the next you-know-what. "Clearly we have here a virtual replay of what the tobacco industry did to our children. Instead of Joe Camel, Hollywood uses Eminem, *South Park*, Doom, and Steven Segal [sic] to seduce children."[16] Six attorneys general announced they were preparing a suit modeled on the tobacco action against pharmaceutical makers over drug pricing.

When lawyers were still assuring the press that "serial litigation" was a figment of defendants' imaginations, Connecticut attorney general Richard Blumenthal was one who detected sinister motives behind the alarm, telling the *Washington Post* that "[t]here is this wave of falsehoods which various interest groups are spreading to undermine the attorneys general," such as "that we're somehow anti-business" or that "we're working hand in glove with the trial lawyers."[17] He stoutly declared that he had no intention of being "intimidated" or "cowed" by such calumnies. But soon Blumenthal was observed to be taking a prominent role assisting the trial lawyers in both managed care and gun litigation. In San Francisco, the municipal administration launched what was called an "affirmative litigation" department, its mission to team up with private lawyers to find grounds to squeeze money out of businesses. Philadelphia soon followed suit with a similar new unit, its city solicitor, himself formerly a private class-action lawyer, saying he hoped the city's pending lawsuit against gun makers "would prove to be just the beginning."[18]

Within months of the tobacco settlement, it was clear that the major plaintiffs' firms were reinvesting much of the windfall in ambitious new suits, often targeting whole industries. Scruggs teamed up with other tobacco-suit veterans to launch a volley of suits against managed health-care companies over various cost-containment practices, though Congress had specifically seemed to authorize some of those practices not long before. "We're going to dismantle the managed care system," declared Russ Herman, a former president of the Association of Trial Lawyers of America (ATLA).[19] The kickoff of the lawsuit campaign made big waves on Wall Street in October 1999, destroying $12 billion of value in managed-care companies' stocks in a single day. Scruggs was not shy about helping this process along, paying visits to stock analysts to inform them that unless the companies played ball with him he could run them out of business.[20] He brushed off complaints from his targets that the tactic amounted to extortion.

Newsweek was soon to nominate Scruggs as "the most influential man in America that you've never heard of," and no wonder: A one-man dynamo, he was demanding billions of dollars from a long list of controversial industries, ranging from defense contractors, whom he was planning to sue for questionable billing, to the makers of Ritalin, the drug for hyperactivity in children, which critics had charged was being prescribed too widely in schools. On a more visionary note, he also teamed up with several noted black lawyers, including Florida's Willie Gary, to map out what was envisioned as the biggest lawsuit campaign in history, demanding reparations for African-American descendants of slaves. The suits would be aimed at private companies, institutions, and perhaps even individuals whose business histories, founding donations, inheritances, or fortunes descended in some respect or other from slave enterprise. (Bequests from slave owners, for example, were early sources of funds for Princeton and Yale.) Though the reparations idea stirred up an immense amount of anger and ill will among white Americans, Scruggs's colleagues claimed—with all apparent seriousness—that it was really intended as a way of bringing "closure" to the nation's history of racial division so that everyone could "move on."

The real problem with trying to identify the "next tobacco" was that there were so many nominees. "Guns have become the next tobacco," crowed an attorney with the Brady Campaign. "I think plaintiffs' attorneys are going to try to make lead paint the next tobacco situation," worried the chief lawyer for the National Paint & Coatings Association (NPCA). Stocks of health-insurance companies had crashed, a Wall Street analyst noted, because of the prospect that they were "going to be the next tobacco industry." "You know what Ralph Nader said. After tobacco, the next target for trial lawyers will be gambling," said the head of the National Coalition Against Legalized Gambling (NCALG). After a key antitrust ruling went against the world's largest software company, lawyers rushed to file consumer class-action suits intended to "turn Microsoft into the next Philip Morris," the *Washington Post* reported. "This may be the next tobacco litigation," boasted the lawyer who filed a whistle-blower suit charging oil companies with underpaying royalties on federal lands. "I view these mold claims [claims against developers and landlords over mold in buildings] as similar to asbestos 30 years ago," said California lawyer Alexander Robertson, varying the formula a bit.[21]

A conference of legal academics held at Pepperdine University in Los Angeles examined the question of which industries should be made the next tobacco, with alcohol companies the favored candidate, while others suggesting hamburger joints and steakhouses.[22] However, attorney John Coale was quoted in the press as dismissing both prospects with a quip: "We'd never do that," he said. "We enjoy liquor and meat too much."[23] But the idea was not really that far-fetched, since an ever more ambitious public health establishment had begun to redefine overeating, drinking, violence on TV, gun ownership, and even suburban sprawl as maladies ripe for medical intervention, as it had done earlier with tobacco consumption.

Increasingly, mass tort litigation was following a fully entrepreneurial model: Big law firms would identify an industry they wanted to sue, and then find and sign up the right clients to do so. There was one major precedent within the American legal system for this model of lawyer-propelled litigation, namely the industry that had formed around class-action suits. And experience with the class-action industry raised many danger signals about the sorts of ethical and practical problems that were likely to arise once lawyers began to manage mass personal-injury litigation as well.

Even as early as the 1920s there had emerged, in recognizable modern form, a class-action sector of the litigation world run by lawyers for their own benefit. When a likely occasion for a lawsuit came along, such as a business scandal or sudden stock price drop, class-action lawyers rushed to sue, identifying and installing as complainants token clients who exercised very little control over the suits that went on in their names. ("I have the greatest practice of law in the world," said one of the most famous of their number, Milberg Weiss's Bill Lerach. "I have no clients.")[24] A typical example was the early-1990s flap over the briefly popular singing duo Milli Vanilli who, after fading in popularity with their teenage fans, were revealed not actually to have been singing at all; they had been lip-synching to tracks prerecorded by others. Most young fans appeared willing to shrug off the affair, but not so many of the nation's most prominent class-action firms. They rushed to file more than two dozen suits against Arista Records charging fraud, deception, and all manner of other illegalities, demanding disgorgement by the company of every penny taken in from the sale of the group's albums, et cetera. The lawsuits invariably sought class-action status. When the cases eventually settled, the record company offered a $3 rebate to any customer who could offer proof of having bought one of the band's albums, while the lawyers requested court-ordered fees approaching $2 million. How spontaneous were the litigants' grievances? "Of the 49 plaintiffs in the Milli Vanilli cases, at least 41 appear to have had pre-existing relationships to lawyers, most of whom worked at firms specializing in class-action cases. And many of the plaintiffs say they agreed to file suit at the suggestion of a lawyer," reported the *Wall Street Journal*'s Amy Stevens. Attorneys "found clients in their own law offices and contacted their friends with teenage children"; one "didn't know she was a plaintiff until she read it in the newspaper." As a matter of fact, the lawyers were doing very much the same thing that the record promoters had done: line up appealing if vacuous faces to lip-synch their own compositions.[25]

Multiply by hundreds if not thousands of actions, and you get the year-in, year-out business of the class-action industry, which today files a more or less continual stream of shareholder and investor actions against big companies, consumer suits over credit card grace periods and bank check-bouncing fees, airline frequent flier programs, magazine sweepstakes and premium promotions that arguably fall short of promises, and so forth. To find likely cases, some lawyers comb through mass-market commercial agreements in search of slipups in the fine print, often

highly technical. Others piggyback on government enforcement actions. Few class members opt out; and when the
case settles, the accepted logic behind the lawyers' payday
is that the suit has created a benefit for the class members,
which entitles the lawyers to deduct a reasonable fee before
the class is paid.

So eager are class-action lawyers to sue that it is common
for their complaints to contain misspellings or inappropriate boilerplate carried forward from complaints in earlier
cases.[26] When a key antitrust ruling went against Microsoft,
for example, the class-action bar rushed to court with various complaints that described the giant software firm as
being in the generic drug business, or said the principal
place of business of the Seattle-based firm was in the state
of Texas, or asserted the right to represent customers injured by past purchases of Windows 2000 (which hadn't
gone on sale yet), or mistakenly described Microsoft's competitor Apple as the nonexistent "MacIntosh Computer
Company." The subsequent settlements often involve
whopping fee bills for the lawyers, even as consumers themselves get the equivalent of the coins found under the sofa
cushions. Thus credit card giant MBNA, charged with misleading ad claims, agreed to refund customers $3.57 each,
while lawyers requested $1.3 million in court-approved
fees; and magazine promoter Publishers Clearing House,
charged with overaggressive promotion of its sweepstakes,
set aside $5.5 million to be divided up as refunds among an
estimated 48 million households, an average of twelve cents
per household if all were to file claims, while lawyers were
set to bag $3 million in fees. The list could be extended
indefinitely with similar cases.

While many cases involve relatively trivial amounts, the class-action device can menace business defendants with gigantic liabilities by the magic of automatic multiplication. An Augusta, Ga. local unit of the Hooters's restaurant chain declared bankruptcy after being subjected to an $11.9 million class-action verdict; its sin was to have bought ads in six "blast fax" circulars each sent to 1,321 recipients, after which it got sued under a federal law applying a $500 penalty per offense to companies that allow their advertising to be included in unsolicited fax mailings.[27] The judge awarded the lawyer himself $4 million in recognition of his endeavors. Similar litigation had erupted in other cities, with lawyers in Houston demanding tens of millions of dollars apiece from mom-and-pop Mexican restaurants and other local defendants. An opposing attorney described the new legal specialty as "Powerball for the clever."[28] Fear of runaway-size verdicts is one reason even a long-shot suit is apt to be bought off with a settlement if a judge has consented to certify it as a class action. (Scruggs, for one, has boasted that his favored strategy to force a settlement is to "[r]aise the stakes so high that neither side can afford to lose.")

Though grudgingly accepted as the least bad way of handling a certain type of legal controversy, class actions were troubling even to many commentators who had little sympathy for business defendants. They often rewarded lawyers with big fees for cases that had been inexpensive for them to prosecute. Class-action suits had a reputation as a magnet for unpleasantly hardball or cynical operators, in part because no constituency of actual clients was looking over the lawyers' shoulders. Equally disturbing, some class-action lawyers had a reputation for striking deals with the companies they sued—some called them sweetheart deals—which provided little benefit to the class but major fees to the lawyer. Judges presented with a settlement to approve found it difficult to verify that lawyers had proved loyal to the interests of their absent clients, since the defendant in the case would have agreed, as part of the settlement, not to contest matters further, while the lawyers had an incentive to exaggerate the benefits they had obtained. In New Mexico, in 1999, a class action against a life insurance company resulted in no payouts to policyholders, though the company agreed to make fuller disclosures. The lawyers got $7.5 million. In another case against a different life insurer, filed in the same New Mexico court and with an overlapping cast of lawyer-characters, Albuquerque lawyer Gary Duncan stood to gain cash and other benefits worth an estimated $10 million. (After the deal drew unfavorable publicity, he backed off.) A famous mid-1990s Alabama case against mortgage lender BancBoston over escrow practices was one of several in which many class members received benefits that actually were smaller than the legal fees deducted from their accounts, leaving them poorer in various instances by $100, $150, or more. Class members do have the legal right to show up at a fairness hearing to proffer objections, but if they do so they must prepare for an acrimonious fight, and the payoff for them if they prevail is likely to be small.

A frequent source of controversy was the kind of settlement that provided "nonmonetary relief" in which a defendant agreed to make fuller disclosures in future or to put an independent member on its board—the sort of steps that might have been taken anyway. Also problematic was the "coupon settlement" in which the benefit for class members is the right to future discounts or rebates. After lawyers sued an airline for making changes in its frequent flier program, class members got benefits typified by a coupon for $75 off air tickets that cost at least three times that amount. The lawyers applied for fees of $25 million. Homeowners in a suit over plastic pipe got a coupon promising 8 percent off the price of new pipe if they replaced their plumbing in the future. The lawyers put in for $38 million in fees. Such settlements often claim to provide large supposed benefits for the class, yet in an economic sense it is obvious that coupons, on average, are not really "worth" their face value; otherwise a Sunday paper with $50 in coupons in it would sell for $50. (And, of course, companies frequently issue coupons entirely for free without having to be sued in hopes of winning customers' business.) The use of settlement coupons is often encumbered with conditions and red tape: The *Washington Post* found that of 96,754 coupons issued as part of the settlement of a case against one big financial services company, only two were redeemed.[29] In another case what was billed as a $10 million settlement fund actually paid out only $60,000.

One sign of the gradual convergence of mass tort and class-action law came in October 1999 when it was announced that the Toshiba Corporation of Japan was agreeing to lay out a staggering $2.1 billion to settle a class-action suit over a flaw in five million of its popular laptop computers. The flaw, involving the machines' floppy drive controller, might cause users to lose data under certain circumstances. The simplest of the steps the company was taking was to post on the World Wide Web, within a few days, a software fix that users could download to rectify the problem. In addition, it would offer coupons worth $100 to $225 off its products to owners, give $600 million in rebates (ranging from $210 to $443) to the owners of 1.8 million newer machines, and donate machines to charity.[30]

Many actual owners of Toshiba laptop machines, including many with much technical sophistication, reacted to the announcement of the settlement with gape-mouthed astonishment. Most had never noticed any such glitch, heard about it, or realized that they were being represented in a lawsuit over it. "We never had problems with the disk drives when we were using Toshiba laptops, and our experience with them goes back pretty far," said Jennifer Winch, an information technology (IT) manager at Pacific Gas and Electric (PG&E). But the lawyers said they had engaged experts who, they said, could demonstrate the data loss happening if you let them set up one of the machines just so. Toshiba, for its part, said it had managed to re-create the flaw only under rather unusual conditions, as when trying to save files to the floppy drive "while simultaneously doing one or two other intensive tasks, such as playing a game or watching a video." This was an unusual combination of demands to place on laptops in real life; in fact, the *Los Angeles Times* reported that "no consumer ever complained of losing data as a result of the glitch."[31] It was also certain that the glitch had not affected the many laptop users who never use their machines' floppy drives at all, relying instead on network or Internet hookups for data transfer. The kicker was that Toshiba had agreed to pay a cool $147 million in fees to Wayne Reaud's law firm of Reaud, Morgan & Quinn, which had filed the class action in its hometown of Beaumont, Texas, known as one of the nation's most plaintiff-friendly venues. The Reaud firm was known for its asbestos and tobacco work but was almost completely unfamiliar to lawyers specializing in high-tech matters.

Which was more than a straw in the wind: By the close of the 1990s, the class-action and personal-injury bar, historically quite distinct from each other, had began to blur if not quite merge. Not only had personal-injury firms like Reaud's jumped into "traditional" financial and product-refund class-actions, such as the Microsoft consumer antitrust suits, but several of the firms that dominated the financial class-action business, like Milberg Weiss and Lieff Cabraser, had plunged into tobacco and other mass tort work. The attraction was clear: If a lawyer could only get himself appointed to represent the right group, he might have more clients/subjects than many a real-world monarch. And a few courts were beginning to abandon completely the old reluctance to use outright class-action methods in personal-injury claims. In the celebrated case of *Engle v. R. J. Reynolds Tobacco Company*, a Miami judge certified Stanley and Susan Rosenblatt as the legal representatives of "All United States citizens and residents, and their survivors, who have suffered, presently suffer or who have died from diseases and medical conditions caused by their addiction to cigarettes that contain nicotine"—no matter what their medical condition or views on tobacco. A state appeals court agreed with Judge Robert Kaye that such a suit could be kept "manageable" in its dimensions, as class-action rules required, but did narrow the class to Florida smokers only.

Each year mass tort litigation has come to share more of the long-distinctive features of class-action litigation. There is the same frenzied rush by lawyers to file cases and stir up publicity at the very beginning of a controversy, not only for the sake of client recruitment, but to minimize the danger that a judge will proceed to certify some other lawyer as the one entitled to manage the action, a right with an economic value often quite out of proportion to the time and effort involved. Mass torts, like class actions, typically lead to the establishment of all-important "steering committees" to coordinate the plaintiffs' side. The custom in class actions is for the firm that wins the lead counsel appointment to divvy up the representational tasks with the others, as Stanford's Janet Cooper Alexander notes: ". . . a wise lead counsel is careful to assign work to all class counsel to permit them to earn fees from the case. They will then be less likely to object to lead counsel's appointment as lead in this and other cases."[32] The same patterns have emerged in mass tort cases.

And mass tort lawyers find themselves operating with considerable independence from their nominal (and passive) clients, just as class-action lawyers have always done. If they are handling a book of one thousand asbestos or breast-implant cases, after all, they can hardly alter their overall strategy to cater to one discontented client; and if they are settling the thousand cases in a batch, the client's right to approve a settlement tends to turn into a right to be handed the indicated settlement, with no back talk indicated. And with mass torts, very much as with class actions, policing attorneys' loyalty to their clients turns out to be no easy task. A suit on behalf of flight attendants who said they'd been harmed by smoke in airliner cabins (when smoking was still permitted) ended in a deal in which class members got zero dollars and zero cents, tobacco companies agreed to waive certain defenses against individual suits and set aside $300 million for a newly formed charity to be run under the lawyers' supervision, and $46 million in legal fees went to the lawyers themselves, husband-and-wife litigator team Stanley and Susan Rosenblatt. A brief by Public Citizen's Alan Morrison charged that the "gargantuan" fee "appears to be grossly excessive" and said the settlement "violates fundamental tenets of fairness and adequate representation," but the Florida courts approved it anyway.[33]

The common practice of settling mass tort claims in batches ("inventory" settlements) tests attorneys' loyalties in at least two ways. Often a defendant is willing to settle the strongest cases in the lawyers' inventory, such as the clients who are sickest or whose illnesses are most likely to be related to its product. But the lawyer may refuse to settle those cases unless the opponent pays a larger sum to settle the whole inventory. Is this a simple reflection of the truism that in unity there is strength, and that claimants will do better overall if they maintain solidarity with each other? Or does it sacrifice the best interests of the clients with the strongest cases for the sake of the overall client roster and the health of the practice? Equally troubling, many defendants are willing to accept a batch settlement that takes the form of having them write one overall check to settle the inventory, after which it's up to the plaintiffs' lawyers to divvy up the kitty among the various clients. The judge in such cases, notes one commentator, does not usually review "the manner in which plaintiffs' counsel allocates the settlement among the claimants."[34] The result is to leave attorneys a great deal of unsupervised discretion to steer money to some clients at the expense of others.

What was striking about the new mass tort lawyers was the extent to which—though not notably successful at putting their own ethical house in order—they were willing to step forward to offer their litigation clout as a substitute for their own judgment and authority of duly elected legislatures. In the tobacco and gun suits, they presented mass litigation as a way of achieving controls on product marketing that Congress and state legislatures had irresponsibly failed to enact. Scruggs and the other lawyers suing managed-care companies portrayed their lawsuits as a way of obtaining the "patients' bill of rights" that Congress had dragged its heels about enacting. Both gun and lead paint suits were pitched to child welfare and minority groups as a way of bypassing legislatures' reluctance to provide adequate funding for worthwhile urban programs. The reparations idea was turned into a plan for lawsuits against private companies after years in which it had made the rounds in African-American communities, without success, as a plan for getting the U.S. Congress to vote general appropriations to compensate the descendants of slaves.

This was the result of a new conception by powerful trial lawyers of their role in society. An article in *American Lawyer* on the origin of the gun suits reported that one of the suits' prime movers, prominent New Orleans trial lawyer

Wendell Gauthier, helped talk his colleagues into joining the effort—some had argued that gun makers didn't have enough money to be worth suing—because of the way the suit "fit with Gauthier's notion of the plaintiffs bar as a *de facto* fourth branch of government, one that achieved regulation through litigation where legislation failed."[35] Nor was he alone in this view. "Ask Scruggs if trial lawyers are trying to run America, and he doesn't bother to deny it," reported *Time* in its profile; " 'Somebody's got to do it,' he says, laughing."[36]

The lawyers were implicitly offering a new kind of deal to those disappointed in the political process. Are you failing to get what you want at the ballot box? Hire a lawyer instead. The linkage soon became quite explicit. Just after the year 2000 elections, the Sierra Club and a number of other big environmental groups announced that they were teaming up with trial lawyers to file lawsuits aimed at wresting the initiative in environmental policy away from the federal government's legislative and executive branches.[37] Fifteen law firms would kick in $50,000 apiece to underwrite the first round of suits, demanding from the Smithfield Companies, Inc., the largest raiser of hogs for the nation's breakfast tables, the remarkable sum of $148 billion (yes, "billion")—something like a hundred times the value of its assets. In order to avoid legal risks of this magnitude, it was reasoned, Smithfield and other companies in its position would agree to accept the sorts of environmental controls that officials in Washington had failed to order into effect. "This is a mechanism to bring an industry to the table," explained Florida tobacco veteran Mike Papantonio of Frederic Levin's firm. Expected later installments of the campaign would target chicken and beef producers, utilities, mining companies and so forth. The motivation for joining the alliance, the environmental groups were quite frank in noting, had been the recent national elections, which by installing the Republicans in power had cast doubt on the likelihood of getting any major expansion of environmental laws in the near future.

Any number of difficult social issues require the striking of some sort of balance among social goods: between, say, the boon of low chicken and pork prices and the tendency of feedlots to constitute a local nuisance, or between the cost-control advantages of managed health care and the danger that patients will be denied access to experimental therapies. Until very recently it had been thought that a duly elected legislature was in the best position to strike the right balance on such questions. Now the fights could be transferred to the courtroom, where the best lawyer could win. With the gun and tobacco suits and similar actions, wrote *The New Yorker*'s Peter Boyer, the new class of trial lawyers found itself "guiding the national agenda—a new means of public–policy making that can't be found in any civics book."[38] The reason it can't be found in any civics book, of course, has a lot to do with Article I, Section 1, of the U.S. Constitution, which specifies: "All legislative Powers herein granted shall be vested in a Congress of the United States, which shall consist of a Senate and House of Representatives."

According to supporters of the suits, that old way of doing things just doesn't work any more. "What has happened is that the legislatures . . . have failed," says attorney Coale.[39] "They failed to regulate tobacco. . . . Congress is not doing its job [and] lawyers are taking up the slack." "I think that, except in areas of the most compelling national interest, the political branches of government are incapable of solving pressing national problems,"[40] Scruggs told one audience. Hence the necessity—in the view of the new litigation elite and some of its admirers—of rescuing the process of lawmaking from the lawmakers. The *New York Times* hailed the gun suits as having "opened a new avenue for regulating the firearms industry without action from Congress,"[41] while a Clinton administration official said it proved "the public good [did not have to be] held hostage to legislative stalemate."[42] "Why was it important for trial lawyers to become this new arm of government?" asked Papantonio. "Because the new arm takes the place of an arm that's not working anymore."[43]

Such disdain for the democratic process has increasingly crept into mainstream debate. Thus the *New York Times* described litigation against gun makers as a response to "partisan gridlock" on the issue of national gun control, an odd choice of phrase since it implied that such measures had stalled despite the wish of all parties to move forward on them, whereas the actual reason for the measures' failure was that most lawmakers of the majority party did not support them in the first place. (As a pejorative description of the normal workings of democracy, "partisan gridlock" had a better sound to it than "We couldn't round up the votes to win no matter how we tried.")[44] A news analysis published in the *Wall Street Journal* is not much more lucid. It describes the new mass suits as having been filed "to try to settle controversies that couldn't be resolved through elective politics." Increasingly, asserts reporter Paul Barrett,

Americans "turn to courts when the traditional avenues of politics or activism seem obstructed," with the result that "[l]itigation has become the preferred route for resolving many political and social conflicts that once would have been handled in the political arena or the marketplace."[45]

All of which manages to beg nearly every pertinent question. "Preferred" by whom? (Not by the ones getting sued.) Has the country really "turned to" the lawyers, or have the lawyers thrust themselves into existing controversies for their own reasons? Are the lawsuits intended to "settle" or "resolve" the controversies, or just to impose one side's will in them? And how was our new elite of litigators planning to detect the point at which a controversy "seems obstructed" and can no longer be "resolved through elective politics," thus entitling it to override conventional methods of representative government, as distinct from the other possibility in the case, which is that the controversy just isn't being resolved in the way *it* prefers?

We were soon to find out.

Gunning for Democracy

In late 1998, when a group of big-city mayors got together to launch a massive campaign of lawsuits against gun manufacturers, they wanted it to be known that they weren't primarily concerned about the money. "Chicago would not take a penny if we could just get the handguns off the streets," said a spokesman for that city, whose suit was demanding a large number of pennies, $450 million' worth, to compensate it for the cost of responding to gun-related crime.[1] A lawyer involved in Miami's suit used almost identical language, saying it wasn't about anything to do with dollars and cents: "It is about getting unsafe guns off the street."[2]

Although the sums of money the cities were demanding in the suits were more than enough to drive every major gun maker into bankruptcy many times over, proponents also proclaimed that there was no reason for ordinary gun buyers to feel alarm. New York attorney general Eliot Spitzer claimed to have no quarrel with "those law abiding citizens who own guns."[3] "This isn't about . . . taking guns away from hunters," added a supporter of Detroit's courtroom action, which also demanded hundreds of millions of dollars.[4] Then-president Bill Clinton, who backed the suits, was quoted as saying his "goal [in doing so] wasn't to 'bankrupt' gun companies, but to reform them."[5] Attorney John Coale, a spokesman for the suits, dismissed concerns that legitimate purchasers might find it impossible to obtain handguns: "It can't be done, and it's not a motive, because as long as lawful citizens want to buy handguns, and as long as the market's there, there's going to be someone filling it."[6]

It used to be that lawyers would go to some lengths to deny the imputation that they had filed a lawsuit for merely tactical reasons, just to strong-arm their adversaries into some unrelated concession, without actually intending to get the "relief" they were asking for from the court. But times had changed, to the point where the public relations campaign on behalf of the municipal gun suits actually made a point of stressing their insincerity: Just because the cities were demanding billions of dollars didn't mean those demands should be taken at face value. "The real goal of the litigation," one news account in the January 6, 2000, *Wall Street Journal* reassured readers, "isn't large damage awards but a settlement under which the industry would agree to more stringent regulation in an effort to keep guns out of the wrong hands."[7] Once Smith & Wesson (S&W), Glock, Beretta, and the rest accepted the needed controls that Congress and state legislatures had so irresponsibly failed to enact, they might be allowed to resume normal commercial life, or so it seemed from the many pious assurances.

It was the tobacco model all over again, the gun opponents said. Once again the machinations of a powerful industry had kept lawmakers from heeding a clear consensus among educated opinion that a dangerous product needed to be restricted and made unavailable to children. "The failure of Congress to address social problems in any meaningful way had left a void," opined litigator Daniel Abel of Florida's Levin Papantonio, active in both the tobacco and the gun rounds.[8] "The legislature has failed," proclaimed spokesman/attorney John Coale. The litigation, Coale commented later, "should be viewed as an invitation to start a discourse about social problems." Harvard's Laurence Tribe noted that "the more natural and democratic alternative of getting the legislature to do something seems to be ruled out by the lobbying power of the industry."[9] As another lawyer high-fived after winning a round in one of the first efforts to achieve gun control through litigation, New York's *Hamilton v. Accu-Tek:* "You don't need a legislative majority to file a lawsuit."[10]

It wasn't as if there was any real debate to be had on the gun issue anyway, the gun opponents seemed to think. After all, there was no point trying to argue with unwashed and uncouth "gun nuts." Everyone agreed that there were far too many shootings in America: How could anyone deny that taking guns out of circulation would reduce the toll? Indeed, advocates were beginning to treat firearms as a public health issue, to "medicalize" the problem, as had worked so well with tobacco and liquor. Thus *The New Yorker,* in its profile of the lawyers behind the suits, described Brady Campaign/Handgun Control, Inc., attorney Dennis Henigan as believing that "it is imperative to steer the argument about guns away from the problematic area of criminal use, with its inconvenient focus on criminals";[11] instead "guns should be thought of as pathogens, and gun ownership, perhaps, as a disease." That certainly cinched the illegitimacy of the other side's position: If gun enthusiasts were disease carriers, then there wasn't any more need to listen to them than if they were running around claiming that polio or cholera had their good points.

The mayors' sudden courtroom onslaught was widely reported as if it was something new and surprising, but in fact it had been preceded by years of careful groundwork. The plaintiffs' bar searches out deep-pocketed institutions to sue for all varieties of human misery and woe, and one of the most prominent categories of such misery consists of the aftermath of acts of deliberate crime and violence. Until fairly recently, however, American courts were relatively hostile to most requests that they shift blame for an armed robbery, drive-by gang shoot-out, or depressive suicide away from the actual perpetrator and onto one or another corporation for not preventing it. Not only did judges hew to old notions of individual responsibility, but they basically doubted the practicality of wide-ranging liability based on failure to prevent. As far as the role of gun makers went, authoritative legal treatises routinely cited guns (as they did tobacco) as a product whose injuriousness was in itself no grounds for liability given its open and obvious quality. Indeed, consumers sought out guns for their injurious nature; you might have a legal claim against a manufacturer if the gun it sold you failed to emit a bullet at high velocity when you pulled the trigger, but not if it did exactly what was promised.

The spectacular expansion of liability law in the 1960s and 1970s gave trial lawyers much more promising material to work with. Judges embraced new doctrines of *negligent security*, allowing victims of mugging or rape on commercial property to sue landlords and mall owners on the grounds that installing better lighting or hiring more parking-lot guards might have prevented the crime. Courts also liberalized product liability law in a great many ways, such as by making it much easier to sue manufacturers over *foreseeable misuse* of their products. Liberal-leaning law reviews published more articles proposing a widening of rights to sue gun makers, nor was much published on the opposite side— the atmosphere in law schools (like that in left-liberal academia generally) being unsympathetic to private gun ownership. Member attorneys of the Association of Trial Lawyers of America (ATLA) maintained a working group on the subject to share information and coordinate suits against gun makers. In 1995, ATLA cosponsored a conference on the subject in partnership with the Johns Hopkins Center for Gun Policy and Research, which had been founded by a personal-injury attorney who quit practice "to educate both the public-health community and trial lawyers" (as one profile put it) about what litigation could do to disarm America.[12] Hundreds of attorneys attended.

The ATLA conference was well timed, because the gun-control movement, as of 1995, had encountered an abrupt end to a long streak of successes in the conventional legislative process. The year 1994, or most of it at least, had been one of impressive gains for gun controllers: Congress passed both the "Brady bill," mandating nationwide background checks of gun purchasers, and a ban on the type of guns controversially labeled "assault weapons." That fall, however, outraged progun forces had mounted their biggest political mobilization ever, which contributed importantly to the Republicans' stunning November 1994 capture of both houses of Congress for the first time in decades. Capitol Hill doors began closing to the antigun cause, not only because the new GOP leadership was disinclined to offend one of the constituencies that had helped it reach office, but because moderate Democrats, unhappy at the way the issue had cost them votes, were extra wary about exposing themselves to more such disasters in future.[13] On top of it all, the federal courts proceeded to strike down key portions of the Brady bill as unconstitutional. It all provided a perfect opportunity to interest antigun activists in litigation strategies that bypassed legislatures.

At the same time, new and media-savvy leadership began moving to the fore in the gun-control movement. A group called the Violence Policy Center (VPC) was formed, its executive director having previously worked as a key Capitol Hill lobbyist against product-liability reform. Among VPC's first projects was an effort to enlist existing gun-control activists into the trial lawyer–backed coalition against curbs on product-liability litigation, on the grounds that such curbs might, at some point in the future, impede suits against gun makers. The lawyers' prize catch, however, was the Brady Campaign–affiliated Handgun Control, Inc.

(HCI), easily the highest profile gun-control group by virtue of the recognizability of its spokesfigures Sarah and Jim Brady, the latter wounded during the attempted assassination of former president Ronald Reagan. The HCI/Brady Campaign introduced a large litigation arm, in 1983 known as the Center to Prevent Handgun Violence (CPHV), which, under the direction of attorney Dennis Henigan, was to throw itself wholeheartedly into the lawsuit campaign, representing many of the cities that were to sue.

As its ties to the litigation lobby multiplied, the gun-control movement began to alter its policy agenda and, in particular, its favored choice of opponents. In the past most of the focus of new lawmaking was on the parties to the sales transaction—that is, dealers and individual buyers. Among key proposals were mandatory waiting periods; sales record keeping, and buyer background checks; identification and exclusion of more categories of unsuitable buyers; and so forth. From the trial lawyers' point of view, however, it was at best a waste of effort to campaign against rinky-dink dealers and near-assetless individual buyers when much deeper pockets could be found among gun manufacturers. As the HCI/Brady Campaign and VPC took over leadership roles within the gun-control movement, manufacturers soon moved from the periphery to the center of antigun demonology. Why did unattended children get into gun accidents? Up until lately the guiltiest parties were thought to be irresponsible parents who had been careless about gun storage, but now we were told by the litigationists that the fault was on the part of the manufacturers for failing to ship the guns equipped with "trigger locks" in the first place. Why did urban gang members find it so easy to lay their hands on guns? We might once have blamed shifty dealers who traded under the counter, but now it was found to be the gun makers' fault for having "flooded" the market with guns and having displayed "willful blindness" to what happened after they left the manufacturers' hands. In fact, the misbehavior of dealers in general really should be charged to the manufacturers' perfidy, since it was within the gun makers' power to insist that their distributors adhere to rigid codes of conduct on pain of cutting off their future supply. With a bit of ingenuity, the litigators could find ways to blame a manufacturer for pretty much the entire later history of a gun after it left the factory.

Historically, there are good reasons why gun manufacturers have never exercised a high degree of control over the eventual disposition of their wares. Since firearms are among the most durable of all consumer goods and are seldom discarded, it has long been the case that a large share of all weapons wind up changing hands in used condition, either in sales between individual owners, by dealers who trade in used guns, or as surplus after use in the police or military. Nor were manufacturers in a position to dictate terms to dealers or consumers when it came to sales of brand-new guns. Gun owners as a group are highly knowledgeable about their product, swap expertise constantly through a multitude of clubs and publications, and readily switch to different brands if one manufacturer tries to foist something on them they don't much care for. Even those of us willing to believe that the marketing wiles of tobacco companies are what lead people to smoke may find it hard to swallow the notion that it is gun ads that account for most decisions to become a gun owner. Gun-advertising budgets, unlike those for tobacco promotion, are relatively small, and most gun ads appear in specialty publications aimed at those already interested in the product.

In fact, gun companies had and have remarkably little in common with tobacco companies, other than being detested by many of the same people. Size? At $61 billion in sales, Philip Morris was one of the ten biggest industrial firms in America, while the nation's gun manufacturers (as firearms scholar David Kopel has pointed out) would not be big enough to qualify for the Fortune 500 list even if you combined them all into a single company.[14] Sophistication? Much of the gun-making business was typified by family-owned Freedom Arms Inc. in the town of Freedom, Wyoming, whose thirty-five employees shipped about two thousand modernized Western six-shooters a year to collectors and enthusiasts who place orders half a year or more in advance. Political clout? Tobacco companies had been major political players for decades, while gun makers counted for little in political circles, and few of them really knew the political ropes even in their home states. (For historical reasons, several big gun makers had their headquarters in Connecticut and Massachusetts, which did nothing to prevent the politicians of those states from being among the most antigun in the country.)

What the gun lobby did have, and the tobacco lobby lacks, is a large body of grassroots consumers, vigilant and organized for collective action as are few groups in American politics. Again and again, the lawyers suing the gun industry failed to understand (or pretended not to understand) that America's intense "gun culture" has little more to do with the companies that make actual guns than its golf culture has to do with the companies that make balls, tees, and putting irons, or than its parenting culture has to do with the makers of diapers and cribs, or than its art culture has to do with the makers of easels and tubes of paint. The "gun culture" is based, instead, on countless clubs, associations, circles of friends, shooting ranges, veterans' associations, and police auxiliaries, instructors, outfitters, hunting guides, farmers, ranchers, outdoorsmen, military and historical collectors and enthusiasts, small dealers, accessory makers, gun magazine publishers, persons in the security trade, and on and on. Dennis Henigan, of the Brady Campaign, denounced the National Rifle Association (NRA) as "mouthpieces" for gun manufacturers, almost as off-base and absurdly as the atheist who accuses organized religion of being a front for the interests of the makers of candles, vestments, hymn books, ewers, and fonts.[15]

Within a year or two of the launch of the municipal litigation campaign, more than thirty cities and counties around the country had signed retainers giving the lawyers wide authority to pursue suits against gun makers on their behalf and generally promising them a share of any damages obtained. As reporters soon established, it was the outside trial lawyers and not the city mayors who had provided the impetus for the suits by pitching the idea at presentations to city officials behind closed doors.[16] The sameness of the rhetoric issuing from city representatives in newspapers around the country suggested that the nationwide talking points were also being issued from a central dispatching headquarters.

Why did the litigators pick mayors as the politicos to work with this time, rather than picking the state attorneys general again? The ostensible reason was that the mayors cared more about crime than anyone else, since their cities suffered from some of the nation's highest crime rates. (Gun maker–bashing, of course, conveniently served to shift the blame for urban mayhem away from their own failures of governance.) More important as a political explanation, perhaps, is that the attorneys general have to run for election before statewide electorates that, unlike the mayors' citywide electorates, contain large progun constituencies who might organize against them at the next election. As if to prove this theory, Philadelphia mayor Ed Rendell made initial signals as if to join the gun suits, then shelved the idea when he decided he wanted to run for statewide Pennsylvania office, gun supporters being numerous in rural parts of the state. His successor as mayor, John Street, with no such ambitions, proceeded to sign the city up. Among attorneys general, only New York's Eliot Spitzer actually joined the litigation, and even he went out of his way trying to reassure upstate hunters that the suits didn't really threaten gun availability. (Connecticut's Richard Blumenthal cheered the campaign on but refrained from filing.) Even had a few more attorneys general been recruited, the number would not have been sufficient, by itself, to create the sort of pile-on momentum seen in tobacco, in which the sheer mass of filings tends to compel settlement in and of itself.

A drawback of using mayors, of course, was that they so obviously did not represent any sort of cross section of American public opinion as a whole. In most instances, they were out of step even with opinions in their own state, particularly in the case of the mayors of such southern cities as New Orleans, Atlanta, and Miami, who stood virtually no chance of convincing the respective state legislatures of Louisiana, Georgia, and Florida to enact sweeping gun controls. But the gun suits' implicit message was that big cities were entitled to obtain certain kinds of nationwide gun regulation no matter what the rest of the country happened to think of the matter. They had a right to bring gun selling in other people's towns and states under control, the reasoning went, because it had an effect on them—some of the guns sold elsewhere wound up being used on their turf.

This logic was remarkable in its implications. Even at the height of prohibitionist fervor, it had been widely assumed that the city fathers of a hypothetical Drytown, Utah, could ban liquor sales only within their own town's limits and had no authority to reach out to close or regulate the saloons of nearby Wetville, Nevada, any more than the government of Uruguay could decree the abolition of the British monarchy. It mattered not at all that Drytown's scofflaw citizenry was slaking its thirst with contraband potables smuggled in from its looser living neighbors. If Drytown wanted Wetville's liquor trade curbed, it would have to appeal to lawmakers at the federal level of our system of government, getting the U.S. Congress to pass a federal law or constitutional amendment or both. It could not just ask the hometown judge in its own courthouse to teach the Wetville saloon keepers a lesson, by way of damage verdicts or otherwise.

But now the cities' lawyers had come up with various new litigation theories aimed at doing just that. There was the theory of "negligent distribution," for example, which allowed the city of Chicago to claim that it had suffered legally cognizable injury from the activities of the suburban gun shops that did a thriving business just beyond its borders. Whether or not these stores were complying with the letter of federal and state law, the city said, gun manufacturers had committed a legal wrong in "oversupplying" them with more guns than the residents of the shops' own neighborhoods were likely to use. The manufacturers should have known, the specious argument went, that some portion of those guns were destined for unlicensed use in the city.

How could a manufacturer live up to a pledge to cease "oversupplying"? Presumably it would need to come with an estimate of how many of its brand of guns suburbanites would be expected to buy for their own account. Then it would refuse to ship any more than that number, even if the result was to cut off dealers by July—tough luck, it would have to say to them (and they to late-coming customers), no more shipments for you till January. Yet such a policy would not in itself prevent many of the guns sold in the first six months of the year from finding their way into the nearby city. At the same time it would deprive suburban buyers of access to guns that it was perfectly lawful for them to buy.

In fact, however, the numerical calculation of annually permitted gun sales would be far more complicated than this, since a gun company does not have a monopoly on the market. An upward blip in demand might simply mean that one company's brand was becoming more popular, winning higher market share at the expense of a competitor, which would not saddle it with the guilt of "oversupplying." How would a company entering the market for the first time, or introducing a new product line, know that it was avoiding the dreaded form of misconduct? The only way companies could know they had behaved legally would be to get in touch with their competitors to compare sales figures and coordinate sales to keep the overall volume to a certain level—and *that*, of course, would constitute a felony antitrust violation for which the executives could be sent away.

Also likely to engender sued-if-you-do, sued-if-you-don't situations were demands in various cities' suits that manufacturers take into account demographic features of neighborhoods, or of otherwise lawful purchasers, which purportedly could serve as tip-offs of future gun misuse. Chicago's complaint alleged that it was an element of manufacturers' misconduct to have sold guns in high-crime neighborhoods. But there have been few offenses more widely denounced by civil-rights litigators in recent years than "redlining" and "profiling," in which companies are accused of refusing to do business in certain neighborhoods or of putting some of their customers under closer scrutiny than others or demanding more documentation for their purchases based on arbitrary characteristics of appearance or place of origin. One expert witness in gun litigation has suggested, for instance, that gun sellers should be on the alert for "buyers who appear in unkempt clothing and have a slovenly appearance."[17] Then there were the demands that gun manufacturers invade their customers' privacy. The Chicago lawsuit, for example (notes UCLA's Eugene Volokh), asked that manufacturers be made to check out prospective customers' residences[18] and if they live in Chicago, demand proof that they have places to store the gun outside of town—the ramifications for privacy being enough to boggle the mind.

All the lawsuits demanded that gun companies adopt practices that were in no way required either by federal or state law; in some cases, lawmakers at both levels of government had considered and pointedly rejected such measures. Florida lawmakers, for example, could hardly have made it clearer that they neither wished to enact major gun controls themselves nor trusted the city of Miami to do so: In 1987, they had passed a law specifically forbidding any city within the state from regulating the gun business. Which did not in the least deter Miami-Dade mayor Alex Penelas, who (reported Reuters) "said he was using the courts in an attempt to crack down on the gun industry because the Florida legislature refused to do so. 'Every year that I've gone to the legislature we have basically been told to take our case elsewhere,' he said"—"take our case elsewhere," presumably being a less blunt way of saying "scram."[19] Mayor Penelas almost seemed to be counting the suits' antidemocratic character as a point in their favor—as if people would think it more natural and understandable for him to run to court precisely *because* the democratically elected officials of his state had declined to give him his way in the ordinary lawmaking process.

Finally, there were all the ways the suits demanded that guns be redesigned to include new features. Thus manufacturers were flayed for not incorporating into their designs "gun locks"—and isn't it a good idea to lock up something as dangerous as a gun? They had unconscionably omitted "child proofing"—didn't we require that kind of protection on aspirin bottles? They had also failed to develop and market a new generation of "smart guns," which would be personalized so as to prevent them from being fired by anyone else.

In each of these instances the cities and their litigators were attempting to punish gun makers for not foisting on their customers features that few of those customers wished to have, and some of which suffered from the further inconvenience of not yet having been invented. It is a trivial matter, for example, to throw in an inexpensive trigger lock when a gun is sold, so long as one accepts that many users, once they disengage the lock, will never get around to reengaging it. (In practice, many gun enthusiasts favor exterior lockable cases for guns they want to keep secure when not in use, as opposed to locks that require the insertion of a device into the gun's mechanism.) What the cities' lawyers had in mind, however, was something far more ambitious: a method of making a gun's mechanism relock automatically when it was left idle, most likely through some combination of an integral trigger block, timer, and combination lock. The obvious problem was that few home owners, on hearing the burglar ascending the stairs, wanted to take the time to tap in a sequence of numbers on a keypad in the dark, assuming they could remember the sequence. The cachet of gun locks began to fade in the press after a 1998 mayors' meeting at which attorney Henigan offered to show how easy it was to activate a gun with a trigger lock in a hurry, but couldn't get the thing to work.[20] Maryland governor Parris Glendening ran into a similar embarrassment at a later press conference when he tried to demonstrate a similar concept, "locking magazines."[21]

To the extent that there is one big institutional influence on the direction taken by gun design, it is the government itself, given the prominent buying role of police departments and the military. In their capacity as major purchasers of guns for police use, the cities filing the gun suits had shown very little interest in the safety technologies their lawyers now had begun claiming were so vital. Even more significant, the cities also filled a role as some of the nation's biggest *suppliers* of guns, releasing onto the resale market large quantities of both police surplus weapons and weaponry seized from lawbreakers.

When the press got wind of this juicy news, as it soon did, the mayors and their litigators ran into some of their worst publicity yet. New Orleans, for example, at the very moment of announcing its first-in-the-country gun suit ("We have been so focused here in New Orleans on getting guns off the street and protecting our citizens," Mayor Marc Morial explained at a press conference)[22] had just finished scoring one of the biggest gun-resale deals ever when it sold through a broker some 7,300 guns, including TEC-9s and various other semiautomatics whose importation and manufacture Congress had banned in 1994. And Detroit unloaded a remarkable thirteen-plus tons of weaponry not long before filing its suit. In these and other cases, the cities had followed few if any of the safeguards that their lawyers now claimed were absolutely obligatory for any responsible

gun seller.[23] One way of lessening the risk that surplus police guns will fall into criminal hands, for example, is to
stipulate that they be resold only to other police departments. But such a stipulation can cut by half the amount
used weapons fetch on the market, so the authorities in
New Orleans, Boston, and elsewhere had not seen fit to
impose it. Safety locks? Only two of the 7,300 guns that
New Orleans sold were equipped with them. If the lawyers'
theories were to be taken seriously, the cities would be in
danger of being dragged to court as defendants, not plaintiffs. The same was true of the state of Connecticut, whose
attorney general Richard Blumenthal took a prominent role
in advancing the gun litigation. As recently as 1990, the
state government had actually been in the business of *subsidizing* gun making, allocating $25 million in state pension
money in a disastrous venture into "social investment" intended to keep locally based Colt in the gun-making business. When Colt guns later were used in shootings, where
was the lawyer to accuse the state of having made it possible?

As in the tobacco case, "recoupment" actions to recover
government outlays served as the centerpiece of the gun
offensive, but an important part of the strategy was to come
up with as many other inventive theories of liability as possible, precedent or no. These included, for example, the
notion that guns were a legal "nuisance" akin to drifting
smoke or stray animals. As attorney Dennis Henigan put it,
"What you really want is a diversity of cases in lots of different regions, lots of different courts to create the greatest

threat of liability."[24] And who was to say one of the new litigation theories could not break through, if assigned the right judge, and then look legitimate in retrospect? The suits, as Kopel noted, were also "cleverly structured to prevent the defendants from filing a motion to consolidate the cases,"[25] thus reducing defense costs; and the cities generally refrained from suing ammunition manufacturers, a much wealthier group of companies (one is DuPont) who, as Kopel notes, "could easily afford to pay for lawyers to handle every case from start to finish."

Among gun makers proper, the cities' attack was quite indiscriminate: They sued companies that made the sort of handguns that often turn up at urban crime scenes but also those that made the sorts of hunting, sporting, and historical weaponry seldom favored by modern criminals, such as Freedom Arms with its Western six-shooters. The cities and their litigators sued companies that had won praise for their efforts to improve gun safety and those that had a strong orientation toward police or military supply. As in the tobacco round, the city litigators also named as defendants such trade associations and industry groups as the American Shooting Sports Council, the National Shooting Sports Foundation, and the Sporting Arms and Ammunition Manufacturers' Institute. Although most courts quickly dismissed the trade associations from the cases, the litigation still served to chill advocacy: Anyone thinking of participating in such associations had to worry that every confidential memo they might write would, in future, have to be turned over to a hostile lawyer.

Naturally, the burden of response faced by gun makers themselves was crushing. Colt CEO William Keys told a

U.S. Senate hearing that his company faced "discovery requests seeking virtually every document in Colt's possession," the result being "astronomical" costs as well as vast distraction of management from the tasks of running a company.[26] "As in the war against tobacco, winning in court isn't necessarily the objective of the lawyers," observed the *New Yorker*'s Peter Boyer in an article on the strategy behind the gun suits.[27] Defending against just twenty suits, "according to some estimates, could cost the gun manufacturers as much as a million dollars a day." (The lawyers soon had thirty such suits going.) "The legal fees alone are enough to bankrupt the industry," boasted spokeslawyer Coale. "The pressure is going to be on."[28]

Indeed, the imbalance in financial resources between the two sides was remarkable. On the one side were thinly capitalized, often family-owned enterprises; on the other side, enormous municipal administrations like those of Chicago, Atlanta, and Detroit, represented by lawyers of extraordinary wealth like Ron Motley, Wendell Gauthier, and Stanley Chesley, men whose trophy investments often included sports teams and who could easily have afforded to buy whole gun companies as Christmas presents for their kids. As if that weren't enough, a number of extremely well-heeled foundations got into the act on the plaintiffs' side, despite the seeming coals-to-Newcastle redundancy of allocating philanthropic funds to a cause that American trial lawyers were already pursuing for profit. Among them was the New York–based Center on Crime, Communities & Culture endowed by billionaire financier George Soros.

Given America's lack of a loser-pays rule, it didn't matter whether the gun companies were completely vindicated at the end: They could expect no restitution from their well-off tormentors. "We are a small company," said the head of a California gun maker who estimated his legal bills were running at $50,000 to $100,000 a month. "We're going to go broke."[29] Indeed, several handgun makers filed for bankruptcy before any of the cases reached judgment on the merits; a lawyer for one said its owner "didn't have even the beginning of the resources to pay the legal fees."[30] (When Southern California's Lorcin closed its doors after having earlier filed for protection from creditors, a Brady Campaign spokesman expressed the pile-it-on wish that its owner would be held personally liable for any judgments against the company.) Strangely, none of this kept the plaintiffs' side from adopting the same brave pose that had worked so well for antitobacco forces, as beleaguered critics of an all-powerful industry. "The courts are the place where David and Goliath can go at it and David can win," said director Nancy Mahon of Soros's antigun project: "That's why the gun industry is so spooked by this suit." The *Washington Post* reported the comment straight up, apparently not moved to laughter at the image of the Soros team trying to pose as fiscal underdogs.[31]

The grind-'em-down strategy had some prospects of working, even if—as soon proved to be the case—most judges found the gun suits unpersuasive. In the first case to reach a decision on the merits, Ohio judge Robert Ruehlman crisply dismissed Cincinnati's lawsuit as "an improper attempt to have this Court substitute its judgment for that of the Legislature," especially egregious given that the risks associated with firearms were "open and obvious and matters of common knowledge." An appeals court unanimously agreed, comparing the suit to the "absurdity" of suing the makers of kitchen matches over arson. Other judges soon threw out the suits by Chicago, Bridgeport, Miami, Camden, New Orleans, and Philadelphia. On the other hand, lawyers representing Detroit, Atlanta, Boston, Newark, and Cleveland managed to dodge early dismissal of their suits, and Ohio's high court reinstated Cincinnati's suit; although most or all of these were expected to go down to eventual defeat, it was hard to be sure that having taken out so many lottery tickets in so many states the plaintiffs' side might not win a couple before the right judges. With each state court system and each jury a new authority free to find worthy of punishment what its predecessors have found not so, our system of mass litigation resembles a firing squad, in which all the lawyers need is for one or two of the sharp-shooters to point as they're told.

The lesson was not lost on liability insurers and lenders, both of which groups were soon observed to be fleeing the firearms market as fast as they could. Vice president Robert Hartwig of the Insurance Information Institute said the unavailability of new liability coverage for the industry was hardly surprising: "It's like trying to insure a house when it's in the path of an oncoming hurricane."[32] New England shotgun maker Harrington & Richardson (H&R 1871, Inc.) announced it would stop making handguns "because of the litigation-driven increases in the cost of liability insurance and shipping."[33] Even Colt, storied in the history books since Sam Colt invented the revolver, found itself unable to line up adequate financing for its operations. It proceeded to lay off a large part of its workforce and drop most of its civilian handgun lines, facing $3 million in legal bills for the first year of the suits alone.[34] (Pentagon officials were worried about the impact of the company's woes on military readiness since it was the sole supplier of the M-4 carbine and one of two suppliers of the M-16 rifle.) Ironically, an early casualty was Colt's venture aimed at developing a smart gun: One of its owners was quoted as saying that "potential punitive damages scared away needed outside investors."[35] That wasn't the only backfire effect as far as safety innovation went: One of the first companies to announce a planned exit from the U.S. firearms market was Switzerland's SIG, which had won plaudits by offering the first handgun with a number-code locking system.[36]

Once upon a time it was considered grossly unethical to inflict litigation costs on an opponent for tactical advantage, but few gun-suit supporters seemed to feel any qualms about it. The *Atlanta Journal-Constitution* approvingly noted that the suits "have already forced some gun makers to the bargaining table" because they "can't afford lengthy courtroom battles."[37] And if the defendants did go broke, wasn't it really their own fault, since they could have chosen to capitulate before that point? In some ways the gun-control advocates had come to embrace a kind of reasoning very similar to that of the gun enthusiasts they so abhorred. The reason to keep a loaded gun in the nightstand, according to the self-defense literature, is not because you want to shoot the prowler but because it lets you "control the situation," getting him to back off or hold still until the authorities can take charge. Some of the city administrations apparently imagined that brandishing their weapons would be enough to prevail, without actually having to use them. In each case, of course, the calculation may go awry, and

the threat of destructive force has to be turned into a reality—the situation not being quite as much under control
as the side with the weapon had hoped.

Irrationally or not, more than a few gun makers vowed
to go down fighting. "It may bankrupt us, but we are never
going to settle,"[38] said Bob Baker of Freedom Arms in Wyoming, who had had to lay off twelve of his thirty-five employees after running up more than $200,000 in legal bills
in little more than a year. Hi-Point Firearms owner Tom
Deeb told a reporter that at one point he "seriously considering going out of business because of the lawsuits, but
has since changed his mind. 'I think what they're doing is
wrong,' he said . . . 'Even if it breaks me, I'm going to stick
it out and do everything I can to keep my people working.' "[39]

If the mighty tobacco industry decided to cut a deal under
similar circumstances, why wouldn't the puny gun industry?
It was a reasonable question, but once again the differences
between tobacco and gun makers were more important than
the similarities.

Tobacco companies, despite their image as unyielding, in
fact resembled other big business lobbies in their willingness to resolve political disputes through compromises
based on pocketbook convenience. Their record was one
of being willing to live with many tinkering sorts of
changes—tax hikes, segregation or banishment of smokers
at restaurants and public places, even a ban on broadcast
tobacco ads—so long as the results were consistent with the
economic viability of their trade. But gun company execu-

tives either believed themselves, or at least were aware that many of their customers believed, in the idea of individual firearms' ownership as a constitutional right reflecting the fundamental human right to self-defense, a position intrinsically less amenable to compromise. The gun issue was far more long-standing, acrimonious, and salient in American politics than the tobacco issue precisely because its grassroots advocates on both sides had never conceived it as a pocketbook matter: It was pure principle.

For a brief moment, nonetheless, it looked as if the cities might be vindicated in expecting a rapid capitulation. On March 17, 2000, Clinton administration housing secretary Andrew Cuomo unveiled, with great fanfare, what he called "the most important announcement"[40] of his tenure: a proposed settlement his department had brokered with the nation's biggest gun maker, Smith & Wesson (S&W). In exchange for getting the cities to relent in their suits, S&W would agree to a long list of demands. On the design side, it agreed to install trigger locks on its guns, whether or not its customers wanted them, and it would finish developing a "smart gun" within three years. The company also agreed to marketing restrictions, the gist of which was to impose tight new regulations on its independent dealers. On pain of no longer being allowed to carry the company's product line, these dealers would have to agree to put their employees through approved training courses, turn away buyers unless they agreed to go through certified safety courses before taking possession of their purchases, allow regulators warrantless access to many of their records despite the likely intrusion that would mean for both their and their customers' privacy, refrain from selling various perfectly lawful weapons put out by other manufacturers, which the Clinton administration disliked but had not succeeded in getting Congress to ban, and avoid selling at gun shows unless the other dealers in attendance had submitted to various controls, which again went beyond anything in federal law.

Dealers and individual gun owners, neither of whom had been represented in the negotiating room, voiced immediate outrage, but S&W CEO Edward Shultz hoped they and other constituencies would be understanding of his company's plight: The alternative, he said, was to "go out of business paying for lawsuits."[41] And it wasn't as if they would necessarily get a better shake from other manufacturers: Clinton administration officials made clear that they expected other companies to surrender on similar terms. Once enough of them did so, the settlement further provided, ordinary gun designs would be withdrawn from the market, leaving consumers no choice but to accept the products and practices the authorities had decided were best for them. Police forces, however, would get an exemption, allowing them to go on buying the old designs; after all, cops need their guns to work reliably.

Ambitiously, the S&W settlement set out a blueprint for a five-member oversight commission that would wield extensive power over industry practices in perpetuity. In effect, it aimed to create a completely new national regulatory agency to bypass the long-established U.S. Bureau of Alcohol, Tobacco and Firearms (ATF), which federal law had already assigned the national gun-regulation beat (ATF got little respect from either side in the gun wars, with antigun forces considering it ineffective, and the progun side seeing it as too ready to trample the rights of owners and dealers).

Of the new commission's five members, the plaintiffs' side in the litigation would get to pick an outright three-member majority: Cities and counties that had joined the lawsuit would pick two, and "state parties," a list that was expected to grow beyond the single entry of New York, would pick one. Of the remaining two-member minority, one seat was to be filled by a nominee of the federal ATF and the other by gun makers.

The structure of the proposed oversight commission is significant for the light it casts on the philosophy of governance of the deal's drafters, who, in essence, installed their side in a role of permanently entrenched sovereignty that might win the envy of a one-party Ruritanian autocrat. Though effectively governmental in its powers, the commission would escape the organization chart of any level of government and thus dodge all need for routine disclosures and reporting about its operations, legislative oversight, and budgeting pressures. Only one of its five incumbent seat holders would even indirectly and theoretically be answerable to a nationwide electorate, namely the one nominated by the ATF, whose director can be replaced at some point by the voters as part of a change in federal administration. The working majority on the panel would be held by the three members appointed by lawsuit "parties," however, and the majority of the American people could not be sure of dislodging these suzerains no matter what combination of votes it chose to cast in the future. Cities like Miami and Bridgeport, whose suits had already been thrown out as meritless, *would* get prominent roles in devising the new rules of the game to govern gun selling; huge and populous tracts of the country that had refrained from suing would be excluded from a role in selecting the ruling junta. The bothers of democratic "gridlock" would be avoided by giving a permanently entrenched minority the power to rule the majority indefinitely.

After market leader S&W surrendered, many gun-control advocates expected a quick mop-up of the rest of the industry, perhaps believing their own rhetoric about how the powerful gun makers really "control" the market and jerk around consumers and dealers. But it didn't work out that way. Customers deserted S&W in droves, vowing never again to buy its guns. Dealers dropped the line rather than have their business practices dictated to them. Shooting-sports organizers told the renegade firm it was no longer welcome at competitions. The company soon lost its number-one position in the market. Adding insult to injury, most police departments spurned appeals from Andrew Cuomo's Department of Housing and Urban Development (HUD) secretary to back up the deal by switching to S&W guns in police procurement. Rank-and-file cops tended to see such brands as Glock, Beretta, and SIG Sauer as more accurate, easy to use, and durable, and were not happy at the idea of making their personal safety just another chip for Cuomo to trade in his wheeling and dealing. "Politics aren't going to enter into how we choose our firearms," said an L.A. County police official. "When you think of what we do for a living, we just can't take chances."[42] The head of the Fraternal Order of Police (FOP) made similar comments.

With the fate of the settlement hanging in the balance, the politicians began to show their most brutal face. Cuomo menaced gun makers, saying that unless they gave up they'd suffer "death by a thousand cuts."[43] "If you don't sign," threatened New York's Spitzer, referring to holdout Glock, "your bankruptcy lawyers will be knocking at your door."[44] (A Spitzer flack later claimed his boss was referring to the costs to the company of losing police business.) Spitzer and his fellow hyperactive attorney general Richard Blumenthal of Connecticut announced that they intended to sue the other gun makers for the supposed offense of shunning S&W in business dealings; they had, for example, halted joint legal defense efforts with the turncoat company given the new divergence between its legal interests and theirs. This was surely the first antitrust action in history aimed at punishing smaller companies for not cooperating with the largest company in the market in an agreement restraining trade. Blumenthal admitted that, in the words of a news account, he "didn't have solid evidence of any illegal behavior"; the point was sheer intimidation.[45]

None of it worked. The attitude of gun buyers was so overwhelmingly clear that other gun makers, after taking a close look at the fire into which S&W had jumped, elected to remain in the litigation frying pan, unendurable though it was. The pact effectively collapsed, with an aftermath of business disaster for S&W: Substantial layoffs followed, as did the departure of its chief executive, and the company's British owners soon unloaded it at a distress price. But the gun settlement failed for a second and very significant reason, quite apart from the opposition of the gun world. As HUD and other go-betweens soon realized, even if they could get other gun makers to sign, they were failing to get enough of the cities. Despite the extensive concessions that S&W had offered, as many as half the cities that were suing, after consulting their lawyers, flatly turned down the deal. Why? A lawyer representing many of the cities said it was because the settlement "does not contain any monetary damages."[46]

Not that it had never been about anything as grubby as the money, of course.

Stacked: The Breast-Implant Affair

Between 1994 and 1996 teams of researchers at the Mayo Clinic, Harvard, and many other leading institutions came out with major studies that found—contrary to what we had been told in one of the great scare campaigns of modern times—no link between silicone-gel breast implants and the rate at which women contract autoimmune or connective-tissue diseases such as scleroderma, rheumatoid arthritis, and lupus. The authoritative studies confirmed what most of the medical community had long regarded as well established, namely that the silicone compounds used in modern medicine are inert and unreactive in the body, and do not cause any sort of systemic illness through inflammation or immune reaction. As PBS's *Frontline* summed up the data: "Women with implants do not have measurably different health from women without implants."[1] Millions of women had been badly scared, it seems, for nothing.

In a rational world this news would have been followed by a huge sigh of relief, then by a round of apologies, and soon thereafter by some quiet retirements from public life. First to apologize would be the trial lawyers who'd stoked

the panic from an early stage, recruited tens of thousands
of anxious women (1-800-RUPTURE was one hotline),
filed lawsuits on their behalf that often shared the same
typographical mistakes, bankrupted the formerly healthy $2
billion-sales Dow Corning Corporation of Midland, Michigan; and pocketed millions in contingency fees from the
rush-to-judgment jury awards.

Next in line to offer regrets would be various public and
media figures manipulated, wittingly or not, by the lawyers.
Connie Chung, who touched off the initial panic in a 1990
CBS news show, would send a producer to accept a Golden
Oops statuette. Food and Drug Administration (FDA) chief
Dr. David Kessler would quit his job after squirming before
a congressional committee probing his decision to order the
implants banned. Public Citizen, the Ralph Nader operation that sedulously spread the scare, would shamefacedly
halt its sale of implant litigation kits to trial lawyers and
disband its clearinghouse for implant law firms; and its
spokesman, Dr. Sidney Wolfe, would find his card tossed
from many a press Rolodex.

Of course this was America in the age of litigation, so
none of the above actually happened. The lawyers and Public Citizen simply denied everything. Dr. Kessler dodged
and weaved. Miss Chung and her producers had long since
moved on to other projects. Studies or no studies, some
juries—enough to keep the game highly profitable—went
right on awarding damages: One in Nevada awarded $14
million. A $4 billion settlement offered by Dow Corning
and other defendants, at that time the largest legal settlement in history, collapsed as too *low*, and the parties went
back to the negotiating table to work out a revised deal that

brought the estimated total of settlements and payouts to $7 billion.

The breast-implant episode bears retelling as a case history in the model of mass tort litigation as a sort of campaign in which psychological momentum and the shaping of public attitudes counts for at least as much as legal argument. With much help from tireless consumer group allies, cothinkers in high federal office, and a (temporarily) credulous press, it hardly seemed to make much difference that the science behind the trial lawyers' crusade ranged from unconvincing to imaginary.

Few advances did as much to usher in the age of modern medicine as the discovery of silicone compounds in the early 1940s. For as long as there have been metal catheters to corrode, wooden prostheses to rot, and rag tourniquets to go septic, the medical profession has felt the need for a stable and biologically nonreactive material for use in the human body. Silicones, inert and sterile to an unprecedented degree, fit the bill admirably, making possible the long-term placement within the human body of effective artificial hips, knees, joints, and lenses; heart valves and pacemakers; fluid-draining shunts for infants with hydrocephalus (water on the brain); and many similar devices. Americans receive millions of silicone implants annually, including six hundred thousand joints alone.

Liquid silicone was introduced as a lubricant for injections and transfusions on World War II battlefields, and in later years considerable quantities of it could be found circulating in the bloodstream of persons who used syringes regularly, such as insulin-dependent diabetics. Safe to eat, silicone was also used in the formulating of prescription and over-the-counter pills and even breakfast cereals. Breast implants employing fleshlike silicone gel were introduced in 1964 and soon became widely popular. Although they could cause localized complications, in particular sometimes painful "contracture" of the scar tissue that grew up around them, surveys both short and long term showed users overwhelmingly pleased with the results. Like other silicone devices, breast implants had a track record that was superior to, and better documented than, that of many or most other medical interventions. Or so practitioners thought.

On December 10, 1990, the American public was abruptly informed that these assurances of safety were not to be relied on, and that silicone implants could in fact pose a deadly peril to the health and well-being of their users. This alarming word came, not from some major scientific journal, recognized body of medical specialists, or other stodgy gatekeeper of traditional medicine, but from the CBS prime-time television series *Face to Face with Connie Chung*. The show profiled five women who had received implants and subsequently fallen ill, some gravely so. Two experts suspected that this had happened because of the implants, which contained, Chung warned, "an ooze of slimy gelatin that could be poisoning" them. The federal government was finally beginning to look into the dangers. "But, for some women, it may be too late." One critic later chided Chung for offering

...no review of the available scientific data; no interviews with medical professionals who might challenge the link between the implants and the women's illnesses; no mention that the two doctors she cited to support a link ... had never published studies on silicone breast implants in a major medical journal. Nor did she mention that both sources were paid medical experts for plaintiffs' lawyers involved in implant litigation.[2]

In the ensuing uproar, women across the country called their doctors to report that they, too, had been experiencing fatigue, headaches, achy joints, and other symptoms like the women on the show. Further media reports followed with names like "Toxic Breasts" and "After Breast Implant, Horror Began."

There was ample reason to be skeptical about these reports. Autoimmune or connective-tissue disease is a still-mysterious family of ailments, including such serious conditions as lupus and rheumatoid arthritis in which the body mistakenly attacks its own tissues. (Some patients with implants also came down with symptoms of other debilitating but poorly understood syndromes, such as chronic fatigue syndrome and fibromyalgia.) For unknown reasons these diseases seemed to strike especially frequently at otherwise healthy women in their prime adult years, the same group that tended to receive implants—but this pattern of disease incidence had been recognized since well before the product's introduction in 1964. So many women had received implants, and so many would have been expected to be struck by illness of unknown origin, that the simple workings of chance ensure that the one event would be followed in thousands of cases by the other. Before-and-after, even with suspicious timing, just doesn't in itself prove cause-and-effect, which is why most clinical anecdotes, as individual case histories of this sort written up in medical journals are commonly called, never lead anywhere as regards the search for new causes of illness.

Trial lawyers, who often complain that their critics are anecdotal, are usually quite happy to proceed with their own anecdotes, which they call cases. All they really need is to find an expert to testify that the selected defendant's conduct more likely than not caused the injury; and since in American law (in contrast to those in most foreign countries) experts are typically hired and paid for by the litigants, it is usually possible to find some who are willing to be team players. Implant manufacturers had their own hired scientists and medics, but many trial lawyers were content to fight the "battle of the experts" to a draw before juries.[3] If scientists couldn't agree whether silicone was dangerous, then the devices were probably too risky to have been put on the market, weren't they? Faced with contradictory if not incomprehensible scientific testimony, a jury might easily conclude that it really came down to whether you wanted to side with sick women or big business.

With the panic in full swing, the next order of the day for lawyers was client recruitment. "Women with Breast Implants" was the boldface head on a quarter-page ad in a Milwaukee paper. "Have you had joint or neck pains or headaches? You may be entitled to compensation." A Denver ad included what one account described as "a sketch of two breasts—one pointing north, the other south." "Are 'dream breasts' to die for?" asked an ad placed by the Houston law firm of John O'Quinn, which hired the biggest public relations shop in town to promote its implant litigation work; one of its attorneys went on a TV news show to inform women with implants that they had "time bombs" in their breasts. Support groups for "silicone survivors" were springing up around the country, and lawyers from the O'Quinn firm attached themselves "barnacle-like" (as Joseph Nocera put it in his landmark *Fortune* account) to these groups, obtaining from them not only a vital source of client referrals but also a vehicle for raising clients' consciousness and stirring up the media.[4]

Lawyers filed cases all over the country, but the road to victory led through Washington, D.C., where the U.S. Food and Drug Administration (FDA) would have to decide whether to order the devices pulled from the market. If it did endorse the view that the product was too risky to remain in continued use, juries would be much more likely to conclude that it should never have been put on the market in the first place and would be more likely to render large awards. For reasons of this sort, trial lawyers comprise a hidden but potent lobby in countless battles over product recalls.

As it happened, the FDA was headed by an unusually ambitious and media-savvy former congressional aide by the name of David Kessler, M.D. After the Connie Chung show, the agency's own advisory panel of experts had conducted a six-month investigation and recommended, in November 1991, that the devices remain available with informed consent for women who wanted them. But less

than two months later, brandishing manufacturer documents from a court case that he said raised new doubts
about implants' safety (and which had somehow reached his
hands notwithstanding a court order keeping them confidential), Kessler demanded a moratorium on the implants'
distribution. The advisory panel went along.

Even aside from the implant controversy, trial lawyers
had many reasons to cheer Kessler's tenure at the FDA. In
a mass tort campaign over the use of implantable bone
screws ("pedicle screws"), a Kessler underling had leaked
raw patient data to plaintiffs' lawyers, in violation of the
agency's own rules and of the confidentiality promised to
doctors to secure their cooperation. (The misstep was said
to be inadvertent.) A House oversight panel later found that
the agency had taken an average of 31 days to respond to
plaintiffs' lawyers' freedom of information requests on the
bone-screw matter compared with 697 days for requests
coming from defendants and reporters. On a far bigger
matter, the tobacco controversy, the enmity Kessler bore
the tobacco companies made him one of the lawyers' key
allies, keeping the companies pinned down under constant
public fire and scrambling to respond to agency initiatives.
"We were in touch with people at the FDA all the time,"
attorney John Coale told the *New Yorker*'s Peter Boyer.
"There were a lot of faxes, phone calls, and other forms of
communication being exchanged."[5]

Finally, Commissioner Kessler had particularly cordial
ties to the Ralph Nader–founded Public Citizen's Health
Research Group and its director, Dr. Sidney Wolfe, who
had lobbied for Kessler's retention in office.[6] Long familiar
to the Washington press corps as the individual to call for

negative comments and leads on pharmaceutical and other health business, Wolfe, from the initial scare onward, assumed the role of chief pot stirrer on the implant controversy, assailing the manufacturers at every turn, blasting the FDA for not taking stronger action against the silicone menace, and, in general, keeping the issue in the papers. Like his mentor Nader, Wolfe had developed a relentlessly accusatory public persona, always on the attack.

At a January 2, 1992, Public Citizen press conference, Wolfe declared, with customary assurance, that "tens of thousands of women with these implants now face life-threatening diseases" because silicone was "causing auto-immune disease, and causing a whole host of other problems."[7] How did he know this? Well, it seemed he had "spoken to a large number of immunologists" who had told him about "a unique syndrome" of "disease in the joints" that women were suffering "and that there are tens if not hundreds of thousands of women in this country that have this syndrome and are really wiped out with it." Two years previously, it seemed, a helpfully anonymous source within the FDA had leaked to his group internal documents from the agency that showed it was aware of problems with implants that had not been made known to the public. Shockingly, even now it had not ordered the devices off the market.

For reporters it all made an impressive, if not easily checked, package. Who had time to speak with "a large number of immunologists," the way Wolfe had, to find out whether tens of thousands of women were "really wiped out with" silicone syndrome? And few seemed overly skeptical about the narrative in any case. *Business Week*, *Ms.*, and the news (though not editorial) side of the *Wall Street Journal* enthusiastically joined in the anti-implant coverage, as did women's service magazines: "A Body to Die For," was *Redbook*'s contribution.[8] And few stories were complete without quotes from Wolfe demanding, for example, that criminal charges be pressed against Dow Corning executives for their supposed withholding of documents (an investigation by FDA staff later cleared the company of this charge, but it was carried as a page B-16 sort of story). It was not actually all that newsworthy for Wolfe or his group to call for prosecution or criminal investigation of major drug companies. Over the years Public Citizen demanded such action against most of the big firms, including Warner-Lambert, Schering-Plough, Pfizer, Upjohn, SmithKline Beecham, and so on.

One of Public Citizen's techniques was to collect case anecdotes from trial lawyers who were suing over alleged side effects from some drug or medical device, then publish the results as a "study," sending it both to the FDA (with a demand that it ban or restrict the product) and to the press. Of course, case descriptions based on lawyers' descriptions of what had happened to their clients were not likely to be fully objective and might well have omitted other possible explanations for those clients' health woes. But the press often used such Public Citizen material as a quickie story-in-a-box, with a headline along the lines of "Drug X linked to five deaths." In addition, Public Citizen openly ran clearinghouses for trial lawyers suing breast-implant manufacturers and other categories of defendant and offered litigation kits for sale ($750 in the implant case), consisting of copies of documents admitted into evidence in earlier cases that lawyers could use as the nucleus of their case. Revenue from such sales aside, Public Citizen generally declined to disclose where it got its money, arguing that its contributors might face retaliation were their identities revealed.

Events in the courtroom were soon going extremely well for the lawyers. In late 1991, a San Francisco jury awarded a complainant $7 million over health problems she attributed to her implants, and more multimillion-dollar verdicts were to follow. In December 1992, O'Quinn won $25 million against Bristol Myers Squibb on behalf of a plaintiff whose own expert had agreed that her symptoms could be compared to those of a "bad flu." The trial was televised on *Court TV,* contributing enormously to the national frenzy. Soon the number of lawsuits had spiraled into the hundreds, then thousands; by the end of 1993, Dow Corning alone faced more than twelve thousand such suits. Juries seemed to view just about all implant manufacturers as equally guilty; and in March 1994, O'Quinn proceeded to hammer 3M on behalf of three women with a $28 million verdict. Manufacturers settled the great majority of cases rather than risk trial.[9]

With docket backlogs mounting, the mass tort industry was beginning to display its tendency toward concentration. As O'Quinn showed his prowess at winning enormous verdicts, more clients signed up with him, more law firms around the country farmed out their cases to him, and his caseload mounted into the thousands. Many were filed in his hometown of Houston, whose liberal venue rules allowed him to bring suit even if clients lived in other states. It did not hurt his efforts in Houston that he had a reputation for being politically well connected, having given $183,000 to political campaigns (including judicial campaigns) between 1990 and 1994. According to Joseph Nocera, the going rate of settlements for O'Quinn's Houston cases as they were called for trial was rumored to have reached $1 million apiece. Later, when it grew harder to win implant cases, O'Quinn's "market share" was to rise still further as other law firms abandoned the field and turned cases over to him.

The firm of O'Quinn & Laminack, despite the impressive verdicts ($650 million, $517 million) to its credit, might have seemed an unlikely standard-bearer for either consumerism (famed for his run-ins with bar disciplinary authorities on the issue of client chasing, O'Quinn over the years attracted a number of unusually vivid client complaints about the handling of their cases) or feminism ("It is considered something of a horny boy's club," *Texas Monthly* noted, "and the gum-chewing O'Quinn is not noted for his polish"). Where he had few peers, as published accounts have made clear, was in grasping the nature of the psychodrama he wished to stage before the jury. To prevail in a breast-implant case, as two of O'Quinn's partners once argued, "you must prove that the manufacturers are evil. They are not good people who make bad decisions, not good people who just did not know, but just plain evil." Psychologist/consultant Robert Gordon, who helped O'Quinn "tailor his jury presentations for maximum emotional impact," found in his research that the ideal jurors for an implant plaintiff were not other women "but blue-collar men who like women with large breasts. 'Our research indicated that implants created guilt on the part of male jurors who put so much emphasis on breast size,' Gordon explains. 'You can bring this [guilt] out at trial.' " *Texas Monthly* credits O'Quinn's success before juries to his understanding that "scientific evidence is nowhere near as powerful as age-old myths about femininity, in particular those of women wronged. Every O'Quinn trial allows the jury to become the plaintiff's rescuer." In one particularly notable win, he "directed a domestic drama for the jury. He put the beefy husband of one of the plaintiffs on the stand, an ex-jock who agonizingly testified that he had ignored his wife's complaints as she had grown progressively sicker. 'He was saying he thought, "Well, she just cain't play hurt. She ain't tough," ' O'Quinn says. Then, in open court, the man apologized to his wife for not having faith in her. The jury awarded $44 million."

Among O'Quinn's contributions to the scientific side of the controversy was to promote the work of a pathologist at the UCLA Medical Center named Nir Kossovsky,[10] who had developed what he said was the world's first test to detect immunological damage from silicone. O'Quinn's firm referred to Kossovsky as the "senior world authority on the biological properties of silicone," and jurors in the *Court TV*–televised Pamela Johnson trial said his testimony played a crucial role in their $25 million verdict. Yet according to Gary Taubes's article in the December 1995 *Discover*, Kossovsky lacks formal training in such specialties as immunology, rheumatology, or epidemiology; and researchers at the Scripps Research Institute's Autoimmune Disease Center deemed his test "invalid."

As implant litigation grew to resemble an assembly line many a client found herself sent, for purposes of diagnosis, to an unfamiliar doctor or clinic favored by her lawyer. In turn, many such medical practices came to be dominated by attorney referrals; some individual doctors handled more than one thousand women. One doctor in Texas made $2 million a year certifying illness in implant recipients, more than 90 percent of whom came in from lawyers. A diagnosis in hand "is of great value to your claim," his brochure explained; "the manufacturers (and frankly, jurors) value a woman's case much lower" without one. Many diagnosis-mill brochures, like many lawyers' ads, were well calculated to scare women out of their wits. Some warned that their children were in lasting danger from exposure to silicone *in utero* or in mother's milk. Among "blatantly unethical" practices among some diagnosis mills, Dr. Marcia Angell of the *New England Journal of Medicine* wrote in her 1996 book *Science on Trial*, were putting patients through "unnecessary, costly and sometimes risky" treatments such as courses of steroids to treat supposed silicone poisoning; one woman was given $90,000 a month in hospitalization and $10,000 a month in therapy. Other litigation-support clinics, meanwhile, prudently disclaimed any use of the diagnoses for any purpose other than forensic use—seeming to admit that their pronouncements were to be taken seriously only as advocacy and not as "real" medicine. But once women had been told that something was drastically wrong with their health, it was impossible to prevent many of them from taking appropriately drastic steps. Others were genuinely sick, but from conditions other than the imagined "silicone illness"—and the misdiagnosis of their very real symptoms might delay the identification of their actual ailment, to bad effect.[11]

Slowly, at its own pace, mainstream scientific research began to catch up with the controversy, as various studies prompted by the early scare were brought to completion. In June 1994, a Mayo Clinic study published in the *New England Journal of Medicine* found no higher rate of connective-tissue disease among implant users. The journal's executive editor, Dr. Marcia Angell, added an editorial critical of the lawyers' claims. The next year the American College of Rheumatology (ACR) found the evidence "compelling" that "silicone implants expose patients to no demonstrable additional risk for connective tissue or rheumatic disease." In June 1995, researchers in the well-known Harvard Nurses' Health Study, again publishing in the *New England Journal*, found no evidence of disease; by the end of 1995, the number of studies and abstracts pointing in the same direction had reached twenty. A brief scare over the possibility that implants might cause breast cancer was among the first to be disposed of: Recipients showed no higher rates of that ailment.

Trial lawyers and their allies reacted with great vehemence, deriding each study in turn as badly designed, or too small in sample size, or having missed new patterns of "atypical" disease because researchers had supposedly checked only for classically defined autoimmune ailments. When the official body of rheumatologists went on record against the new disease theory, Wolfe was contemptuous: "It basically shows how ignorant the people in the college are about the fundamental processes of epidemiology."[12] At the same time, as the lawyers' original position grew less and less tenable, they retreated—"bunker by bunker," as Dr. Angell put it—to theories quite different from those they had put forward initially. And it was hinted, at every opportunity, that the new studies had been tainted by financial influence. Implant makers, in response to the expectation by the FDA and other parties that they pay for new safety studies, had financed some of the studies directly, while in other cases the responsible researchers were attached to universities or hospitals that had gotten grants from drug companies in the past (indeed, it wasn't easy to find top-flight researchers who lacked such entanglements).

Press coverage, favorable for so long, began to turn sharply against the lawyers,[13] led by *New York Times* reporter Gina Kolata, whose June 13, 1995, article was headlined: "A Case of Justice, or a Total Travesty?" Two weeks later the *Los Angeles Times* followed suit in a scorching editorial: "Judges and juries have often overlooked rational evidence" in finding implants responsible for disease, it said: "Tort lawyers have managed to use anecdotal evidence . . . to persuade juries that there is a causative link." Public opinion showed signs of swinging in the same direction. Breast cancer survivor groups, whose members had been deprived of silicone implants for reconstructive mastectomy by Kessler's moratorium, called for them to be made available once again. With silicone off the market, the only available option for most women had been saline implants, which were much less popular because they did not have a natural feel. Wolfe, implacable as ever, demanded a halt to the use of saline implants as well, though their contents consisted merely of saltwater, the same substance routinely infused directly into patients in need of hydration. Kessler, however, finally letting a bit of daylight show between himself and Public Citizen, turned down this demand and also allowed a resumption of silicone use for those relatively few mastectomy patients who were enrolled in clinical protocols; others were out of luck.

The lawyers did not sit still while events turned against them. PR firm Fenton Communications, which worked for O'Quinn as well as for Public Citizen, sent out packages attacking *Times* reporter Kolata; hatchet jobs attacking her wound up running in several widely read publications.[14] "Another Fenton press release," remarked a *Wall Street Journal* editorial, "jumped the gun and announced that a University of Michigan study had linked silicone implants with disease. Just two days later, the researchers proclaimed the connection wasn't statistically significant, but Fenton continues to give the wrong impression about the study's findings. 'I'm burning mad,' says Jim Moody of the American College of Rheumatology. 'The study, presented at our conference, said the complete opposite of what Fenton claimed.' "

Dr. Angell, when she published the pioneering Mayo Clinic report, discovered how hazardous it could be to get in the lawyers' way. "Almost immediately," she writes, "I received phone calls from reporters who had spoken with plaintiffs' attorneys eager to discredit the Mayo Clinic, the *New England Journal of Medicine*, and me personally." Dr. Sherine Gabriel, principal investigator of the Mayo study, said an onslaught of subpoenas and highly burdensome document demands from the lawyers had "severely compromised my ability to do research" and also scared away other scientists from the field, who told her they wouldn't risk a similar ordeal by undertaking research that could draw law-yerly fire. A panel of the American College of Rheumatol-ogy found that "rheumatologists who have expressed opinions or published work viewed as contrary to the in-terests of plaintiffs and plaintiffs' attorneys in implant-related litigation have been subjected to various forms of harassment in the workplace or even at their homes. Much of this has been attributed to plaintiffs' attorneys."[15]

Certainly the trial lawyers' luck had not run out in the courtroom. In 1995, a Nevada jury awarded $14 million to an implant plaintiff; the state's high court upheld the $4 million compensatory portion of the award, though it over-turned the $10 million punitive. In early 1999, a jury in Washington state voted $10 million against Bristol Myers-Squibb. To be sure, implant manufacturers were beginning to do much better at beating cases at trial—better, but still not well enough. When the trend in federal courts turned against letting implant cases get to the jury, lawyers began taking their cases to friendlier state courts. Manufacturers might win 80, 90 percent, or even more of the trials and still face ruin.

Some defenders of our litigation system are accustomed to argue that companies seldom get sued successfully unless they have done something very wrong, and that defendants that feel sure of their factual ground should simply sit tight and refuse to settle, confident of eventual vindication at jury verdict or at least in post-trial motions or appeal. None of the implant manufacturers shared this blithe view, no mat-ter how good the science looked from their point of view. So Dow Corning, 3M, and other makers cut a deal in which they agreed to set aside $4.25 billion to compensate claimants; the trial lawyers would get a cool billion. The settlement promised substantial sums to claimants, from hundreds of thousands of dollars to as high as $2 million each. At the insistence of plaintiff's lawyers, however, it did not restrict eligibility to women with objectively verifiable symptoms. As Angell observes, "A woman could claim joint and muscle aches, disturbed sleep, fatigue, and burning pain in the chest, none of which can be objectively verified by her doctor or anyone else, and collect up to $700,000."[16]

Trial lawyers now redoubled their recruitment efforts and helpful paralegals were ready to explain which self-reported symptoms on the "grid" of compensation categories were most popular. The number of claimants had been expected to reach 60,000, but in a little more than a year it had mounted to an astonishing 440,000, an estimated half of all women with current implants, including more than 100,000 who claimed current illness. Four billion dollars was now clearly not enough, and the deal collapsed as too low. After a return to the drawing board, manufacturers cut new deals with plaintiffs, agreeing to lay out more money overall than had been offered before—$7 billion or so—although with far lower amounts offered per claimant than in the first settlement try. And with thousands more suits backed up waiting for trial, on May 15, 1995, Dow Corning filed for Chapter 11 bankruptcy.

Public Citizen, accustomed always to play attack, was in all the papers to flay the giant company for having the temerity to tell a court it was going broke. Nader himself called the bankruptcy filing "outrageous" and an instance of "corporate welfare," and *Multinational Monitor*, one of the publications in his stable, described it as a "new moral low" in tactics "to skirt responsibility." And the filing was certainly unwelcome to trial lawyers, who found their inventory of cases against the Michigan firm, such a rich asset the day before, suddenly frozen. "The solution," proposed *Multinational Monitor*, "is to make corporate executives responsible for egregiously harmful products. Executives found guilty should be criminally prosecuted and jailed."[17]

If implanted silicone was really injurious to human health, it stood to reason that patients with other kinds of implant and prostheses must be suffering from it, too. Soon lawsuits were raging against makers and suppliers of a wide range of other medical devices. The biggest of these campaigns was waged against the contraceptive device Norplant, which consisted of tiny hormone-releasing silicone rods inserted under the skin of a woman's upper arm, the idea being to dispense with the need for the pill and its scheduling demands. There was no real evidence that its side effects were any different or worse than those common to the pill and all other hormone-based contraceptives, but Norplant, like breast implants, had been marketed to a population of young and otherwise healthy patients, the most legally dangerous kind. A campaign including lawyers' billboards and TV ads, as well as media campaigns, helped enlist no fewer than 50,000 women to sue its manufacturer, American Home Products. The litigation did not go well for the plaintiffs, the lack of solid science being only one of its problems; too many of the women were suing on vaguely described side effects they'd never reported to their doctors, while others, even after signing up to sue, had continued to recommend the device to friends, said they were glad they'd used it, and went back to their doctors to have a replacement set put in. In August 1999, effectively throwing in the towel, lawyers for 36,000 of the plaintiffs—the leading law firms were O'Quinn's and Ness Motley, with 3,500 and 17,000 cases respectively—cut a deal with the manufacturer to settle most of the suits for only $1,500 per claimant, a mere pittance by usual mass tort standards, but still adding up to a not-unimpressive $50 million-plus.

Worse yet was the surge of litigation against makers of other implanted devices that in many cases were more medically crucial to recipients' health than either breast implants or Norplant had been.[18] Some were sued over joints and prostheses they supplied which, though working uneventfully, were made from silicone. In other cases, a heart valve or mechanical jaw had failed, and lawyers then made a practice of suing the various component and material suppliers, all of which might furnish deep pockets to help fund a settlement. The result was that a supplier that had originally contributed a few cents' worth of resin, metal, or polyester yarn to the overall assembly might find itself a defendant in a series of million-dollar lawsuits. DuPont spent an estimated several million dollars fending off lawsuits on behalf of 1,600 jaw-implant recipients who named it as a defendant because it had supplied about five cents' worth of Teflon to the maker of the implant. Inevitably, major materials suppliers began to extricate themselves from the medical implant market. In 1992, DuPont, Dow Chemical, and Dow Corning all announced they would forbid use of their products in implantable applications. Other companies were fleeing as well: A manufacturer of grafts testified that fifteen other suppliers had turned down her requests to fill the gap after DuPont cut off her supplies of polyester yarn. By 1994, *Science* magazine was reporting that "materials shortfalls are forcing unwanted design changes on new devices," neonatologists were expressing alarm about the continued availability of shunts for hydrocephalic infants, and other medical professionals warned that, unless addressed, the crisis would soon endanger human life. Despite fierce resistance from trial lawyers and Public Citizen, Congress, in 1998, passed—and Pres. Bill Clinton found it advisable to sign—a Biomaterials Access Assurance Act providing modest liability protections for raw material suppliers that had met recognized quality standards, and the crisis eased.[19]

The breast-implant affair was in no sense isolated or flukish: Lawyers and their allied consumer groups had stoked (and continued to stoke) a long series of unfounded health scares about other products, from the Audi 5000, with its supposed "sudden acceleration," to cell phones and power lines that are said to cause brain cancer and leukemia, and mercury dental fillings that are alleged to cause a variety of toxic woes. According to correspondent Atul Gawande in the July 5, 1999, *New Yorker,* serious medical consequences have followed the litigation-driven withdrawal of Bendectin, which had been the only pharmaceutical compound aimed specifically at nausea in pregnancy (and which continues to be sold uneventfully in Canada under the name Diclectin). After the drug became unavailable, he writes, hospital admissions for hyperemesis (extreme nausea and vomiting in expectant mothers) tripled, putting women at risk of serious complications, "including rupture of the esophagus, lung collapse, and tearing of the spleen" as well as "significant dehydration or starvation." Peter Huber, in his book *Galileo's*

Revenge, has documented some of the adverse public health consequences of overlitigation in such areas as childhood vaccines, the use of caesarean sections in obstetrics, and the epidemiology of supposed immune-system damage from low-level chemicals in the environment. In a very real sense, lawyers and their allies are themselves committing acts of medical malpractice when they spread medical misinformation to vulnerable clients.[20]

"Panel Confirms No Major Illness Tied to Breast Implants," reported the *New York Times* on June 21, 1999. It might have seemed anticlimactic—hadn't the controversy been resolved a few years earlier?—but the fact is that the trial lawyers had never stopped hammering away at their side of things, not for a moment. "An independent panel of 13 scientists convened by the Institute of Medicine at the request of Congress has concluded that silicone breast implants do not cause any major diseases," wrote the *Times*'s Kolata, still on the beat.

The panel had reviewed seventeen epidemiological studies and found them "remarkable for the consistency of finding no elevated risk or odds for an association of implants with disease." Nor was the theory of "atypical" illness, much bruited by lawyers, borne out either: "There is no novel syndrome." "It is a very strong statement," George Mason University law professor David Bernstein told the paper. "It would have been nice to have had this $7 billion ago."[21]

But it hardly seemed to make a difference. Trial lawyers were still vehemently dismissing all the studies as virtually fraudulent, just as they have stoutly refused, years after the fact, to concede the safety of the Audi 5000 or Bendectin or power lines or any of the other products wrongly assailed. Because our legal system, unlike most countries', lacks a loser-pays principle, they never did have to worry that there would be any price tag for them to pay for the damage done by unfounded litigation. Whatever the merits of this assurance of impunity, it seems to have operated on a practical level to make them feel that they have no particular obligation to apologize over the wrecked careers, ruined companies, and wrongfully extracted billions either; they have a right to try whatever suits they like and a right to keep whatever money falls into their lap as a result, according to the general view. In the tenacity with which they admit nothing and dispute everything, many of today's trial lawyers have come to resemble no one so much as their opposite numbers, the old-line tobacco executives who still insist that this business about cigarettes causing cancer is an open question.

Trial Lawyer TV

In most big litigation campaigns these days, the ginning up of publicity damaging to the targeted defendants is as vital a part of the lawyers' efforts as anything that goes on in court. "We understood this just wasn't a legal case," plaintiffs' lawyer John Coale explained, regarding the tobacco suits. "We had to have the public and the media and the political world on our side."[1] Thus it was, as Boyer put it, that "the plaintiffs' lawyers became the prime creators and marketers of a national narrative entitled 'Big Tobacco.' 'Oh, hee-hee-hee, we just started in on Big Tobacco,' says Coale, delighting in the memory. 'You know, it was "let's just refer to 'em as Big Tobacco," Big Tobacco, Big Tobacco, Big Tobacco! Pretty soon, everybody's talking Big Tobacco.' "[2] The plaintiff's side granted regular exclusives to friendly voices in the press, trickling out the flow of internal tobacco company documents at a careful pace so that some new indication of the companies' perfidy could appear in the papers every couple of days.

Of course the present generation of litigators did not invent the idea of trying cases in the press. Familiar with the workings of power and privy to a large amount of inside information, lawyers have been among reporters' and editors' most valuable sources for a very long time. In turn, even relatively conscientious reporters regularly find themselves writing pieces that serve lawyers' objectives in various ways. Hostile coverage inflicts reputational and privacy damage on an opponent, who may offer a concessionary settlement in hopes of stanching the flow of bad press. Even relatively neutral coverage can influence trial atmospherics and jurors' preconceptions, helping establish a case as the kind of big, symbolic and important one that might merit a send-'em-a-message award. Not incidentally, it can also spread the fame of the lawyer handling the case.

The press plays a particularly powerful role in client recruitment and conciousness raising. For mass tort lawyers, mass media publicity is by far the best way to grab the attention of asymptomatic persons with past exposure to such products as silicone breast implants, asbestos, or Fen-Phen, who might otherwise have had no notion of suing. Scary publicity about the products themselves conveniently help generate the basis for arguing that these future claimants are being reasonable when they say they fear future disease. Rapid client recruitment itself is vital in turning scattered cases, which a defendant might repel singly, into the sort of litigation campaign that overwhelms its resources. And as lawyers have discovered over and over, by far the most powerful medium for reaching their intended audience is television.

"To the frustrated channel surfer," wrote Tad Friend in the May 7, 2001, *New Yorker,* "it often seems that there is only one show on television, 'Dateline NBC: 48 Hours of

20/20, PrimeTime Thursday,' and that this show endlessly repeats one basic story: The Thing That Went Horribly Wrong.

> In the codified newsmagazine vernacular, what kind of thing went horribly wrong becomes instantly clear. If it was a consumer product, you get something like the following: "Little did they know that a pepper grinder . . . *could kill!*"; an old photo of a young girl eating, her mother saying, "Mary always loved pepper"; a montage of an out-of-focus ambulance weaving through traffic, an I.V. drip, and a flatlining heart monitor; shoppers browsing for appliances as we pan down to the correspondent, who says, "Could it happen . . . in *your kitchen?*" a shot of a document, then a snippet enlarged against it (". . . failed to meet safety standards . . ."); an expert who is identified in voice-over as his hands tap at a keyboard and who is then asked, "Just how dangerous are these condiment-delivery devices?" "*Profoundly* dangerous, Bob"; an empty playground swing rocking gently.[3]

As a summary of the formula for sensationalist consumer TV journalism, this misses only one essential element, namely the family's pending lawsuit. There almost certainly will be such a lawsuit, since the elements of the Story of the Thing That Went Horribly Wrong almost invariably track those of the narrative a plaintiff's lawyer is preparing for trial. The jury—like the television audience—will be given the same heart-tugging introduction to the victim's family and its happy life before the injury; the same line-up of details evoking pity, horror, and indignation; the same pronouncements from impressive-looking experts and dramatic highlighting of document excerpts revealing Things the Defendant Didn't Want You to Know; and a closing argument in the same relentlessly accusatory tone. Only trial lawyers, or those they work with, can provide the network with all the modular elements from which the Story is assembled: the family (to which the lawyer will normally control access); the experts (well-compensated members of the litigation team, more likely than not); the opponent's internal memos and correspondence (cherry-picked from a much larger number of documents obtained by way of compulsory discovery); and so forth. If the network wants to get this story—and future stories like it—it will need to rely on the continued cooperation of the lawyers and litigation consultants who compile these sorts of visuals-cum-narratives.

These stories require the network to conduct much less original research than viewers may assume they've had to do. By the time the helpful folks from the litigation community drop the horror narrative on the producer's desk, the package may practically be tied up with a ribbon and bow, though the network will still probably want to add the "balance," consisting of an interview with forlorn-looking executives of the company or institution being sued. The television producers have one considerable advantage not available to the trial lawyer conducting a cross-examination of those executives in a live courtroom: on TV, you can shoot a long, repetitive interview and then edit it down, removing the overbearing or accusatory questions and leaving only a few hapless or evasive-sounding replies.

The TV networks' heavy promotion of safety exposé stories, sometimes during competitive "sweeps weeks," inevitably leads to suspicions of calculated sensationalism. (Exec. Dir. Don Hewitt has boasted that CBS's *60 Minutes* is "the biggest moneymaker in the history of broadcasting.")[4] But the better explanation for their durable appeal is that they make network news personnel feel good about themselves. The prestige is often reflected in Emmy awards, not to mention the peer admiration due them for having proved their courage by defying some powerful interest in the form of a manufacturer that may also be a big advertiser. Deborah Norville, asked what made her proudest about her years with *Inside Edition*, unhesitatingly named the show's exposé of Chrysler's minivan latches.[5]

Soon after NBC's November 17, 1992, airing of a *Dateline* episode on alleged gas tank flaws in General Motors trucks, it began to become evident that the Story of the Thing That Went Horribly Wrong could itself go horribly wrong. By the time it was over, *NBC News* president Michael Gartner had resigned, and *Dateline* anchors Stone Phillips and Jane Pauley had read over the air an apology that went on for an excruciating three minutes of airtime, an eternity in a medium in which even simple one-sentence corrections are a rarity. *Los Angeles Times* TV critic Howard Rosenberg called the *Dateline* blowup "an unprecedented disaster in the annals of network news and perhaps the biggest TV scam since the Quiz Scandals."[6] Former *NBC News* president Reuven Frank deemed it "the worst black eye NBC News has suffered in my experience, which goes back to 1950."[7]

"Waiting to Explode?", watched by 11 million households, followed the usual formula with relentless precision. First, viewers were introduced to Shannon Moseley, a seventeen-year-old who died in a fiery 1989 crash at a Georgia intersection when a drunk driver broadsided his full-size GM truck at nearly seventy miles per hour. Shannon's grieving parents, interviewed on screen, were convinced that their son's death needn't have happened: GM had put the truck's gas tank in too exposed a location. The Moseley family, it soon developed, had a suit just about to go to trial against the giant automaker. GM's lawyers planned to argue that young Shannon Moseley could not have survived a crash of that high a force no matter what had happened, but lawyers for the young man's family disagreed with that assessment.[8]

There then appeared on screen one of the family's lawyers, who announced that the tanks on the youngster's truck "were placed in about as stupid a place as they can possibly be placed." The company's full-size 1973–87 pickup trucks, unusually for a passenger vehicle, had utilized a "sidesaddle" tank configuration more typical of larger commercial trucks, one that placed twin gas tanks on each side of the vehicle. Not only did this leave the vehicle too vulnerable (the lawyers charged) to high-force broadside collisions, but the company's designers had compounded the problem by placing the tanks outside rather than inside the vehicle's protective "frame rail." The Moseleys' was one of a number of such lawsuits trial lawyers were pressing after such accidents, demanding that GM be subjected to punitive damages for not issuing a recall of the trucks.

The next interview was with Clarence Ditlow, director of the Center for Auto Safety, who was, if anything, even more scathing, calling the truck a "rolling firebomb"; NBC, summing up his charges, termed it the "most dangerous vehicle out there on the road." Then there appeared another expert, safety consultant Byron Bloch, and he agreed with the lawyer and Ditlow. In a "side impact or a sideswipe impact," he explained to all-ears NBC reporter Michele Gillen, "the fuel tank gets crushed. . . . There is an immediate holocaust." If viewers were still not convinced, they could watch and make up their own minds: It seems NBC had filmed a real-life demonstration of what happened when one of those trucks got hit in the side at a moderate speed. Although one such staged collision didn't result in a fire, the viewer was told to watch the results of a second one. Another vehicle was shown heading into the side of a GM truck, there was a collision, and the truck appeared to burst into flames. Reporter Gillen said that, upon inspection after the crash, a hole was found in the gas tank. And GM's side of the story? Two representatives of the company had granted NBC's editors a four-hour interview of which two and a half hours were taped; from this, the show's editors utilized a minute and three seconds of airtime. The show mentioned in passing GM's contention that the trucks' overall safety record was good, but de-emphasized this bit of information almost to the vanishing point.

The effects were as you might expect. GM sputtered that the show was "grossly unfair, misleading and irresponsible"—but then you'd expect a big company to react that way, wouldn't you? As for the Georgia jury that heard the Moseley case a few weeks later, it awarded the family a record $105 million, most of that in punitive damages. Juror interviews suggested that the huge size of the award was based, in part, on anger at GM's apparent unrepentance. Given the damning facts, how could the company go on denying there was a problem?

GM engineers were at once suspicious about *Dateline's* crash simulation, since they knew the vehicle's gas tanks had been engineered to withstand impacts at speeds far higher than the one the program said it had used. But when the company asked the network for more details about the staging, it got the brush-off: Following usual network practice in such cases, NBC said it was nobody's business how it went about gathering news. (Network execs, like trial lawyers, can natter on all day about the People's Right to Know when it comes to everyone else's obligations to disclose, then get huffy about their Right to Privacy when inquiries are made about their own doings.) NBC producer Robert Read further informed the automaker that since the tests took place, the vehicles "have subsequently been junked and therefore are no longer available for inspection by anyone."

The whole matter would likely have worked out smoothly for NBC at this point, but for one thing: People at the test scene had talked. The network's Indianapolis-based consultants, in their plans to stage the crash fire, had brought in local firemen as observers to make sure nothing went wrong. Those firemen began telling friends about the discrepancies between what they saw and the way NBC presented the tests on screen. Indianapolis has a large automotive community, and word soon reached editor Pete

Pesterre of *Popular Hot Rodding*, who realized the significance of what he was hearing and contacted GM's attorneys. The GM attorneys, in turn, knew that the firemen's account would be easy to dismiss unless physical evidence were found to back it up, and they launched a search for the four vehicles used in the tests, the two trucks and two "striking vehicles." It took a search of twenty-two junkyards around central Indiana, but in the end they finally located them; contrary to what the NBC producer had said, they had not been destroyed. Then the real revelations began.

To begin with, an X-ray inspection of the fuel tank found it fully intact, contradicting NBC's assertion that a hole had been discovered in it. If the tank had not burst, where had the fuel for a fire come from? The crash truck, investigators learned, had been fitted with a wrong-size gas cap that popped off on impact. Moreover, the stagers had overfilled the gas tank. Bashed in the right spot by the crash, they concluded, the tank had squirted a little stream of gasoline out of its filler tube.

Gasoline by itself does not ensure a fire, but NBC's stagers weren't taking any chances. On the truck's underside, in a location not visible to viewers, they had strapped incendiary devices: A freeze-frame analysis of the film revealed puffs of smoke visible a moment *before* impact. Not only were the igniters themselves hidden, but they had been detonated by remote control. Visible wires would have signaled to attentive viewers that something unusual was going on.

Editing and camera work had helped, too. The firemen on the scene are reported to have chuckled at the network's failure, for all its strenuous efforts, to get any better fire than the relatively puny one obtainable by coaxing a little gasoline out of the truck's filler tube. NBC's camera angle, however, made it hard for viewers to see that flames were not coming from inside the truck itself, and the network chose to show only a brief snippet of the fire, so that viewers had no way of knowing that it burned itself out in about fifteen seconds, after it exhausted the ejected fuel. For good measure, GM concluded that the network had given viewers serious underestimates of the actual crash speeds.

What happened next? Although word had begun to circulate about the incendiary devices, NBC dug in and refused to apologize, even after GM said it intended to sue. NBC News head Gartner insisted that the segment was "fair and accurate" as a whole—igniters or none, apparently. And the experts the network had put on screen during the segment, Bloch and Ditlow, vocally defended the test methods. The use of igniters was "among accepted test procedures," contended Ditlow, raising eyebrows.[9] "There was nothing wrong with what happened in Indianapolis," Bloch told Reuters.[10] "The so-called devices underneath the pickup truck are really a lot of smoke that GM is blowing to divert you away from the punitive damages in the Moseley case."

But by this point GM had too much proof in hand. At a spectacular press conference, general counsel Harry Pearce walked reporters step by step through a demonstration that the network and its stagers had not only taken extraordinary measures to portray the truck as defective but had actively concealed those steps from both viewers and the automaker. Moreover, Pearce pointed out, actual highway statistics did not bear out the trial lawyers' and NBC's intuitive and anecdotal case against the trucks. The federal government's safety agency, the National Highway Traffic Safety Administration (NHTSA), had issued standards for automotive design that specifically addressed the danger of gas tank breakage in side crashes, and the GM design had not only complied with but far exceeded those standards. While *Dateline*, summing up Ditlow's charges, had called it the "most dangerous vehicle out there on the road," federal statistics over the nearly two decades the truck had been in service showed it to be among the safest vehicles of its era. Specifically, the federal crash database showed the GM truck to have a fatality rate of 1.5 per 10,000 vehicle years, markedly superior to passenger vehicles in general, which mostly showed fatality numbers in the 1.6 to 2.5 range. Overall, the GM vehicle's safety record was quite similar to that of its main competitor, a Ford truck, and it actually scored better than the Ford in avoiding fatalities following side-impact collisions, its presumed weak point. (It took about four thousand side-impact crashes in a GM pickup to get one fire with a major injury or fatality.) In a postscript, the defect-investigation staff of the NHTSA filed a sixty-page report in September 1993 concluding that the trucks were not defective, did not pose an unreasonable risk, and provided better crash protection than many other vehicles that had not been subject to controversy.

The network folded its hands, and an apology and Gartner's resignation followed. After his departure, Gartner explained that NBC's capitulation had not simply been coerced by the prospect of the lawsuit from GM. "I realized we were just plain wrong."[11] "And he blamed those whom the network had called on for advice during the production of the segment and afterward: "I saw that I had been too ready to believe our so-called experts, without trying to find out who they were."

Who, exactly, were NBC's experts?

Consultant Byron Bloch, who had both appeared on screen and been active at the Indianapolis crash scene, had for years been a consultant to trial lawyers regarding alleged product defects. Bloch has testified about products ranging from coffeepots to railroad cars. He'd also mounted $400-per-person seminars for trial lawyers, promising the scoop on such topics as "Key Graphic Exhibits for Trial." Bloch was the one who had rationalized to NBC the policy of keeping mum about the igniters by assuring the network that the fire had been set off by a headlight filament; a later analysis for GM found that the fire had started near the igniters, not the headlights.[12]

Clarence Ditlow, president of the Center for Auto Safety, was one of the safety lobby's most recognizable faces, ever ready to dispense a quote critical of Detroit. Like Bloch, Ditlow also did consulting work for trial lawyers, and his center, like the Public Citizen Health Research Group, makes a practice of selling kits to attorneys who file product-liability suits, comprised of documents that had proven to be of use in earlier cases. One of its price lists includes "Air Bags and Crashworthiness," at $750 for three volumes, and "GM Sudden Acceleration," at $595 for two volumes ("As Seen in *TRIAL* Magazine"). An ad for a Ditlow kit on state "lemon laws" promised to help attorney readers "win fast settlements and court awarded fees." Like Bloch, Ditlow had gotten into the auto-safety field through connections with Ralph Nader, as had Joan Claybrook, president of Public Citizen, the other most prominent media figure when it came to criticizing automakers' safety efforts. Both the Center for Auto Safety and Public Citizen had, in fact, been founded by Nader; both groups, like virtually every group in the Nader orbit, refuse to divulge their sources of financial support.

For the actual staging of the test, the network had hired Bruce Enz, a relative newcomer to the field who ran something called the Institute for Safety Analysis, a for-profit litigation consultancy that had no engineers on its payroll. Later, another figure with much experience as a network source on auto safety stories, Ben Kelley of the Maryland-based Institute for Injury Reduction, boasted of having recommended to NBC that it hire its crash testing out to Enz. Kelley, too, had served as a litigation consultant to trial lawyers, and his group, too, sold kits to lawyers; his product line included the "Seat Belt Injury Source Book" at $1,200.[12]

Kelley's institute is also less coy about its sources of support, its letterhead proclaiming that it was "founded by trial attorneys." ("We are made up of trial attorneys," he readily acknowledged in a 1993 interview. "This is like saying that the Democratic Party is a front for Democrats.") In a fundraising letter sent out after the *Dateline* filming, Kelley proposed conducting a new series of crash tests on the GM trucks, the results of which could be distributed to the public and submitted as evidence in litigation, something that could not be done with the proprietary NBC tests. The tests would follow "a modified design further enhancing the likelihood of a real-world impact resulting in fire."

As a group, Ditlow, Bloch, Claybrook, and Kelley have been extremely successful at shaping the agenda of the television networks as well as much of the prestige print media on issues of auto safety. In 1992, *AutoWeek* quoted an unnamed NHTSA official as estimating that 90 percent of the press inquiries the agency received were prompted by leaks from Ditlow, Claybrook, and Kelley. Which is not to say that any of them have a great success rate in identifying problems the agency agrees need fixing: Of the twenty-three petitions Ditlow's center had filed with NHTSA since 1988 asking it to open investigations, "seven were granted and two still remain under active consideration. But only one resulted in an actual recall, covering 554,910 Toyotas for automatic door lock failure."

In turn, Ditlow often flays NHTSA as soft on automakers, which has led to friction with the agency's staff. In 1989, fifty career, nonpolitical staffers at NHTSA's Office of Defects Investigation signed an open letter taking him to task. It stated that "after many years of quietly ignoring your many attacks on the safety defects program," the staff "wants to go on record that we believe your organization frequently goes beyond legitimate disagreement with the program and may, in fact, be seriously undermining it." In particular, they said, Ditlow had been "unfairly and inaccurately charging us with closing investigations under pressure from the auto industry." They added that such attacks weakened the public confidence in the agency's work that, in turn, led consumers to submit information to it on suspected safety defects and failures.

> We rely heavily on this information to initiate and pursue investigations and you hinder these investigations substantially by your attacks that discourage the public from contacting us. It is ironic that the effect of your actions may be to diminish a source of information upon which you rely heavily to raise money for the Center for Auto Safety. The Center periodically requests all of the complaint data we receive regarding potential safety-related defects. As we understand it, the information is then sold to attorneys. The amount and quality of the data made available to us, and subsequently to you, will suffer if the public believes what you have said about our program.[13]

While none of the four (Ditlow, Bloch, Claybrook, and Kelley) has a background in automotive engineering, they do have something even more valuable for some purposes: the ear of assignment editors. Kelley, who once worked at the Insurance Institute for Highway Safety (IIHS), has been an active network source at CBS and elsewhere; his institute has been known for developing "video news releases" decrying auto hazards that it sent out in quantity to local TV news operations, which often ran them on air with little, if any, change. Bloch has worked with all three networks, with a particularly close relationship to ABC, for whom he began to serve as a regular outside consultant on auto-safety matters as early as 1978. In the subsequent years he brought the network seven different exposés, two of which won Emmys.

When *Dateline* came to grief, many saw its fakery as a bizarre departure from normal and responsible network standards. Both CBS and ABC put out word that "their standards forbid the sort of staging that got NBC into trouble," to quote the *Los Angeles Times*,[14] and *60 Minutes* executive producer Don Hewitt was particularly emphatic that such things were unheard of at *his* show. "If that had happened at '60 Minutes,' " he said of NBC's failure to disclose its use of incendiary devices, "I'd be looking for a job tomorrow." Hewitt claimed not even to know why NBC might have wanted to plant the rockets. "I can't for the life of me figure out why anybody would do that," he said on CNN's *CROSSFIRE*. "It's not something anybody at '60 Minutes' would do."[15]

Which practically invites a closer look at *60 Minutes*'s own dubious history of auto-safety coverage. Most famous, perhaps, is its November 23, 1986, episode, "Out of Control," attacking the Audi 5000 for its propensity to "sudden acceleration." The Audi, it will be recalled, was a car possessed by demons. It would back into garages, dart into swimming pools, plow into bank teller lines, everything but fly on broomsticks, all while its hapless drivers were jamming the brake—or so they said. That's what had happened to, the Bradoskys, the middle American family featured in the *60 Minutes* episode. They happened to have a lawsuit going against the automaker. Clarence Ditlow, of the Center for Auto Safety, had been campaigning on the issue.[16]

"Sudden acceleration" had been alleged in many makes of car other than the Audi, and from the start many observers were inclined to view it skeptically. A working set of brakes, they pointed out, can easily overpower any car's accelerator, even one stuck at full throttle. After accidents of this sort, the brakes were always found to be working fine, nor could anything else be found to be wrong with the car. Such mishaps happened most often when the car was taking off from rest, and they happened disproportionately to short or elderly drivers who were novices to the Audi.

The Audi's pedals were placed farther to the left, and closer together, than those in many American cars. This may well offer a net safety advantage by making it easier to switch to the brake in high-speed emergencies; that would be consistent with the Audi's exceptionally good safety record as measured by federal highway statistics. But it might also allow inattentive or novice drivers to hit the wrong pedal. *60 Minutes*, however, scoffed at the wrong-foot theory. It showed a filmed demonstration of how an Audi—as fixed up by, yes, an expert witness testifying against the carmaker—could take off from rest at mounting speed. The expert, William Rosenbluth, was quoted as saying that "unusually high transmission pressure" could build up and cause problems. "Again, watch the pedal go down by itself," said Ed Bradley.

Bradley did not, however, tell viewers why that was happening. As Audi lawyers finally managed to establish, Rosenbluth had drilled a hole in the televised car's transmission and had attached a hose leading to a tank. That fact, however, was brought to light later. In the aftermath of the *60 Minutes* show, Audi sales plunged from 73,000 cars in 1985 to 23,000 in 1988, dealers were hit hard, resale values plummeted, and lawyers piled on. Eventually, at much expense, the company prevailed in most of the litigation, and NHTSA, along with its sister safety agencies in other countries, confirmed that the reason cars were accelerating was "pedal misapplication"—drivers stepping on the gas pedal when they thought they were hitting the brake.

The rest of the show was up to the standards of the filmed demonstration, so far as impartiality went. The heartbreaking story of Mrs. Bradosky, a minister's wife who had accidentally run over her own son, would have appeared in a different light had viewers been told about the police report in which she had informed officers that her foot had slipped off the brake onto the accelerator. (A jury, unlike CBS viewers, did get to hear about the police report and found Audi not liable.) And the show interviewed another sudden-acceleration victim who worked as a policeman, supposedly the sort of person unfoolable about such matters; but CBS did not choose to add that (as a VW official later told *Automotive Industries*) the cop had an exceptionally bad driving record and "had gotten the car a day or two before [the accident]."

In December 1980, *60 Minutes* had found its attention on the small army-style CJ Jeep, which it warned was dangerously likely to roll over "even in routine road circumstances at relatively low speeds." Again there was footage, this time of Jeeps flipping in single-car crash tests run by the IIHS in collaboration with a CBS film crew. Correspondent Morley Safer described the first of what appears from a distance to be standard maneuvers. "It is something called a J-turn: a fairly gentle right-hand turn that a driver might make if he was going into a parking lot." The Jeep flips over. Safer concedes that "it does not happen every time," and a good thing, too, since if it did the nation's parking lots would be cluttered with overturned Jeeps spinning their wheels helplessly like so many June bugs.

The camera then went on to show a second test run, "an evasive maneuver, as if the driver is trying to avoid something on the road." An unwanted object is shown obstructing a roadway, lending a you-are-there touch. "The driver would pull out of his lane to the left, go around the obstacle, then pull back to the right into his lane," explained Safer. The Jeep flips over again. Dummy occupants, outfitted in plaid shirts and farmers' caps, tumbled out to their doom. American Motors Corporation (AMC), which then made the Jeep, was, as usual, not allowed to attend the test or inspect the vehicles afterward, but its representative was quoted as saying the company suspected the tests of being "contrived to make the Jeep turn over."[17]

And once again, the details emerged only later, when experts were deposed in litigation. Viewers might have profited by knowing, for example, that testers had to put the Jeeps through 435 runs to get eight rollovers. A single vehicle was put through 201 runs and accounted for four of the rollovers. Put a car repeatedly through extreme maneuvers, AMC said, and you predictably degrade tire tread and other key safety margins.

Was the J-turn, or for that matter the evasive maneuver, "fairly gentle"? The Jeep was occupied by robot drivers that were twisting the steering wheel through more than 580 degrees of arc, well over one and a half full turns of the steering wheel. (Do not, repeat *not*, try this in your own vehicle.) More striking yet was how fast and hard the robots jerked the steering wheel—in one case, at a rate in excess of five full revolutions a second. A study for GM, apparently unrelated to the Jeep affair, found that average drivers' maximum steer rate in emergencies reaches 520 degrees/second, while expert drivers can reach 800; rates above 1,000 degrees/second seem to happen mostly when drivers lose control. The robots used rates of from 1,100 to 1,805 degrees/second in the obstacle-avoidance maneuver. They were also gunning the accelerator—not what you or I might do if a crate of hens suddenly fell in front of us on the highway. (An Insurance Institute internal memo had proposed arranging the conditions of the simulations "to ensure rollover.")

A NHTSA investigative engineer later wrote that the tests' validity was "questionable" given their apparently "abnormal test conditions and unrealistic maneuvers," and also found signs that the vehicles' loading had been "manipulated in combination with other vehicle conditions to generate worst-case conditions" for stability. The "vehicle loading" issue was clarified by the testers' own internal report, which was not disclosed at the time of the broadcast but emerged later in litigation. In their report, the testers said that at the request of Insurance Institute personnel, they had taken the step of *hanging weights in the vehicle's corners*—inside the car body, where they were not apparent to the camera. Presumably this was for much the same reason that the *Dateline NBC* rockets were strapped out of sight underneath the GM truck rather than conspicuously on its side, and detonated by remote control rather than by a visible wire, and the same reason the *60 Minutes*'s cameras managed not to pick up the tank with its attached hose on the front passenger seat of the doctored Audi.

Or consider the Emmy-winning *60 Minutes* segment in March 1981, revealing how the most common type of tire rim used on heavy trucks can fly off, killing or maiming tire mechanics and other bystanders. Again CBS relied on film from the Insurance Institute, this time showing an exploding rim shredding two luckless dummies, one of them representing a child. Such footage, said Mike Wallace, "shows graphically what can happen when a wheel rim explodes." Ben Kelley, at that time an Insurance Institute spokesman (he had also appeared on the Jeep segment) then explained that a truck tire is under enormous pressure. "And if that metal, for any reason, dislodges, it fires off like a shell out of a cannon."[18]

Though *60 Minutes* did not see fit to tell viewers exactly why the metal happened to dislodge in the film clip, the Insurance Institute made no secret of the fact. In order to get the rims to explode, it had been necessary to have them "modified," specifically by deliberately shaving off their locking mechanism. In a later deposition, an Insurance Institute employee said the testers had to go back and shave off more and more of the metal in stages before finally removing enough—an estimated 70 percent—to cause the rims to explode.

Dateline couldn't even manage to be original on the use of undisclosed incendiary devices. Back in June 1978, at the height of the Ford Pinto outcry, ABC's *20/20* reported what it called "startling new developments": evidence that full-size Fords, not just the subcompact Pinto, could explode when hit from behind. The show's visual highlight was as exciting as *Dateline*'s: Newly aired film from tests done at UCLA in 1967 by researchers who had earlier performed contract work for the automaker showed a Ford sedan being rear-ended at fifty-five miles per hour and bursting into a fireball.

"*ABC News* has analyzed a great many of Ford's secret rear-end crash tests," confided correspondent Sylvia Chase. And the tests showed that if you owned a Ford—not just a Pinto, but many other Ford models—what happened to the car in the film could happen to you. The show's tone was unrelentingly damning, and by the end popular anchorman Hugh Downs felt constrained to add his own personal confession. "You know, I've advertised Ford products a few years back, Sylvia, and at the time, of course, I didn't know, and I don't think that anybody else did, that this kind of ruckus was going to unfold"—the sort of bad publicity it's hard for money to buy.

If ABC really analyzed those UCLA test reports, it had every reason to know why the Ford in the crash film burst into flames: There was an incendiary device under it.[19] The UCLA testers explained their methods in a 1968 report published by the Society of Automotive Engineers (SAE), fully ten years before the *20/20* episode. As they explained, one of their goals was to study how a crash fire affected the passenger compartment of a car, and to do that they needed a crash fire. But crash fires are quite rare; in fact, the testers had tried to produce a fire in an earlier test run without an igniter but had failed; hence, their use of the incendiary device (which they clearly and fully described in their report) in the only test run that produced a fire. The "Beyond the Pinto" coverage gave plenty of credit to the show's on- and off-screen expert, Byron Bloch, who "worked as a consultant with *ABC News* on this story, and provided us with many of the Ford crash-test records."

It would be easier to forgive networks after these episodes had they at least apologized, corrected their mistakes, and resolved to do better. But of the three old-line networks, only NBC, after its *Dateline* debacle, made any gesture toward doing so. At CBS, Hewitt, Mike Wallace, and Bradley have heatedly defended even the show's egregious Audi segment, nor is the network any more apologetic about its decision making in the other episodes. ABC is close behind in the competition as to who can regret the least. On June 1, 1990, it ran its own exposé of the Jeep, one of whose themes had been that many rollovers (contrary to Chrysler/AMC's insistence) do not arise from driver error. It cited Carl Cook's fatal one-car accident, and showed Mrs. Cook reciting the details of his blamelessness: "There was no speed, there was no drinking, there was no drugs, there was no falling asleep"; he had been "operating a Jeep vehicle in an off-the-road situation, exactly what it was designed to do." Summing it all up, *20/20* reported flatly that the jury in the resulting lawsuit said that "the fault was not Carl Cook's." Flatly and wrongly: In fact, the jury had voted Cook's own negligence 50 percent responsible for the accident. When Chrysler called ABC on this palpable error, network exec Richard Wald wrote back that "we made a judgment that this was not significant" in light of Chrysler's having been found liable for the other half of the fault. Thus do some network executives deflect criticism: Lest someone think they made an inadvertent slip, they claim to have misstated things on purpose.[20]

For a while it looked as if NBC's 1992–93 igniter fiasco might lead to soul-searching, if not a complete change of course, in relevant journalistic circles. Some heads besides Gartner's did roll at NBC. In a keynote speech to the Society of Professional Journalists (SPJ), *Dateline* coanchor Jane Pauley surveyed the sorry history of crash-test journalism and suggested that all three networks needed to do better.[21] It even seemed, for a brief while, that the newsmagazines were being a bit more cautious about accepting prepackaged safety stories. But what was perhaps more significant is the reaction the *Dateline* episode drew from the ethical arbiters of the journalism business, namely, not much of a reaction at all. The *Columbia Journalism Review* persistently averted its gaze from the GM/NBC story, which just didn't "fit" its preferred template for the danger to media integrity, which is supposed to come primarily from owners and advertisers. Few, if any, retrospectives, books, or conferences were held or done in later years that might have kept memories of the episode fresh or raised the question of whether anything had improved.

Before long, Ditlow and the others were right back at work just as if nothing had happened. Byron Bloch's Web page lists late-nineties' consulting work for shows including *Nightline* and *Primetime Live* (ABC), CBS network news and *Public Eye with Bryant Gumbel* on automotive topics ranging from airbag hazards to the Princess Diana crash. Another litigation consulting firm that made inroads during the 1990s, *Safetyforum*, explicitly cited its ability to manipulate the media in its pitch to lawyer clients: "Our research, ability to define issues and present our findings are well known for the results they create: product recalls, record-setting jury awards, and award winning print and broadcast news stories." Among its associates, Cindy Raffles was formerly with the Institute for Injury Reduction, where she "worked extensively with producers and reporters of national news programs including *20/20*, *Primetime Live* and *Street Stories* to develop stories that expose dangerous products."[22]

20/20 was completely unapologetic after its October 27, 1995, segment on Chrysler minivan latches ("Open to Danger") was flayed by a correspondent for *Brill's* as "unfair because it failed to inform viewers that Chrysler vans were still generally safer in crashes than competing vehicles," and specifically safer on ejection rates and fatalities.[23] (Two years after the segment aired, a South Carolina jury returned a $262 million verdict against Chrysler in one such case, later thrown out on appeal.) And in 2000, many of the familiar advocates were presented with almost a dream opportunity when an automotive hazard was revealed that actually was worth calling to the public's attention: Some models of Firestone tires showed a high rate of dangerous blowouts when driven over long hauls at high temperatures under heavy loads, especially when mounted on Ford's Explorer sport-utility vehicle. Ditlow, Claybrook, and others enjoyed a field day of media coverage, helping ensure that the story stayed in the papers for months. Whether or not their efforts improved public understanding of the safety issues was another matter: They seemed eager to publicize almost every theory that might reflect discredit on Firestone or Ford, including theories soon rejected by investigators, and they kept demanding the widest possible immediate recall of tires, at the cost of slowing the process of getting replacement tires onto the much smaller subset of vehicles at more serious risk. Nor could they or their trial lawyer friends claim any credit for bringing the blowout pattern to public attention. That credit went to a claims watcher at the State Farm insurance company.

And tellingly, not Ditlow nor the trial lawyers nor the network producers were yet willing to give up on the seemingly lost cause of sudden acceleration. Stung by the embarrassment of the Audi round, lawyers had huddled with new experts and emerged with yet more theories as to how sudden acceleration might be a genuine mechanically induced phenomenon. One Arkansas plaintiff's lawyer petitioned NHTSA to reopen its probe of the phenomenon, which did not have the intended effect: The agency flatly denied the request in a scathing thirty-four-page memo, saying proponents of the theory "have never produced credible evidence" for it, that a plausible explanation of the phenomenon due to mechanical malfunction had "never been published nor is there any literature in the automotive engineering field supporting it."[24]

The renewed sudden-acceleration campaign did, however, win converts at the one show you'd think of all shows would have learned a healthy skepticism about these issues, namely *Dateline NBC*. In February 1999, it built an episode around a then-recent development in a Cleveland sudden-acceleration case against Ford. The local judge, in marked contrast to most of the judges to rule in such cases, had bought the plaintiff's contentions that Ford had been concealing data about sudden acceleration and condemned the company in sweeping, even vehement language. Four months later, in June of that year, Ford emerged with a total victory on appeal, the higher court throwing out the lower court opinion and ruling that the company had not been shown to have been concealing anything. Despite entreaties from Ford, *Dateline* never ran a word about the reversal, and NBC's affiliated *MSNBC* Web site continued to run the original story without a hint that it had been overtaken by later events.[25]

Despite the epic embarrassment of the scandal over the simulated GM truck explosion, it was hard to avoid the conclusion that nothing, in the end, had been learned at all.

Asbestos Memories

Had you set out twenty-five years ago in search of the places in America where the wealthiest and most powerful private lawyers in the history of the world would spring up over the following quarter century, you would have done well to skip the centers of high-powered law practice in Manhattan, Chicago, and Washington, D.C., and turn your back on the freshly minted classes of grads from places like Harvard and Yale Law. You would instead have been well advised to start paying visits to the decrepit dry-docks and derelict piers of the nation's once-dynamic shipbuilding industry in such cities as Baltimore, with its vast Sparrows Point complex; Brooklyn and Philadelphia with their historic navy yards; Hampton Roads, Virginia; San Francisco; Oakland; New Orleans; Charleston, South Carolina; and Bath, Maine. Last but not least, you would have stopped off at a string of small industrial cities on the Gulf Coast that included Pascagoula, Mississippi, and the communities of Beaumont, Port Arthur, and Orange, Texas. A call or two to the local unions that represented shipyard, steel, oil, and insulation workers could have put you in touch with one of the ambitious young attorneys willing to represent rank-and-file workers in compensation claims for exposure to the dust from the mineral fiber asbestos—such men as Peter Angelos in Baltimore, Dickie Scruggs in Pascagoula, Wayne Reaud and Walter Umphrey in Beaumont, and Ron Motley in Charleston.

Back then the courts were just beginning to give the go-ahead for workers to sue over asbestos exposure, and many products using the fiber had only recently been pulled off the market. Few predicted that the new legal field would develop into by far the largest and most complex body of injury litigation in history. As mass tort topics went, asbestos was novel in that it was if anything underpublicized. It was bigger by an order of magnitude than breast-implant litigation, for example, and it involved a genuine rather than trumped-up health menace, but it was always easier to get the press to focus on the silicone sorority, young women's bosoms being an intrinsically more interesting subject than old men's lungs. Indeed, asbestos litigation was bigger than most other areas of product liability combined—guns, tire blowouts, diet pills, contraceptives, toxic shock, aircraft, you name it.

The conventional account of the asbestos story, as given in works like Paul Brodeur's *Outrageous Misconduct: The Asbestos Industry on Trial*, presents it as a straightforward morality tale of innocence on the one hand and greed on the other.[1] Workers had no idea that inhaling asbestos dust was dangerous to their health; manufacturers knew about its hazards but managed to cover them up until 1964, when Dr. Irving Selikoff of New York's Mount Sinai Hospital published research showing that workers who had spent years installing asbestos insulation suffered a higher death rate and a much higher rate of pulmonary disability than other workers. A public outcry grew, and by the early 1970s most products containing asbestos had been pulled from the market. By that point, however, researchers had begun to realize that millions of workers in construction and industry had been exposed for years to the deadly fibers—on the face of it an enormous public health catastrophe that might easily have been avoided had the manufacturers only been more responsible.

One of the complications with this account is that many of the dangers of working with the fibrous rock had been documented for a very long time before 1964. The ancients marveled at the natural occurrence of a mineral in fibers that could be worked like those of wool or flax, yet were as fireproof as stone or brick and highly resistant to rot, acid, damp, and decay. (The word *asbestos* comes from the Greek for "inextinguishable"; asbestos cloth could be thrown into a fire and pulled out unharmed.) At the same time, ancient medical writers noted that workers who spun asbestos cloth suffered diseases of the lungs. By the early twentieth century, asbestos workers' lung ailments were classed as part of the family of workplace dust diseases known as pneumoconiosis, which included such serious and even fatal conditions as black lung among coal miners and silicosis among glass, pottery, and stone workers.

Also by the early twentieth century, life insurance companies were charging a steep hazardous-occupation premium to cover the lives of workers who routinely handled raw asbestos—such a practice being one that could hardly be kept secret from workforces themselves, of course, since individuals often applied for insurance on their own lives. Studies in Britain in the late 1920s, which drew considerable American attention, began to quantify the hazards faced by asbestos workers. In 1931, Britain made asbestosis a compensable disease, and most U.S. states followed by the early 1940s.

By 1940, in other words, it was well established that occupational exposure to asbestos dust was a hazard to life and health, and that only the actions of responsible employers could ensure that it did not become an undue peril. Asbestos was a standardized material, after all, arriving in generic condition from a distant supplier, like coal or turpentine. It was the employer who could control the volume of dust kicked up in the workplace reaching workers' nostrils and throats, just as it was the operator of a filling station (as opposed to a remote refinery operator) who could make sure station employees were not exposed to noxious levels of petroleum fumes. Employers occupied positions along a wide spectrum of safety consciousness: Some took meticulous precautions—ventilation, respirators, frequent wipe downs of surfaces—to intercept dust, while others didn't seem to notice or care if their workers ended their day coated like snowmen. During the 1930s, a number of widely noted exposés in the national press had pointed the finger at employers who, through incompetence, negligence, or worse, had sentenced workers to disability or death by tolerating appallingly high levels of asbestos dust in enclosed spaces.

Why not cease using the stuff entirely if it was so dangerous? The question never came up (at least until major advances had been made in the development of synthetic substitutes) because the advantages of the material were so compelling. Aside from being light, durable, and of low heat conductivity—which made it perfect for insulation, especially in conveyances such as ships—asbestos was above all, for whatever this is worth in ironic retrospect, the archetypal *safety* material: No substance ever partook less of frivolity or mere ostentation. Since the beginnings of human culture, fire in man-made structures had taken an immense toll of suffering, loss, and death. One of the first industrial-era applications of asbestos was the famous fireproof stage curtain to check the spread of theater fires. With modern methods of mass production, fireproofing could develop from a luxury for the rich to something the ordinary citizen would come to expect in his schools and gathering places, passenger vessels, and apartment buildings.

It was easy for safety engineers to become enthralled with the mineral's versatility. As an ingredient in roofing and siding shingles, it guarded against fire communicated by cinders from one structure to the next. As a covering on cables and wires, it worked to prevent electrical fires. It was also used in large quantities in boilers, furnaces, gaskets, and related products; work gloves, mitts, aprons, and utility blankets; in joint compounds, putty, waterproofing, spackle, adhesives, wallboard, and plaster; brake linings and many other components for cars and locomotives; packing material; and even in the early plastic Bakelite, beloved by collectors of art deco. Aside from the fact that fire codes often specified its use, employing it was a way to show you cared about your customers' and, yes, workers' safety. Following the logic of safety pursuit, a dollop of the ubiquitous substance could be mixed into every component and surface capable of protection, from wallpaper and paint to ceramic tiles and ceiling panels.

With asbestos exposure, as with smoking, the most insidious aspect of the health risk is its latent and slow-developing nature. Most heavily exposed asbestos workers, like most heavy smokers, function well enough for years with little or no evident impairment. Eventually, they may discover that they have contracted asbestosis, a buildup of scar tissue inside the lung that impedes pulmonary function and can even be fatal in extreme cases. Asbestos exposure can also cause a distinctive, otherwise rare and highly deadly cancer known as mesothelioma, which arises in the "pleura" or lining of the lung. And it increases the rate at which victims develop fatal lung cancer, especially in combination with cigarette smoking, with which it shows a particularly deadly synergy: The combination of heavy asbestos exposure and long-time smoking increases lung cancer rates more than fiftyfold compared with persons who have been exposed to neither risk. And the same groups of blue-collar male workers who were most likely to encounter high asbestos exposures also smoked at a high rate.

As in the case of smokers who rationalize to themselves that one more pack can't make the difference, the hazard's extreme latency also tended to lull all parties—management, unions, and individual workers—into ignoring the need for safe practice. Through the 1950s and 1960s, asbestosis was included on state lists of compensable diseases, union magazines ran full-page ads urging members to wear respirators when working with the substance, and many in-house employer publications published cautionary articles. Yet both workers and supervisors widely disregarded employers' dust-control rules. Immediate benefits—keeping up production, steady work at good pay, freedom from cumbersome respirators or constant wipe-down breaks—seemed more important, and unions themselves tended to ignore the dust issue in contract negotiations in favor of concentrating on better pay and benefits. In fact, during the last years before most asbestos products were withdrawn from the market, workers were in no great rush to refuse to handle them, despite frightening news reports and the placement of prominent warnings on their packaging.

A further grim aspect of latent occupational diseases is that workers' compensation systems were very poorly set up to cover them. Since their development in the late-nineteenth and early twentieth century, these systems had concentrated on compensating (at modest benefit levels, but with no need for a showing of fault) persons injured by sudden or acute accidents at work—explosions, falls off ladders, the mangling of limbs in machinery, and so forth. With such injuries there's seldom much doubt about how serious an injury is, when it happened, or at which workplace. Latent occupational disease introduced doubt and problems of proof along all three dimensions. An older laborer, after stints with a dozen or more employers in heavy industry or construction over his working life, reports feeling short of breath and fatigued. How seriously ill he is may be quite unclear: Symptoms could be the first signs of a fatal or disabling illness or could reflect the advance of age or could be transient and soon reverse themselves. They might reflect influences other than those at work, such as smoking. And it was not safe to assume that all (or any) of the harm traceable to the man's employment had been inflicted by his most recent employer—it might have been one or more of the earlier ones, or all combined. Workers' comp systems incorporated aspects of insurance intended to ascribe responsibility for injuries accurately to particular employers or at least their industries ("experience rating"), partly on the principle that riskier lines of industry should pay their own freight so as to have an incentive to improve, partly because other, safer employers objected to having to pay for the less safe.

Because of these difficulties of proof, and not wishing the common fund to run out, all workers' comp systems placed limits on coverage of latent occupational disease. Benefits were low. Some systems declined to provide compensation unless a worker could demonstrate which job had caused the injury. Some would pay only for diseases that manifested themselves within a few years of exposure. Some started a short statute of limitations running on the worker's right to file a claim on the first appearance of even a mild symptom, though serious disease might not set in until years later. And because of the "deal" that underlay workers' comp—in exchange for coverage, workers give up the right to sue their direct employer for damages—workers could not expect to go to court to bring up their employer's negligence in hopes of an alternative route to compensation.

Until, that is, some lawyers came up with what was probably the single most profitable legal concept devised in trial lawyers' offices in the third quarter of the twentieth century: They would sue asbestos *suppliers* instead.

This was far from an obvious or an inevitable notion. It was, after all, the employer and not the distant supplier who had decided to use the substance and had had the power to control dust and exposure levels. Nor was it consistently true that suppliers were knowledgeable about the safety issues while employers were not: Some employers were highly sophisticated and ran well-staffed industrial hygiene departments, while some suppliers (as it was to turn out) were both small and poorly informed.

Pursuing lawsuits rather than workers' comp had a big attraction: If successful, they would bring far more money than comp awards, including payment for categories like pain and suffering. And helpfully, courts were fast relaxing long-standing legal rules that had until recently barred many product-liability claims. In 1965, the American Law Institute (ALI), an influential body of law professors and other authorities, in its Restatement (Second) of Torts had momentously announced that manufacturers could be held liable for failure to warn of dangers associated with the use of their products, even if the dangers were intrinsic to the nature of the product. Moreover, the legal change held out the possibility of imposing retrospective liability on manufacturers who, in accord with the previous state of the law, hadn't warned of such intrinsic dangers. That is what soon began to happen. In the 1973 breakthrough case of *Borel v. Fibreboard Corp.*, a federal appeals court ruled that a Texas insulation worker could sue asbestos manufacturers for *failure to warn*: Had they only affixed warning labels to their products, Borel's lawyer argued, he would undoubtedly have acted to protect himself.[2] In virtually all the hundreds of thousands of asbestos suits that followed, lawyers asserted that their client had been quite unaware of the hazards of asbestos dust and would certainly have taken steps to avoid those hazards had a warning label been provided.

The installing of commercial insulation was not the only way in which Borel, the plaintiff in the landmark case, had been exposed. He had also worked in the crash U.S. government shipbuilding program of World War II, in which vast amounts of asbestos were used. Nor was this coincidental or isolated: Lawyers on both sides of the asbestos wars have stated that of claimants with serious disease arising from the mineral, half or more may have been exposed to it while working on World War II ships.

The U.S. government's 1939–45 Liberty Ship and Victory Ship programs turned the somewhat sleepy American shipbuilding trade into the engine of perhaps the most intense construction program in history. "One hundred and thirty-one shipyards operated on a 24 hour a day, 7 day a week schedule, building 7,000 ships and performing 67,000 repairs," notes one account. The shipyards at Orange, Texas, for example, turned out four hundred minesweepers, destroyers, amphibious landing boats, and other vessels during the war. From first to last, speed was of the essence: The time needed to complete new ships was shaved to mere weeks. The sense of urgency and the tremendous effort of will went far in meeting the challenge of supplying Britain and winning a two-ocean war. The same haste, however, also led to a vast relaxation of the sense of caution with which asbestos was approached.[3]

Asbestos was a vital war material: On the Navy's heavily industrialized modern ships ("floating factories") there were simply no alternatives to its use in large quantities. Even decades later, when litigation had broken out and asbestos suppliers were fast fleeing the business, Defense Department procurement officials refused to consider the use of substitutes and turned down a manufacturer's offer to reformulate its product without the mineral. During the war itself, naval officials tightly controlled the distribution of the mineral, ordered it delivered to government specifications, used powers of requisition to direct purchase from private companies, and stockpiled the results at the government's General Services Administration (GSA) facility at Baton Rouge, Louisiana.

Like other experienced participants in industry, the Navy was under no illusion that the substance was somehow safe. "Asbestosis is an industrial disease of the lungs incident to the inhalation of asbestos dust for prolonged periods," observed the Navy's surgeon general in a 1939 annual report on health conditions at New York's Brooklyn Navy Yard; the report pointed out that the yard's pipe coverers and insulators were exposed to such dust. Two years later, with the Liberty Ship program in high gear, it was proposed to have an outside inspector visit the yard to inspect health hazards. Navy brass, however, vetoed the visit. Comdr. C. S. Stephenson wrote to an Admiral McIntire on March 11, 1941: "I told him [a Mr. Bard] that I had spoken to you and that you had indicated that President Roosevelt thought that this might not be the best policy, due to the fact that they might cause disturbance in the labor element.... None of our foundaries [sic] would pass the necessary inspection to obtain workers' compensation insurance from any of the insurance organizations. I doubt if any of our foundaries would be tolerated if the State industrial health people were to make surveys of them."[4]

Asbestos shipped by the federal government from its General Services Administration (GSA) stockpile came in burlap sacks bearing no warning labels whatsoever. As federal judge Jack Weinstein later put it: "The Navy, though aware of the hazards posed by asbestos dust, in its urge to build its warships as quickly as possible, did not inform workers of the dangers and neglected to make available protective precautions." Indeed, the judge noted, "The evidence produced indicates that these risks were known to Government officials at least as high as the highest Navy personnel and probably known to the President of the United States."[5]

Eventually, 2.5 million civilians worked in the wartime shipbuilding program, and a high percentage of them were exposed to asbestos in the stiflingly close conditions of ships' interiors under conditions that fell far short of safe industrial practice even by the standards of that, let alone our, time. From many it was to exact an ultimate sacrifice less immediate and visible, and less gratefully received by their countrymen, but as remorselessly certain in the end, as that of soldiers, sailors, and merchant seamen who rode the ships into enemy fire. And it is easy to imagine as well that the lax habits of industrial hygiene acquired during the war years must have taken a further toll as they were perpetuated in practices of the postwar veteran-staffed civilian industry, in which neither managers nor workers were likely to have treated with adequate respect a danger they had so recently seen treated so lightly.

Unlike servicemen, civilian defense workers have no automatic right to public compensation for losses sustained in the course of serving the nation, nor can they sue the government itself unless it chooses to waive its "sovereign immunity," which it had (and has) not done in this instance. When former Brooklyn Navy Yard workers began growing ill in considerable numbers, they discovered as much, with Judge Weinstein ruling against them on the legalities even though he said "there's no doubt" in his mind "that the Government is primarily responsible as a factual matter." The U.S. Congress showed little interest in saddling taxpayers with a substantial new burden by enacting a legislated compensation program taking federal responsibility for the shipyard workers.

That left the supplier companies. And as trial lawyers examined the files of large asbestos suppliers, especially dominant industry player Johns Manville (later known simply as Manville), they found that the U.S. Navy was not the only institution that had found it convenient to avert its gaze from the risks. Manville had sought to minimize concern by relying heavily on prewar standards as to allowable dust levels put out by the U.S. Public Health Service (PHS), despite mounting data indicating that those standards were too lax. It had permitted its lawyers to argue in court that it was unaware of there being risks at the federally prescribed level of exposure, though its own files showed that workers at its own factories had long been developing high rates of pulmonary disability. Perhaps worst, it had flagrantly breached medical ethics by instructing doctors in its employ not to inform workers that they were developing early symptoms of chest disease. Infuriated juries began awarding punitive damages. The number of claims against Manville rapidly mounted into the thousands, and on August 26, 1982, the company filed for bankruptcy, one of the larger insolvencies in the history of American business to date. The company's failure raised relatively little alarm among other businesses, who assumed that its situation was unique.

Manville's bankruptcy froze all pending claims against the company, which came as a major jolt to the growing ranks of plaintiff's lawyers who had entered the asbestos field. "It required a whole rethinking of our case strategy," a Ness Motley associate told *The American Lawyer.* "We had to find some new targets."[6] Topping the list, not surprisingly, were lesser players in the asbestos industry. Under our courts' famously liberal principle of "joint and several liability," a worker who'd been exposed to many companies' products over the years could sue them all and collect the full judgment from whichever were still solvent. Secondary producers were soon regularly hit with big verdicts on this basis. The evidence against them was often not nearly so damning as it had been against Manville, but they could at a minimum be accused of not providing adequate warnings. Some courts, unconcerned about the dangers of guilt by association, even ruled that a particularly damning set of letters between executives of Manville and another bankrupt company could be admitted into evidence against *other* participants in the industry.[7]

It did not matter that only a minute portion of a company's overall product line had consisted of asbestos-containing goods; its entire asset base was still subject to confiscation. Many relatively small companies that made asbestos products had, over the years, been bought by or merged into much larger firms; and under another of our law's liberal conceptions, "successor liability," the full assets of those larger firms, could be tapped to pay judgments. Thus in 1968, the Keene Corporation bought a company that made asbestos products; it almost immediately realized that it didn't want to be in that business and managed to get out of it within four years—too late. Hundreds of millions of dollars in claims later, it filed for bankruptcy in 1994. Roofing-maker GAF, in 1967, put itself on the road to eventual courtroom ruin when it bought a company that sold $1 million a year in asbestos insulation. In 1963, Crown Cork & Seal (CC&S), the big Philadelphia-based packaging maker, bought a New Jersey firm that made cork bottle caps; in addition to that business, the one it was interested in, the firm also produced an asbestos insulation line. CC&S disposed of the insulation line three months later, but those three months were enough to put it on the hook for hundreds of millions of dollars in later claims, bringing it to the verge of ruin.[8]

The first wave of asbestos claimants were, for the most part, suffering from serious disease. Some lawyers restricted their practice to representing that class of workers, but others were less picky. What soon enabled the caseload to begin expanding more or less without limit was the realization that there was serious money to be made in bringing cases where illness or impairment was mild or scarcely detectable. These cases typically claimed either mild asbestosis, based on subjective or unverifiable symptoms, or what are known as pleural plaques, an asymptomatic thickening of the lung lining detectable by X-ray and associated with asbestos exposure. "In virtually all pleural plaque and pleural thickening cases," observed a federal court in 1990, "plaintiffs continue to lead active, normal lives, with no pain or suffering, no loss of an organ or disfigurement due to scarring. . . ."[9] Lawyers would nonetheless sue for fear of future disease, reasoning that their client—whom they would probably describe to the jury as having a "time bomb" inside his chest—deserved money at least for worry and emotional distress, and perhaps for the cost of the not-yet-materialized illness, too. According to *The American Lawyer,* one attorney with Ness Motley "says the firm tries to stall cases in which illness is not far advanced on the chance that the client will become sicker and fare better in court."[10]

In plaintiff-friendly jurisdictions, juries have returned enormous sums on pleural plaque and marginal asbestosis cases. Thus, one Philadelphia jury gave out $315,000 for nondisabling pleural thickening, and another $1.2 million; a shipyard machinist who suffered no disability got $875,000. A Beaumont, Texas, jury awarded an average of $5 million apiece, $115 million in all, to twenty-one plaintiffs whose asbestosis ranged in severity from "mild" to "asymptomatic." An executive with auto parts maker Federal-Mogul said "90% of [its asbestos] claims are now paid to people who show no serious ill effects." The "vast majority" of its $275 million annual payouts, said wallboard maker USG, were to workers who were not in fact ill. All evidence is that most asymptomatic claimants will never contract asbestos-related disease at all.[11]

With proven rewards to be had from asymptomatic cases, lawyers stepped up recruitment efforts: Asbestos became a staple of law firm advertising in every medium from television to the Internet to the hiring of small planes to pull ad banners through the skies over retiree communities. Among favorite recruiting grounds were union halls and factory gates, where the lawyers could station a van or trailer with hired medical screeners operating X-ray machines. In one famous episode, plaintiffs' doctors said they found evidence of pleural thickening or worse in 65 percent of tire workers screened through such methods; by comparison, a 1987 study by the federal government's National Institute for Occupational Safety and Health (NIOSH) found evidence of asbestosis in only 0.2 percent of tire workers and symptomless pleural changes in an additional 2.3 percent. If the case proceeds to trial, doctors hired by the plaintiffs will typically find a great deal of worrisome stuff on the plates: Doctors hired by the defendants will say they see little or nothing amiss, and a bewildered jury will be left to decide whom to believe.[12]

At the same time, lawyers were steadily working their way downward from early round litigants who had worked for long periods amid large quantities of asbestos dust, to those who had had much lower exposures. It had been known for decades that the relatively small number of workers engaged in asbestos mining, or in the fabrication of raw asbestos into products, faced a definite risk. Selikoff's 1964 study had caused widespread alarm because it had demonstrated that serious risks also extended to workers whose job was to install insulation, an occupational specialty that then, as now, employs a fairly large number of workers and in which working conditions are not easy for outsiders to monitor. What many had been slow to take into account was that insulation, being a naturally loose and crumbly ("friable") substance, tends to release fibers into the air when disturbed, adding up to a cumulatively large dose for those whose job, year after year, requires them to move, cut, and push the material. By the same token, most medical authorities agreed that persons whose dose was low—say, those who simply worked down the hall in a building where asbestos was used—had very little to worry about. This was particularly true if the mineral had been fixed or encapsulated, as in applications like firebricks and gaskets, for the same reason that, while you might contract silicosis from making china dishes, you did not have to worry about serving dinner off them.

As some of the lawyers saw it, however, no exposure was too low to justify legal action. You might catch cancer from a single fiber, and how could the company lawyers stand there and deny that you had breathed in many more than one fiber? As for products where the asbestos was fixed or encapsulated, the solution was simple and elegant: They must have given off deadly fibers while being cut, bent, or scraped during installation. The concentrations of asbestos in a given brand of floor tile or shingle might be only 1 percent or 3 percent, but the client had still doubtless been exposed to more than one fiber. Cements, paints, adhesives? Doubtless cut into after they had dried. Vermont-based Rutland Fire Clay, a century-old maker of stove and fireplace equipment, went broke after being hit with fifty thousand lawsuits, having manufactured a cement containing a small amount of encapsulated asbestos for use in repairing furnaces and wood stoves.[13]

Asbestos-laden brake linings? Don't just sue Detroit automakers and parts makers, sue "friction defendants" like Alcoa for making metal brake components that cut into the soft padding, thus causing fibers to be released. "You have to look under every stone,"[14] as one lawyer put it. Then there were distributors: hardware stores, home-remodeling centers, and family-owned wholesalers that handled thousands of standard industrial products back in the 1940s. And lawyers opened up loopholes in workers' comp laws themselves so as to sue companies in their original role as direct employers of workers exposed to the substance. By century's end, lawyers were suing an estimated 2,400 companies: Campbell Soup, Colgate-Palmolive, AT&T, IBM, Kodak, Ericsson, the Gallo wincry, Gerber Products, Sheraton hotels, Chiquita Brands, and on and on. Viacom, best known as the corporate parent of the CBS network, as of 2000 was facing more than 140,000 pending claims inherited from one of its predecessor companies, Westinghouse Electric.

The "product identification" phase of the lawsuit came to be quite stylized. Either the client, or another of the law firm's clients who had worked at the same job site, would remember that a particular product had been used there, and the workings of complainants' memories on these matters was not left to chance. "We can help you recall possible exposures to asbestos," one lawyer's Web site promises.[15] A common technique is to employ picture books containing page after page of product labels from still-solvent defendants for workers to peruse and "remember"—the more, the better, since all will be expected to chip in toward a settlement. Since records have typically been lost as to which products were used at which workplaces, named defendants cannot readily disprove that their products have crossed a worker's path.

As Manville and other major players in asbestos went broke, a curious thing happened: Many newly recruited complainants abruptly ceased remembering working with those makers' products. Like teachers who notice that many members of the class are handing in identically worded essays, defendants had long suspected that testimony was being mass-produced. Companies with specialty products, whose original market share had been minuscule, found themselves "remembered" and named in nearly as many suits as the leading companies. Workers recited in near-identical language the same representations about their now typically unverifiable symptoms and other elements in the case.[16]

Many of the suspicions were confirmed on August 27, 1997, at an otherwise routine deposition in Corpus Christi, Texas. The plaintiff in the case, Willie Ray Reathy, was being represented by the giant Dallas-based law firm of Baron & Budd, one of the biggest asbestos specialists, and one that has grossed hundreds of millions of dollars in settlements (name partner Fred Baron, a leading Democratic fundraiser, was known for hobnobbing regularly with Pres. Bill Clinton). Baron's firm, which had forty or so lawyers on staff, on this occasion had sent a first-year associate who proceeded to hand over to the opposing lawyer a stack of papers without realizing that it contained an extra document he certainly did not intend to hand over. The document was a twenty-page memo with the title "Preparing for Your Deposition."

When defense lawyers studied the memo, they found it explained a lot. "It is important to maintain that you NEVER saw any labels on asbestos products that said WARNING or DANGER," the memo advised. "Do NOT say you saw more of one brand than another, or that one brand was more commonly used than another. . . . You NEVER want to give specific quantities or percentages of any product names. . . . All the manufacturers sued in your case should share the blame equally!"

Product identification came in for a lot of attention in the memo. "How well you know the name of each product and how you were exposed to it will determine whether that defendant will want to offer you a settlement," the document explained. "You must be CONFIDENT about the NAMES of each product, what TYPE of product it was, how it was PACKAGED, who used it and HOW it was used. . . ." What if defense lawyers get skeptical? "You may be asked how you are able to recall so many product names. The best answer is to say that you recall seeing the names on the containers or on the product itself. The more you thought about it, the more you remembered!" And quit worrying: "Keep in mind that these attorneys are very young and WERE NOT PRESENT at the jobsites you worked at. They have NO RECORDS to tell them what products were used on a particular job, even if they act like they do. . . . The best way to respond to this kind of question is 'Yes, I am SURE I saw it there!' or 'I KNOW it was that brand because I saw the name on the container.' "

"Remember to say you saw the NAMES on the BOXES," the memo said of pipe covering and block insulation—the problem here being that workers might "remember" seeing brand names on these products themselves when, in fact, they weren't stamped with makers' names. Although some of the highest dust exposures occurred during demolition work, "Unless your Baron & Budd attorney tells you otherwise, testify ONLY about INSTALLATION of NEW asbestos material, NOT tear-out of the OLD stuff. This is because it is almost impossible to prove what brand of material was being torn out. . . ."

Defense attorneys may try to ask trick questions about products that weren't in use during your time on the job, but your lawyer will object: "[L]isten carefully to your Baron & Budd attorney's suggestion. Some examples are: 'You didn't see that product before the 1960s, right?' Your attorney will not ask you to say something wrong." That's why you should pause after any question: "Make sure you give your attorney TIME to object before blurting out an answer!"

Make sure to keep your lawyers' options open. "You should name all the products YOU RECALL, but be sure to say there were others, too. This way, your co-workers can testify about brands you cannot remember yourself. . . . It is VERY important to say that there were LOTS of other brands. You just cannot recall ALL the names!" And while you may have to let the opposition see your work history sheets, "any other notes, such as what you are reading right now, are 'privileged' and should never be mentioned."[17]

What happened when this document came to public light? Baron & Budd reacted with a strategy worthy of the successful lawyers they are: not only refusing to apologize for anything, but proposing that *they* were the real victim. To begin with, attorney Baron declared that the artfully written document—which was prominently marked "Attorney Work Product," and reflected close knowledge of the legal impact of possible testimonial content—was, in fact, the production of a rogue, unsupervised legal assistant. In fact, Baron maintained, none of the firm's lawyers knew of the document's use; it had only been used in a small number of cases by this one paralegal in the past year or two, besides which he would never knowingly employ anyone he caught suborning false testimony. (The memo itself, incidentally, amusingly anticipates this tendency to lay the blame on the firm's nonattorney employees: "If there is a MISTAKE on your Work History Sheets, explain that the 'girl from Baron & Budd' must have misunderstood what you told her when she wrote it down.")

There followed a ditch-by-ditch, and quite successful, defense, in which Baron & Budd proceeded to block or outlast one investigation after another, claiming that its doings were protected by lawyer-client confidentiality and refusing to let its clients answer questions about whether they'd seen the memo. One judge referred the matter for possible prosecution, but the charges were eventually quietly buried without indictments. Baron lined up law professors to sign affidavits averring that they saw no ethical violation in the use of the memo. The state bar of Texas, far from disciplining the firm, declared the memo to be just fine and dandy in its view. Soon, the firm was saying that the real scandal was that its privacy had been violated by public attention to a purely internal affair. "Baron & Budd takes the position that any public use of The Document is a breach of B&B's privileges, and we will retaliate against any attorney who uses it," Baron told a newsletter. Making good on his word, Baron struck back with a barrage of legal actions aimed at an opposing lawyer named William Skepnek who had called the attention of courts and the public to the memo.

How typical were the techniques used by Baron & Budd? When the "Preparing for Your Deposition" memo drew critical coverage in the alternative-weekly *Dallas Observer,* Baron had this to say: "You know, there are probably 350,000 of these [asbestos] cases that have been filed over the last 15 or 20 years. You're asking me to say what we do, which is what everyone else does, and which is the way these cases are handled—and it is the way every product-liability case is handled—is wrong." Evidently many of his fellow plaintiff's attorneys agreed that Mr. Baron was a worthy representative of their tribe: Well after the memo reports had stirred national discussion, the members of the Association of Trial Lawyers of America proceeded to elect Mr. Baron to their highest post, as president of the organization for the 2000–01 term.[18]

Had there been any will to do so—had it not contradicted the interests of some businesses and many lawyers—it would most likely have been feasible to revamp workers' comp in some way that liberalized its inhospitable treatment of occupational disease. The chaotic litigation that

eventuated instead makes no sense whatsoever as a means
of providing surrogate social insurance. Very similar cases
fare differently depending on where they get filed, who the
judge and lawyers are, and at what point in the evolution
of the asbestos docket they got settled. Cases often take
years to reach trial, as gravely ill claimants wait in line behind those with no disability whatsoever. The large number
of defendants named in each action, each of whom may
have to send a lawyer to a hearing, adds greatly to the expense and duration, as does the medical squabbling over a
long list of recurring issues, including not only X rays and
symptomatology but also the role of tobacco and other
workplace exposures. Counting all the different transaction
costs, a famous study by the RAND corporation found that
at least 60 percent of the money spent on asbestos litigation
was chewed up in the process; if a private charity were
found to be operating at that sort of overhead, it might get
prosecuted for fraud.[19]

For a long time, the impact on the U.S. economy was
cushioned in part by the extent to which much of the ultimate liability could be fobbed off on insurance providers
abroad, since defendant companies (with help from pro-
policyholder court interpretations) were highly successful in
tapping liability insurance policies. That success, however,
hardly came without a price. Between the 1930s and the
1950s, the discernible threat of product-liability litigation
had been so low that carriers charged nominal rates to insure against it or even threw it in as a bonus coverage to
companies that bought general liability insurance of the sort
that paid for recognized legal risks, like being sued by
someone who slipped in your lobby. Now insurance com-

panies were suddenly ordered to pay tens of billions of dollars to cover legal risks for which they had neither charged premiums nor set aside reserves. Much of the ultimate risk had been laid off through reinsurance on the London insurance market, with its unusual tradition in which Lloyd's "Names" pledged their entire personal fortunes to pay claims, a danger that had seemed mostly theoretical before asbestos law came along. Many "Names" lost everything, and one or two dozen of them (the number is uncertain in part because many surviving families are reluctant to talk) chose to face ruin by ending their own lives. Meanwhile, a hardening unwillingness to underwrite types of insurance vulnerable to U.S. legal risk guaranteed that American businesses would be paying steeply higher premiums into the indefinite future.

Past estimates of the scope of asbestos liability have all had one thing in common: They have been far too low. Most mass torts peak and then subside, but asbestos litigation just grows and grows—though the amount of latent asbestos-related health damage newly manifesting itself each year is almost certainly going down, not up. A common estimate during the 1980s was that the eventual costs would reach $30 billion, a figure that has been revised upward to $100 billion and will undoubtedly be revised upward some more. (As of mid-2002 a figure of $200 billion was circulating.) By the time giant power plant producer Babcock & Wilcox threw in the towel and declared bankruptcy, it had laid out $1.6 billion to settle 349,000 cases and anticipated another $1.3 billion, minimum, looming ahead. Johns Manville's compensation fund, created with the assets of its bankruptcy, badly underestimated the demand for its future payouts: It ran out of money and had to be reorganized. Owens Corning, known for its Pink Panther brand of home insulation, kept assuring shareholders that it could see legal daylight in the distance; in late 1998, for example, having already laid out large sums, it agreed to pay another $1.2 billion to settle what were billed as 90 percent of the claims then in its pipeline. But the pipeline soon filled up again, and its outlays for the year 2000 alone approached $1 billion, with a bankruptcy filing coming the next year.

Companies that made a point of settling cases generously and early, so as to avoid wasting money on lawyers' fees, went broke. And so did those who followed the opposite strategy. Most companies insisted to shareholders that they had reserved adequately on their balance sheets against asbestos liability, then found themselves coming back for one more supposedly final new reserve, and then at length appearing in the financial pages one morning as another smoking crater where pension money had once resided. Besides Owens Corning, other large companies bankrupted in 2000, and 2001 included a roll call of leading companies in the building materials industry: Armstrong World Industries, the leading maker of flooring; GAF, the largest maker of roofing materials; conglomerate W. R. Grace, which made fireproofing and many other products; and United States Gypsum (USG), the largest maker of wallboard. And each removal of another solvent defendant shifted more pressure onto remaining defendants in what was nicknamed a "last-man club."

The litigation, like the mineral, had indeed proved inextinguishable.

The Jackpot Belt

For much of its history the Deep South, despite its fabled hospitality, has also been known for having certain bayou and backcountry sections where a visiting Yankee or foreigner wouldn't set out poking around on his own without being on very good terms with the local powers that be. Disturbing things had been known to happen to strangers on those Dixie back roads, and it was unwise to rely on the local sheriff or county judge to protect you. They might even be among the people you needed protection from. H. L. Mencken may have had something of this sort in mind when, in his famous essay, "The Sahara of the Bozart," 1920, he declared of a certain southern state that a "self-respecting European, going there to live . . . would actually feel a certain insecurity, as if the scene were the Balkans or the China Coast."[1]

For many lawyers representing international business, things haven't really changed that much. When they get together, they swap the latest stories about seemingly routine disputes in the South that suddenly ignited, to the utter shock of the people back at the home office, into massive damage awards. There was the British explosives company that lost an unfair-competition case in Texas in 1995 and was told to pay $488 million, later settling for $36 million. A locally influential Louisiana family sued ExxonMobil over contamination to a small portion of its land after long-standing industrial operations there. The oil company said the cost of doing a cleanup was $46,000, and the overall parcel of land as a whole was worth either $500,000 or $1.5 million, depending on who you believed; but in 2001 a jury ordered ExxonMobil to pay the family $1 billion. In North Carolina, jurors mulcted the British-owned Meineke Muffler chain for $196 million, trebled by the court to nearly $600 million, in a franchisee dispute after a lawyer invited them to "send a message to foreign companies." Sooner or later in these discussions someone will probably bring up what happened to that funeral-home chain from Canada back in 1995 in Mississippi.[2]

Even by the standards of commercial disputes, the case of *Loewen v. O'Keefe* had seemed more than usually uneventful and unlikely to be of interest to anyone beyond the immediate participants. The Loewen Group, based in suburban Vancouver, British Columbia, had grown into a substantial company by buying locally owned funeral homes throughout the United States and then revamping their operations to take advantage of centralized purchasing and other efficiencies. When it bought a number of local funeral homes in Mississippi, it proceeded to give the cold shoulder to competitor Jerry O'Keefe, a former mayor of the city of Biloxi, by terminating his exclusive right to sell funeral insurance through the homes. O'Keefe sued for breach of contract, and he later added charges of fraud and antitrust

violations following the collapse of an attempt to settle the
suit by restoring him to a part of the business. The only
thing that looked even slightly out of the ordinary about
the case was that O'Keefe had engaged Willie Gary of Stuart, Florida—one of the South's most prominent trial lawyers—to argue his case. The son of a sharecropper, Gary
has parlayed more than a hundred victories in $1-million-
plus cases into a private jet named *Wings of Justice* and a
forty-room villa where he hosted then-president Clinton at
a $500,000 Democratic fund-raiser.

Loewen had already turned down, as exorbitant, an offer
to settle the case for $4 million—not a smart move, as it
became apparent in retrospect. On stepping into the case,
one of Gary's first moves was to raise his client's demand
to $125 million. That this sum vastly exceeded any con-
ceivable valuation of the family businesses being fought
over should have tipped off the folks back in Vancouver that
this was no longer going to remain an ordinary controversy.

The trial came on in Hinds County (Jackson), with
Judge James Graves Jr. presiding. It lasted seven weeks.
Over that time Gary's team explored many matters that
seemed only marginally relevant to, sometimes even at odds
with, their client's actual legal case. For example, they made
sure the jury heard at length about Loewen's practice, when
it entered a market by buying up local funeral homes, of
raising prices and introducing more expensive caskets and
the like—"[t]aking advantage of the needy and downtrodden," as one of Gary's fellow counsel later put it. It was
perfect for angering the jury, though it was much less clear
how O'Keefe, who was a competitor, had lost anything by
it, the way he might have lost money if Loewen had started

slashing prices instead. Gary took pains to establish, re-
turning to the point again and again over three pages of
trial transcript, that what company founder Ray Loewen in
his testimony had modestly referred to a company "boat"
would more properly be called a yacht. Later, a Loewen
exec said the strategy was to "incite" the jury. "Much of the
plaintiff's case was . . . an attempt to paint our company as
ruthless predators oppressing the poor people of Mississippi." "Gary's presentation at trial," contends law professor
Michael Krauss in his account of the case, "was almost entirely devoid of any legal argument regarding the law of
contract."

That was just the beginning. With his client on the
stand, Gary drew out that O'Keefe had joined the U.S.
armed forces after Pearl Harbor and won military honors.
The relevance became clear later when Gary told the jury
that a man who had "fought for his country" was now willing to "stand up for America" against this rich foreign company. Foreign? Canada doesn't count as a particularly exotic
or sinister locality in most Americans' minds, but O'Keefe's
lawyers hammered away at the nationality issue so persistently that Loewen's lawyers wound up lodging more than
fifty objections to digs at its Canadian-ness, consistently
overruled by Judge Graves. Men like O'Keefe "fought, and
some died for the laws of this nation, and they're [Loewen]
going to put him down for being American." Nor was the
foreigner-baiting confined to the courtroom. Wrote Krauss:
"One ad placed by O'Keefe in local newspapers during the
trial juxtaposed the Mississippi and American flags on one
side of the page, and the Japanese (!) and Canadian flags on
the other. Under the two foreign flags was written 'NO'

and 'Loewen/Riemann' [Riemann was the local firm Loewen had bought in entering the local market]; under the domestic flags, 'YES' and 'O'Keefe.' " By the time the plaintiffs' side had finished, you'd have thought we'd fought World War II against the Mounties.

As if all this were not bad enough, there was the matter of race. Though the parties to the case were white, the jury consisted of eight blacks and four whites, and both sides engaged experienced black as well as white lawyers. When Loewen added two black former state legislators to its team, O'Keefe's original attorney reportedly advised his client, "We've been out-blacked," prompting them to recruit Gary, who is black. At trial, Gary called former agriculture secretary Mike Espy and other witnesses to testify that O'Keefe was admired and respected by blacks. Loewen, for its part, irrelevantly tried to score points by pointing to a funeral-services deal it had struck with the black National Baptist Convention. Gary's response was simplicity itself: He just demonstrated that Loewen expected to clear a profit on the deal, and since a good deal for one side naturally implied a bad one for the other (or so went the implicit premise), that was proof it had schemed to enrich itself at black people's expense. "This is money they're going to get off 8.2 million African-Americans, a contract that was clearly without question unfair to those members, and you know it."

At the end, even Gary's opening-gun demand for $125 million seemed a thing of the distant past: He told the jury his client deserved a cool billion and invoked a "promise" he had extracted from them. "You said you'd do it, you did, members of the jury. . . . I asked if anyone here, if you felt comfortable sitting on a case that could exceed $850 million, raise your hand; and without hesitation, all 12 of you, you raised your hands." In the end the jury, probably thinking itself moderate, wound up splitting the difference and giving him about half that, deciding that Loewen should pay O'Keefe $500 million, consisting of $100 million in compensatory damages, including $75 million for emotional distress, plus a staggering $400 million in punitive damages.

Judge Graves declined to set aside or reduce the verdict, which left appeal. Contrary to what is sometimes imagined, there is no general right of appeal from a state court to the federal courts, so Loewen needed to hope for the best in the Mississippi state court system, which was and is considered extremely friendly to plaintiffs' interests. Of most immediately pressing concern, the state had an unusually onerous bonding rule, which provided that a defendant wishing to appeal a verdict must first post a bond amounting to 125 percent of the size of the judgment, in this case $625 million—and Loewen had only a week to raise the money. Unable either to meet the bond or pay the judgment, the Canadian firm's only remaining bargaining chip was the threat to declare bankruptcy and thus make O'Keefe wait in line with other creditors. Instead, he agreed to settle, for a sum variously estimated at $130 million and $175 million, depending in part on how one evaluates securities that changed hands. Loewen's stock, previously a favorite on Wall Street—with most of it being owned by American, as distinct from Canadian, investors—plunged in value by 80 percent. The legal setback dealt the company a blow from which it never recovered; it filed for bank-ruptcy in mid-1999.[3]

The Loewen case was the sort that makes and breaks reputations. For attorney Gary, it secured his buzz as a "hot" lawyer, as well as a reported $69 million share of the case's contingency fees, and he soon went on to assume a prominent role in suits demanding hundreds of millions and even billions of dollars from such companies as Coca-Cola, Burger King, Anheuser-Busch, and Disney; he also took a high-profile role among the group of lawyers planning a lawsuit over slavery reparations. The episode likewise made a big impression on the Canadian press: the Montreal *Gazette* observed that "Mississippi and Alabama have developed reputations as dangerous places for out-of-state corporations," which repeatedly turn in "large punitive damages in seemingly minor cases." Indeed, a string of decisions against companies from Great Britain, Germany, Japan, and elsewhere had provoked similar discussions in many American trading and investment partners, leading to comparisons of the U.S. legal system to that of a banana republic. The British financial press said the series of adverse decisions was likely to discourage investment in the United States, inducing investors to hold out for higher interest returns as a way of compensating for legal risk. "The U.S. has, without comparison in the developed world, the highest degree of systemic risk posed by frequently arbitrary, severe and unquantifiable litigation," said one British financier.[4]

———

Just as some towns and counties across rural America are speed traps, so others are tort traps. Perhaps the most famous plaintiff's paradise is Beaumont, Texas, whose courts and juries for decades have had a scary reputation among defendants: "If you study class-action cases in the past, especially in Beaumont, we were in a terrible position," said one official with the Toshiba corporation, explaining his company's decision to fold its hand on the laptop suit.[5] Mobile, Alabama, is an important center for the filing of national class actions. Then there's Barbour County, Alabama, whose favorite son is the state's most successful trial lawyer, Jere Beasley, who served as the state's lieutenant governor under George Wallace. In one year alone, 1994, Beasley coaxed $100 million in punitive damages out of juries, including a $50 million award against a finance company over practices that had allegedly inflated costs to his client by $1,000. (The case reportedly settled for less than a million, though.) Beasley has filed scores of cases before county judge William Robertson, who happens to be his former law partner.

Mississippi juries hearing consumer financial disputes are famous for the enormous masses of punitive damages that they balance in teetery fashion atop a small base of routine "actual" or compensatory damages. One such jury was presented with a dispute over $9,000 worth of the expensive auto insurance that lenders take out if a borrower fails to keep up coverage; it hit the bank with $38 million in punitive damages, later cut by the judge to $5 million. A charge of sales misrepresentation in life insurance resulted in actual damages of $22,000 and $32.5 million in punitive damages; a dispute over the sale of credit life insurance packaged with auto loans resulted in actual damages of $637.99; and punitive damages of $36 million, later cut by the judge to $6 million. A chancery judge in Jones County, Mississippi, incensed at the sales practices of a company that financed consumer purchases of satellite dishes, ordered it to cough up $167 million in punitive damages; it filed for bankruptcy protection.[6] Twenty-three customers of a finance company claimed actual damages totaling less than $50,000 and got a punitive award of $69 million.[7] In Copiah County, Mississippi, jurors handed in a $75 billion verdict, but discovered they'd put too many zeroes on the form by mistake, having only intended to award $75 million.[8] And Mississippi was just following in the steps of neighboring Alabama, which made its name earlier in spawning enormous punitive damage awards that far outstripped those in other states. In the years starting in 1985, the U.S. Supreme Court began hearing a series of cases on the question of whether punitive damages can be unconstitutional in their magnitude and application, and a high proportion of the cases it chose were drawn from the Alabama courts. Among them was the most famous of all, 1996's *BMW of North America, Inc., v. Gore* in which a jury had voted $2 million against the German automaker to a doctor who had not been told about a $601 touch-up paint job done before delivery on his new luxury car.[9]

It would be wrong to assume that the regions of heavy Moon Pie consumption are the only ones civil defendants have to worry about; both Los Angeles and Miami, for example, have made notable contributions to the list of outrageous verdicts. But there's still an unmistakable geographical pattern: Around the curve of the nation's Gulf

Coast, with forays into rural areas inland, stretches a Jack-pot Belt that accounts for far more than its share of massive jury awards, egregious class-action settlements, anything-goes jury-selection practices, confiscatory appeals bond rules, and, not by coincidence, many of the richest lawyers in the world. For the most part, the Jackpot Belt is poorer and less white collar than the rest of America, its economy more dependent on non-sought-after industries such as shrimping, logging, oil, chemical refining, and paper mills. Generalizations about the racial angle are perilous: Majority-white counties and juries, as well as those that are majority black, produce outsize verdicts, and most top trial lawyers know how to play to either audience. "They draw on the same school of thought the George Wallaces and the Huey Longs tapped into," Birmingham defense lawyer Gere White told the *Washington Post.* "It's us against them. It's the idea that the reason you're downtrodden is these big northern corporations are taking advantage of you."[10]

There is a paradox here, of course, at least an apparent one. Louisiana, Mississippi, Alabama, and the rest of the Deep South are widely seen as the most politically conser-vative part of the United States. All tend to vote Republican at the level of national politics, and it is Republicans who have generally campaigned for curbing litigation. Hitting business defendants with massive damage awards is not sup-posed to be a conservative thing to do. If regions lived up to their stereotypes, why wouldn't we expect the outlandish verdicts to come mostly from such northern cities as New York, Chicago, Detroit, or Philadelphia, where juries are known as generous with money and distrustful of business?

For many categories of litigation—car-crash claims

against individual motorists, slip-and-falls, and medical malpractice cases, for example—northern urban juries do still set the pace of generosity. ("The Bronx civil jury," New York attorney Ron Kuby once commented appreciatively, "is the greatest tool of wealth redistribution since the Red Army";[11] but affluent Long Island is considered litigious territory, too, so something about it transcends the rich v. poor divide.) By the same token, much of the Jackpot Belt, until recently at least, was known for modest levels of many of these same categories of suit. With the notable exception of Florida with its retirees, for example, southern states tended to have lower rates of medical malpractice litigation than the national average. (This has been changing recently in states like Mississippi, where awards against doctors have skyrocketed.) Most lawyers pursuing a wrongful-firing action against a local employer, a high-speed-chase crash case against a police department, or a sports-injury case against a school system, would still rather pick a jury from a northern city than from a southern small town.

So the patterns are not as simple as all that. When it comes to claims against local neighbors and institutions, juries in the Jackpot Belt have never been known as particularly keen to hand out large damages. But the pattern shifts when the suit is couched as a chance to "send a message" to arrogant businessmen in some distant city. In cities like Philadelphia, Cleveland, and Newark, by contrast, most jurors and judges are acquainted with many people who hold down white-collar jobs at big companies, even at company headquarters. The courts, though more liberal in a hundred ways than those in rural Alabama, are also places where there is considerable familiarity with the realities of ordinary commercial life. Moreover, the legal establishment in states with large white-collar workforces may perceive itself in having a stake of not letting its system be viewed as so hostile to business that companies stop wanting to locate there. New York's highest court, for example, the Court of Appeals, while regarded as liberal on a long list of issues, has also caused much teeth-gnashing among trial lawyers, who perceive it as committed to a longtime policy of rolling back verdicts on appeal that it sees as irrationally large.

No such inhibitions trouble the presently constituted Mississippi Supreme Court, which is one reason a cluster of poorer counties in the Magnolia State have emerged as a national hub for product-liability suits and pharmaceutical litigation in particular. In Fayette, Mississippi, one jury deliberated for about two hours before voting $150 million in compensatory damages to five plaintiffs claiming damage from the weight-loss compound fen-phen in December 1999. (The case settled, in a batch with 873 others, for a figure estimated in the press at $400 million.) At least four-thousand fen-phen cases have been filed in Fayette, most settling in large batches. In 2001, a jury in adjacent Claiborne County awarded $100 million, $10 million apiece, to ten plaintiffs who said the heartburn drug Propulsid had caused them to suffer anxiety, heart problems, and other ills. Given how friendly the Mississippi Supreme Court is considered to be to plaintiff's interests, many defendants deem it more prudent to settle than to risk an appeal.[12]

Fayette, an impoverished community down the road

from Natchez, might seem at first glance the sickest little town in America. Jefferson County, of which it is the seat, has a population of 8,385, yet since 1995 more than 21,000 persons have filed lawsuits in its courthouse, most claiming injury from widely used prescription drugs or from asbestos. That works out to a rate of more than two and a half product-related suits per resident. Defense lawyers say most of the litigants on the Fayette docket have never set foot in Mississippi in their lives. Under the state's wide-open procedures, once lawyers file suit on behalf of a local resident, they can then add allegedly similar cases from elsewhere, including from other states. Then the entire group can benefit from the deliberations of Fayette's jurors, half of whom have not completed high school and nearly half of whom live below the poverty level.

With the pharmaceutical cases, as with asbestos and breast implants, defendants say lawyers' intensive recruitment efforts have pulled in enormous numbers of plaintiffs whose symptoms are vaguely described and did not result in medical attention, as well as many who lack good records of what drugs they took, or should not have been on the drug in the first place. A spokesman for defendant Johnson & Johnson, for example, was quoted as saying that upwards of five out of six users who reported problems on the anti-heartburn medication Propulsid had taken it despite contraindications in the form of adverse health conditions or conflicting medications. The drug is contraindicated, for example, in persons with heart problems, yet one of the cases the company faced in Fayette was that of a sixty-year-old woman who took the drug despite a history of coronary artery disease and congestive heart failure; she also reported having taken the diabetes drug Rezulin and was suing over it too, in both cases on the theory that the drugs made her rather grave preexisting health problems even worse.

In her local courtroom, she was among friends and neighbors in a very literal sense. According to the Jackson *Clarion-Ledger*, the ten plaintiffs in the big Propulsid trial included the mayor of Fayette, Rogers King, as well as the sister-in-law of the court clerk in charge of summoning jurors. (Johnson & Johnson did manage to persuade Judge Lamar Pickard to move the trial up Route 61 to adjoining Claiborne County, which has a reputation among lawyers not much different from Jefferson County's.) To make sure the case stays in state court, trial lawyers need a local defendant, so they commonly name the town's independently owned Main Street pharmacy. Pharmacist Traci Swilley told the *National Law Journal* (NLJ) that although she eventually gets dropped from the suits, every new filing triggers another claim on her liability insurance, making it hard to get her coverage renewed, as she must legally do to operate. "The people don't realize they're suing me," she said. "They're told by these big-time trial lawyers, 'You're not hurting the pharmacy. This isn't against Traci.' "

For towns like Fayette, litigation helps drive the local economy, with the law office complexes tending to be just about the spiffiest places in town and prosperity radiating outward from them, or so it is hoped. Even the $100-per-plaintiff filing fee that Judge Pickard charges is a significant money raiser, bringing in an estimated $2.1 million-plus to the threadbare little community. The evidently proud chamber of commerce of the town of Texarkana said the Texas tobacco Medicaid suit brought $6.1 million to local hotels and other businesses.[13] After filing suit in Orange County, Texas, on behalf of 1,700 out-of-state asbestos complainants, the plaintiffs' lawyers told the Beaumont newspaper that the suit would do wonders for the area: "Lawyers, expert witnesses, doctors from all over the world will be flying in and staying in Orange motels, eating at Orange restaurants and buying gas at Orange stations."[14]

The Jackpot Belt has played a disproportionate role in virtually every mass tort episode. Asbestos? Draw an arc from Beaumont and Houston through New Orleans, Pascagoula, and on to Pensacola, Florida, and you corral perhaps half the nation's most successful asbestos lawyers. Tobacco? The same group of lawyers engineered key breakthroughs in the Mississippi, Texas, and Florida tobacco suits. With breast implants, Houston was the epicenter. Guns? Louisiana's Wendell Gauthier helped recruit his hometown of New Orleans as the first municipal client. Lawyers often pick the Jackpot Belt as a place to file pilot cases; once a jury in a place like Corpus Christi or Brownsville, Texas, has made headlines with a $10 million verdict against some controversial product, juries in conservative places like Kalamazoo and Roanoke find it easier to start giving money, too.

Houston and New Orleans aside, the Jackpot Belt is not much visited by the national press, a fact that can actually be an advantage in cases in which trial lawyers are not looking for publicity. When they decided to couch Mississippi's tobacco suit as a Chancery claim in their hometown of Pascagoula, for example, Michael Moore and Dickie Scruggs instantly transformed Chancellor William Myers, who presided over the case, into one of the most powerful judges in world history. Their confidence was well merited since, as Martha Derthick of the University of Virginia writes, Myers "could hardly have been more supportive" of their claims.[15] Not only did he turn down the tobacco companies' demand for a jury trial, but some of his most crucial rulings in favor of the plaintiffs were made with almost no explanation: He rejected the companies' motion to dismiss in a one-page opinion, and later rejected the companies' all-important cost-offset defense in an eight-line ruling devoid of explanation or analysis. Had the case been taking place in a major media center, the novelty and obvious importance of the issues it raised would almost certainly have led to a higher level of press scrutiny. Instead, with Moore and Scruggs not going out of their way to encourage reporters to treat the doings in Pascagoula as a big story, it barely appeared on the radar screen of the national media and Chancellor Myers himself remained almost entirely obscure, the subject of next to nothing in the way of media profiles.[16]

With class actions, too, the remoteness of some counties is sometimes an attraction in itself to the lawyers who operate there. Boston University law professor Susan Koniak, who has written about the abuse of class actions, describes it as "common" for such suits to be filed "in the middle of nowhere." Opponents may stumble as they try to familiarize themselves with courthouse byways and identify qualified local counsel. A major class action over defective plastic pipe was filed in the 10,500-population burg of Union City, Tennessee, a two-hour drive from the nearest big city, Memphis. Involved in its filing were big-name class-action lawyers from San Francisco and Washington, D.C., who prevailed on the local judge to grant a preliminary certification of class status the very day the suit was filed, leap-frogging it ahead of its competitors, who were not pleased: "No one could get there, you couldn't fly in to object . . . [you couldn't get] access to the documents," as Koniak put it.[17] Later, another set of lawyers chose the same little courthouse to file in a second competitive class-action situation, this time an antitrust suit over herbicide sales.[18]

Some judges in the Jackpot Belt make no bones about their willingness to dish out what lawyers call "home cooking." One factor that sometimes seems to be at work is the southern custom of making a position as county judge something that lawyers do early in their careers, rather than a culminating honor, as is more often the case up north. The judge who himself has only lately been admitted to the bar may be more inclined to let seasoned counsel run the process with little interference. Plaintiffs' lawyers benefit, too, from the enduring rural institution of the one-judge courthouse. In a big city you may be spinning the wheel on the question of which judge hears your case, but if you go to Fayette you know exactly who'll hear it: Judge Lamar Pickard, whose rulings are dreaded by out-of-town defendants. He's the only judge for civil cases in Jefferson, Claiborne, and Copiah Counties. According to another *NLJ* account, the Texas tobacco suit is just one of a long succession of high-stakes cases that plaintiffs have brought to remote Texar-kana at the northeast corner of the giant state, and they do so "for only one reason: Judge David Folsom." Since the

Clinton appointee is the only federal judge in Texarkana, "every suit filed here goes before him." Hapless defendants often request a change of venue, but Folsom, an old pal of Clinton's since his Arkansas days, said he couldn't recall ever granting one.[19]

One appreciated element of "home cooking" is the ability to get quick court dates (or sometimes slower ones, depending on which is more discomfiting to the opponent). In the breast-implant cases, for example, Joseph Nocera found in his *Fortune* investigation, that John O'Quinn and other local plaintiffs' lawyers seemed to enjoy an uncanny ability to get cases docketed for trial in the Houston courts at the exact times most inconvenient for defendants, such as while a settlement was pending that might be blown apart by a large verdict. The defense would learn only days in advance which of the many cases would be called up for immediate trial: "They control the docket," complained Dow Corning's general counsel.[20]

In the case of Houston, as with many communities throughout the Jackpot Belt, the breast-implant lawyers had been important contributors to the election campaigns of many of the judges hearing their cases—which had also been true in the Texaco-Pennzoil case and, indeed, in most big cases coming out of Houston. In most state court systems, judges are appointed by the governor, often in combination with "retention elections" afterward that are typically less hotly contested than elections conducted from scratch. But the norm in the Jackpot Belt is for judges to be elected on a direct partisan line. Judges up north, too, often take campaign contributions from lawyers who practice before them, but there is something particularly bold and breezy about the acceptance of the practice in the Jackpot Belt states. Texas judges, for example, have attended election-night celebrations at the law offices of attorney supporters. When the trial lawyers' association threw a convention bash to honor friendly judges, Louisiana Supreme Court justice Pascal Calogero rose to thank the group's president for "helping me continue to win elections."[21]

And then there's Alabama, whose supreme court not too many years ago affirmed a punitive damage award of $12.9 million against Northwestern Mutual in a case in which economic losses had been $8,500. Afterward, it was noted that one of its justices had accepted $15,000 in campaign funds from the winning lawyer (together with his wife and partner) while the case was pending—especially notable, remarked *Forbes*, because the justice "was not on the ballot and had no opponent at the time." The Alabama high court has changed composition in recent years, but for a long time its chief justice was a former president of the Alabama Trial Lawyers Association named Sonny Hornsby, among whose most noteworthy accomplishments on the bench was to help strike down a package of tort reforms that had passed the state legislature in 1987. Hornsby made no apologies for sending handwritten notes to lawyers with cases pending before his court inviting them to "FedEx" their campaign contributions and helpfully providing his FedEx number. (The ABA Model Code of Judicial Conduct says judges should not personally solicit contributions, but that code is not legally binding.)[22]

When *The American Lawyer* investigated plaintiffs' firm donations in Alabama, it found they were "breathtakingly generous." By the 1990s, the state had secured what the

ABA Journal called a "reputation as a plaintiff's paradise" and hard-hit defendant interests finally began organizing resistance, which led to a grueling series of high court election battles. In a 1994 ultrasqueaker, Hornsby was at first declared winner over Republican challenger Perry Hooper, whom he outspent three to one, but Hooper was left with a razor-thin margin of victory when a federal court later invalidated two thousand irregular ballots that had never been properly notarized or witnessed.[23]

The more money is thrown at races, the more expensive it becomes to keep up the capacity to wage a competitive judicial campaign, especially in states like Texas, where active candidates must advertise in many different media markets. By the mid-1990s, campaigns for the Texas Supreme Court were rivaling U.S. Senate races in expense, with war chests of $5 to $6 million. But even in Alabama, a far smaller state, heads turned when a race for the state supreme court hit $5 million. Judges who cross the lawyers might as well walk around wearing painted bull's-eyes: In 2000, the plaintiff's bar solidified its grip on the Mississippi high court by defeating moderate chief justice Lenore Prather in her reelection campaign. Many judges feel that they have no choice but to get on the campaign-spending treadmill: If they don't shell out for two, three, or four hotshot local consultants at $15,000 a pop, some challenger might.

And then there is the most basic electoral fact of all: In-state plaintiffs vote and out-of-state defendants don't. "As long as I am allowed to redistribute wealth from out-of-state companies to injured in-state plaintiffs, I shall continue to do so," wrote Justice Richard Neely at a time when he was chief justice of the West Virginia Supreme Court. "Not only is my sleep enhanced when I give someone else's money away, but so is my job security, because the in-state plaintiffs, their families, and their friends will reelect me." The out-of-state defendant, Neely writes, "can't even be relied upon to send a campaign donation." A study of more than seven thousand personal-injury cases by Eric Helland of Claremont McKenna College and Alex Tabarrok of the Independent Institute found civil awards ran substantially higher where judges faced partisan election than where selection was nonpartisan. Significantly, partisan election was associated with only relatively modest boosts in award levels for lawsuits against in-state defendants, at $208,000 versus $276,000 (34 percent), but widened considerably for suits against out-of-state defendants ($385,000 where selection is nonpartisan, $652,000 for partisan selection). This suggests a vindication of the commonsense notion that an election-driven system has a built-in tilt toward dumping costs on outsiders who lack a voice in its deliberations.[24]

Will state legislatures in the problem states step in to rein in their runaway courts? Friends of the trial bar are often very well situated to prevent any such thing from happening. In Mississippi, for example, one of the two judiciary committees in the lower house of the legislature is chaired by a notably successful trial lawyer, Rep. Edward Blackmon Jr. (D-Canton). (Blackmon's victories include a $145 million verdict against Ford Motor Company and a $71 million award in a consumer finance case.) The clout that trial lawyers wield in the political process generally is hard to overstate: In the 1998 election cycle, the Texas Democratic Party raised more than three-quarters of its contributions from trial lawyers alone.[25]

How did things get so bad? One factor is simply that in the Deep South, ambitious Democratic politicos looking for local backing are more likely to find the trial lawyers the only game in town. In northern and western states, a rising "progressive" politician can assemble a financial and organizational base from among many constituencies: unions, ethnic "cradle Democrats," liberal academics, civil libertarians, teachers, feminists, a social welfare establishment, environmentalists, gun-control enthusiasts, and on and on. It may not be necessary for them to get especially close to the litigation lobby. Across much of the rural South, on the other hand, there are relatively few groups to fall back on: there are blacks and teachers, who don't sign big checks, and trial lawyers, who do.

In recent years opponents of the litigation lobby have successfully challenged the trial bar's hold on politics across much of the Jackpot Belt. Texas governor George W. Bush, before he became president, made legal reform a top priority and, after a concerted effort by the state's large and sophisticated business community, secured a significant package of reforms restricting litigious excesses. In both Texas and Alabama, following epic struggles, voters replaced extravagantly plaintiff-oriented supreme courts and also ousted some other elected officials identified with the trial bar's interests. But the action, like an old-time medicine show, simply picked up its tents and moved to nearby Mississippi. Until that point, the state's jurisprudence had been known as anything but liberal: Before 1995, according to the Jackson *Clarion-Ledger*, there had never been a punitive damage award higher than $9 million in the state. In the six years that were to follow, however, as lawyers began to gin up a machine of remarkable efficiency, there were nineteen such verdicts, totaling more than $2 billion. Six individual jury verdicts came in above $100 million during the same period. Reports from Alabama were that many plaintiffs' lawyers who had been practicing there were cramming for the Mississippi bar exam.[26]

The implications are national in scope, since the home-cooking courts are favored destinations for class actions over nationwide business practices. (Given a sizable class-action suit, there will be class members living just about everywhere, which gives lawyers a wide choice of which state and county in which to file.) By the 1990s, Alabama had emerged as the nation's hot spot for consumer class actions, with just a handful of counties accounting for its huge caseload. One survey found that over a two-year period, a single Alabama judge had granted class certification in thirty-five-cases; it could not find any instance in which he had turned down such a request.[27] By comparison, at around the same time, the entire bench of nine hundred federal district judges had granted a total of thirty-eight class-certification requests over one year.

Especially noteworthy was the practice of so-called drive-by class certification, prevalent in Alabama until that state's new supreme court called a halt to it.[28] (It is still carried on in some other states.) In that practice, as attorney Stephen G. Morrison has described it in congressional testimony, the state court judge grants the request for class certification "before the defendant even has a chance to respond to the motion (or, indeed, in some instances has even been served with the complaint)." Thus one plaintiff's attorney filed two proposed class-action suits only a few days apart from each other before the same Tennessee state judge, one purporting to represent 23 million vehicle owners in a suit against a big automaker and the other making antitrust claims against the recorded music industry. The judge obligingly granted certification of both cases on the very day they were filed, before anyone could put together a counterargument.

For newcomers to the subject, it may seem almost incredible that nationwide class actions filed against, say, a California lender, and composed overwhelmingly of complaints over non-Alabama transactions, could belong in the Alabama courts. Why would such cases not belong in federal court? And on paper, at least, present law seems to embody the commonsense idea that federal courts should assume authority over this sort of large case between parties from many states, while state courts remain the normal resort for smaller cases between locally present parties. Lawsuits filed in state court can be "removed" to federal court if the amount in controversy exceeds $75,000 and if the action "is between . . . citizens of different states"—so-called diversity jurisdiction.

But today's plaintiffs' lawyers, most of the time, greatly prefer state court to federal court. State court judges tend to run a less tight ship at trial, allowing lawyers more leeway in jury selection, more use of emotional argument, and so on down the line. And, of course, state court judges offer more home-court advantage: Federal courts answer to a constituency of the nation as a whole, and one of the reasons the Constitution set them up in the first place was to provide a more neutral and objective forum for substantial disputes between parties from different states. The upshot is that plaintiffs' lawyers employ skillful gamesmanship to block defendants' efforts at removal by exploiting loopholes in the law. Most strikingly, if with little apparent logic, courts have decided that the diversity-of-citizenship grounds for removal should apply only in cases where *every* defendant is from a different state than *every* plaintiff. As in the Fayette pharmacy case, trial lawyers simply name a local business as an extra defendant for purposes of "defeating diversity," whether or not they are serious about pursuing the case against that defendant.

Other stratagems, equally artificial, are pressed into service as well. For example, courts have ruled that the $75,000 amount-in-controversy threshold applies not to the aggregate size of the suit, as would be logical, but instead to the claims of individual class members. Moreover, and arbitrarily, once a suit has been pending for a year in state court it can no longer be removed to federal court for any reason. So lawyers "plead around" federal jurisdiction by claiming, for example, that they have no intent of demanding any more than $74,999 for any member of their client class or by vowing to waive certain legal claims that might be valuable and otherwise worth pressing but which can be pursued only by consenting to federal court removal. After waiting 365 days, as attorney John Beisner explained to a congressional hearing, it's hey, presto: "The one-year re-moval period passes, counsel delete these restrictions, and the real lawsuit reveals itself."[29] The bizarre result is that while a simple one-on-one lawsuit between parties from different states over $80,000 worth of spoiled kumquats goes to federal court, a nationwide class action demanding $79,999 each for a million class members, or $80 billion in all, stays in state court because it's seen as too *small* for the big (federal) leagues.

The U.S. Constitution contains a number of provisions ex-plicitly overriding the authority of state courts; for example, it authorizes the federalization of bankruptcy, and it pro-hibits states from impairing the obligation of contracts. The common theme is not simply a desire for uniformity in commercial law; it is also more specifically a distrust of the tendency, well known even back then, of state courts to favor local citizens in their disputes with distant merchants and lenders. While defending state courts in general, Al-exander Hamilton warned in *Federalist* No. 81 that "the prevalency of a local spirit" might be found to "disqualify the local [i.e., state] tribunals for the jurisdiction of national causes."

Article IV, Section 1 of the Constitution specifically grants Congress a broad-ranging power to take measures aimed at ensuring that each state yields to the appropriate authority of its sister states: "Full faith and credit shall be given in each state to the public acts, records, and judicial proceedings of every other state. And the Congress may by general laws prescribe the manner in which such acts, records and proceedings shall be proved, *and the effect thereof.*" (Emphasis added.) If this means anything, it means that the farmers gave Congress authority to stipulate the manner in which states must accord due effect to other states' legislation. One implication is that it is a proper subject of congressional legislation to prevent the courts of one state (say, Alabama) from imposing punitive damages on economic transactions taking place in other states whose law would not have subjected those transactions to such damages.

Since then, of course, the federal government has intruded its presence into a host of matters that would have been reserved purely to local authority in Hamilton's day. Federal law now prescribes labor and employment matters in picayune detail, down to the operation of vacation and family-leave policies at small-town employers. It mandates environmental measures of purely localized scope and effect, as when a three-hundred-family drinking water system in a small town is told to filter out impurities at staggering expense. It instructs the local police force when it is permitted to ask officers to take retirement, and it commands the local beauty salon to install a wheelchair ramp. The Founding Fathers would be spinning in their graves with the velocity of jet turbines if they knew about most of these developments. But on one of the few matters where we know they *did* contemplate a strong federal supervisory role—attempts by state courts to impose their will in high-stakes interstate disputes—we suddenly are treated to lectures about the virtues of decentralization and federalism from such litigation lobby figures as Ralph Nader and Joan

Claybrook, who have spent whole careers pushing for expansion of federal government power on matters from amusement park regulation to corporate chartering.

It is a patently false federalism. To allow courts in Fayette, Beaumont, and Mobile to inflict arbitrary expropriation on national businesses is not a necessary corollary of the federalist principle of respecting the right of each state to self-rule because it ignores the rights of other states—who do not wish to have their businesses expropriated—to live unmolested. When the confused, demagogue-led, or corrupt rural county hands down its ruling in one of these cases, it not only makes law that the rest of the country is then obliged to live with but effectively engages in interstate commerce itself, siphoning fortunes across state lines in an essentially commercial and profit-driven process.

Which leads to the question: Why should this be the one form of interstate commerce the federal government is thought unfit to regulate?

The Art of the Runaway Jury

If a drunk driver plows into you from behind at seventy miles an hour while you are stopped at a red light, you are not likely to live long enough to talk to a lawyer about it: The impact, according to David Boldt of the *Philadelphia Inquirer*, is "the equivalent of dropping the car from the top of a 16-story building."[1] However, Patricia Anderson and her passengers were lucky enough to be riding in a 1979 Chevy Malibu, a car much more solidly built than most of its competition. Six victims survived, but with severe burns because the immense force of the crash had burst the Malibu's gas tank and ignited a fire. Although the U.S. NHTSA did not (and does not) deem the Malibu's gas tank to be defective in its placement, design, construction, or any other way, lawyers for Mrs. Anderson disagreed and proceeded to sue GM, saying the fire might have been averted had the company located the tank somewhere other than toward the rear of the Malibu. (Their expert also estimated the speed of the crash at fifty miles per hour, rather than seventy). A Los Angeles jury agreed, and in 1999 awarded the plaintiffs $4.9 billion—a figure that exceeded the annual gross domestic product of eleven UN member states combined.

The award in *Anderson v. GM*, which Judge Ernest Williams of L.A. County Superior Court later reduced to $1.2 billion, caused something of an outcry.[2] The *Washington Post* said in an editorial that it "makes the tort system into a kind of lottery in which clever trial lawyers and a few victims get very rich at the cost of society's confidence in the justice system."[3] The conduct of the trial had been open to question as well. It turned out that, at the plaintiffs' request, Judge Williams had agreed to exclude from evidence various matters that GM wanted to introduce. Among them were federal government statistics from twenty years of real-world highway experience showing the Malibu to be among the safest cars of its time, with an unusually low crash-fatality rate. Nor was the company permitted to introduce crash-test data raising safety concerns about the alternate placement of the gas tank that the plaintiffs maintained would be better. Most remarkable of all, Judge Williams had excluded from evidence the fact that the driver of the other car, a man named Moreno, had been drunk (having alcohol in his bloodstream amounting to 0.20 "several hours later") and had been sent to prison.

As late as the 1980s, jury verdicts higher than, say, $50 million still counted as sensational and unusual, but by the end of the century only a billion-dollar verdict could be counted on to merit front page treatment; an award in the mere hundreds of millions from L.A., Miami, or one of the Jackpot Belt states might barely qualify for the fine print in the back of the business section. Within days of the Los Angeles jury's decision in *Anderson v. GM*, a rural California jury voted $290 million over a Ford Bronco rollover accident;[4] like the Chevy Malibu, the Bronco more than exceeded the federal safety standards of its day. Later, another L.A. jury voted $3 billion in punitive damages in a tobacco case filed by an individual smoker who testified that he had had no idea the habit was dangerous until congressional hearings in 1994.[5]

And even that paled alongside what happened in July 1999 in a Miami courtroom. Following a trial that took two years, a jury deliberated for a mere five hours before deciding that the tobacco industry should pay $145 billion in punitive damages—a sum more than twice the gross domestic product of New Zealand—for having behaved badly toward Florida smokers. One of the individual plaintiffs, a forty-four-year-old nurse, said she "had no idea there was anything wrong with cigarettes at all." The verdict, in a case styled *Engle v. R. J. Reynolds Tobacco Company*, had followed a series of rulings by Judge Robert Kaye highly favorable to the plaintiffs' side. The *Engle* verdict was greeted with a less than respectful reception in much of the press: "Ridiculous . . . outrageous . . . A ruling that completely ignores personal responsibility is a joke" *(Cincinnati Enquirer)*. "Monstrous . . . outlandish" *(San Diego Union-Tribune)*. "The biggest damages here may be to the reputation of the legal system." *(Washington Post)*. "Falls somewhere between confiscation and robbery" *(Indianapolis Star)*. A "fantasy verdict" *(Cincinnati Post*/Scripps Howard News Service). In November 2000, Judge Kaye upheld the verdict, and the tobacco companies announced their intent to appeal.[6]

Defenders of the legal system typically dismiss cases like *Anderson* and *Engle* as atypical. And it is true that only a tiny number of juries return from deliberations having approved the kind of numbers too large to fit on the calculator readout. Moreover, in many of these cases, judges subsequently cut the size of the damage award, though usually to a level that still counts as stratospheric. But the mere possibility that an extreme outcome will emerge from the process, and perhaps survive review and appeal, gets factored into the valuation of the majority of cases that settle before final verdict. With breast implants, asbestos, and many other mass tort episodes, a rash of arrestingly high verdicts helped educate recalcitrant defendants about the need to pony up substantial settlements. While the press sometimes refers to these as "runaway" verdicts, the term is more often than not misleading, since it suggests that the juries in question are racing off madly on a tear of their own, like a horse that is defying, or ignoring, the signals that humans are trying to send it. But quite the contrary is true: Most "runaway" juries are behaving precisely as one set of lawyers has been carefully coaching and skillfully inciting them to do. They are, for the most part, not running *away* from anything, but running *toward* some resolution of the case that trial advocates have portrayed to them as reasonable. Which is why, in seeking to account for exorbitant or unjust verdicts, the most relevant question to ask is usually not, "Why did these jurors behave so irrationally?" but rather, "How did the lawyers manage to portray this outcome as rational?"

Among the most powerful ways in which American lawyers can shape the outcome of trials is by exercising their rights of juror selection. Typically, they can launch an unlimited number of *for-cause challenges* to oust prospective jurors who supposedly cannot approach the case objectively, to which they can add an often substantial number of *peremptory challenges*, which let them dismiss prospective jurors without offering any reasons at all. The upshot is that jury selection in high-stakes cases has emerged as a protracted and expensive stage of trial all by itself, its results often seen by both sides as vital to the outcome. In the O. J. Simpson case, selection alone lasted ten weeks, which in most countries would be a remarkably long time for a murder trial itself to last. The *Engle* tobacco class action in Florida went it one better, with the tweezing and fluffing of the jury pool going on for three months; in the end eight hundred prospects were sent home in search of the perfect eighteen, after having been quizzed on such matters as their reading habits and their views on seemingly unrelated issues, such as gun control.[7] A busy industry of consultants, how-to seminars, and jury-selection handbooks offer advice to lawyers on whether or not to boot jurors based on such characteristics as hair style, hobbies, brand of car, favored kind of reading, and so forth. The "impartial juror" is just a fiction, declares an ad for one primer that promises to show "how to assemble your winning jury, step-by-step."[8] By the mid-1990s, the jury-consulting business was estimated to have passed $200 million in annual revenues, mostly catering to lawyers handling civil as opposed to criminal cases (that being where the money is).

The whole point of the process, of course, is to engage in discrimination: Should the lawyer use his remaining peremptory challenge to kick the childless Presbyterian senior citizen off the panel or the divorced wheelchair user who has lived abroad? What makes the hypocrisy so complete is that trial lawyers themselves make a very handy living suing when unwary people in other walks of life—employers, landlords, private clubs—engage in the same kinds of discrimination. For most of the rest of us, explicitly considering someone's religion, age, or disability status when considering him as a job applicant or tenant is strictly against the law, and even inadvertent acts of bias—resulting from unconscious stereotyping, for instance—can potentially cost us everything we own in a private lawsuit. But if we ever have to face such a discrimination suit, it will practically count as malpractice when it reaches trial for both side's lawyers *not* to engage in age, religion, or disability discrimination during the jury-selection phase.

The group stereotyping in the literature advising lawyers on jury selection is anything but unconscious or inadvertent. Women "are often prejudiced against other women they envy, for example, those who are more attractive," is one groaner from *The Art of Selecting a Jury*, published as recently as 1988.[9] Mexican-American jurors are "passive" and "Orientals . . . tend to go along with the majority," we learn from a manual in recent use by Texas prosecutors.[10] Although the U.S. Supreme Court has lately instructed lawyers not to employ race (and even more recently sex) as a factor in jury picking, lawyers continue more or less blatantly to engage in "jurymandering" of both sorts.[11] The edicts are difficult to enforce given that lawyers need offer, in the words of Brandeis's Jeffrey Abramson, "no justification, no spoken word of explanation, no reason at all beyond a hunch, an intuition" for their peremptory choices.[12]

One can imagine what would happen to the employer or landlord who claimed such a right to base its selection decisions on subjective hunches.

Demography aside, a major goal of the selection process is the removal of any jurors with too strong a base of experience, knowledge, or opinion about the case's subject matter. If a case presents important medical or accounting aspects, for example, one or both side's lawyers are likely to want to get rid of jurors with expertise in those areas. Manuals emphasize the importance of excluding potential "opinion leaders" for the other side. "You don't want smart people," said a Philadelphia prosecutor in an old training tape.[13] "[They'll] analyze the hell out of your case." Even before selection begins, busy people have often dodged service, leaving a pool comprised disproportionately of retirees, the unemployed, and workers who can be spared from their jobs.

To make matters worse, judges in high-profile cases may bounce juror prospects for cause simply for having followed press reports about the events at issue. In the 1989 trial of Oliver North, for example, the judge flushed out more than two hundred potential jurors for knowing too much about the case, which had been on the front pages for months. ("I don't like the news," said the eventual forewoman. "I don't like to watch it. It's depressing.") One panelist, to quote a *New York Times* account, said of North that "she had seen him on television," but added, "It was just like I was focusing on the Three Stooges or something."[14] Another woman, asked what she knew about the Iran-Contra scandal figure, replied, "I don't know, something about overseas." To get on a big case, as a series of such cases has shown, it helps a lot *not* to read a newspaper, or, if you must read one, to read it only for the horoscope and funny pages. In the 1990 obscenity trial over a Cincinnati museum's exhibition of Robert Mapplethorpe's work, the only prospective juror who regularly attended museums was dismissed for cause, it being felt that actual familiarity with those institutions put an "unnecessary burden" on her objectivity.

Remarkably, some courts exclude jurors for expressing fundamentally political opinions about the state of the law and the courts. "There are too many high jury awards these days: AGREE/DISAGREE." Would giving either answer disqualify a citizen from sitting fairly in judgment on a particular suit? Not at all. To hold an overall opinion is not to prejudge a single case. Yet the juror who answers the question in one way can expect to be excused. In effect, citizens with the "wrong" views can simply be prevented from contributing to jury deliberations. Representative? Democracy in miniature? It's to laugh: According to coverage of the *Engle* trial in the local press, the most frequent reason for dismissing jurors was that they were considered to harbor unacceptable prejudices on the subject of tobacco company liability—apparently typified by a former smoker of three decades who said, "I just think people are and have been well aware of the detriments of smoking. . . . To come back after the fact, I find that somewhat ridiculous."[15]

It is all a strange inversion of the once widely held premise that the courts should actually draw by preference on jurors who are civically engaged and aware of the events of the day. Juror prospects have historically been drawn from rolls of such groups as registered voters, owners of real property, and literate persons, all likely, on average, to display a degree of civic awareness exceeding room temperature. (In the really old days, it was considered an actual plus in local jurors that they were personally acquainted with the parties or witnesses in the dispute—that way they could take their reputation into account in assigning proper weight to their stories.)

In much-publicized cases a vast army of recruit material—1,017 in the trial of the Menendez brothers—must now be screened in search of the few, the proud, the ill-informed. With hundreds of persons sitting for hours filling out vast questionnaires—seventy-nine pages in the Simpson case, forty-five pages for the trial of Reginald Denny's attackers—it can take on the air of a giant college-entrance exam on awareness of current events, albeit with reverse scoring. And the more exhaustive the questionnaires, the more power the lawyers will have to shape the panel, since if enough questions are put to a panel of prospects, you might find a majority willing to give you some answer that can be seized on as evidence of their bias for challenge purposes—despite the uncomfortable implication this might leave that most members of the public are not objective enough to serve on juries. Trial lawyers accuse their opponents of not trusting juries, but their own practice could scarcely convey greater distrust of jurors as individuals.

One consequence of both the questionnaires and of face-to-face *voir dire* grilling of prospects is a massive sacrifice of juror prospects' privacy: They are compelled to answer under oath questions concerning their views on such matters as religion and politics that they might regard as overly intrusive if coming from their own spouses. Their responses may wind up as matters of permanent public record; and if they resist, they can be held in contempt of court and jailed. The Simpson trial's questionnaire contained 294 entries— What was your least favorite subject in school? How important would you say religion is in your life? Have you ever belonged to Alcoholics Anonymous, the Sierra Club, or the National Rifle Association?—to mention a few. In some cases, lawyers have even been known to hire gumshoes to drive around prospective jurors' homes interviewing neighbors about their private lives—this from the same profession whose avidity in filing invasion-of-privacy suits is almost as great as its avidity in filing discrimination suits.

One reason pretrial questioning takes so long is that lawyers routinely use it as a way to begin arguing their cases, planting assumptions and factoids that might or might not be admissible later at trial. One injury lawyer, quoted in Stephen Adler's 1994 book *The Jury*, said he planned to linger over the otherwise standard questions about whether prospects had ever been an employee of the defendant company by reciting its subsidiaries one after another—had they ever worked for this one? That one? "That will make it clear that it's a big corporation."[16] Jurors "must not be aware that an attempt is being made to persuade them" during *voir dire*, suggests another how-to book for lawyers. "They are convinced that they have changed their minds by themselves."[17] Worse, some courts permit lawyers to "get a promise" from jurors: If I show A, will you agree to conclude B?[18] Adler quotes one trial lawyer who got jurors to assure him that they could return a "substantial verdict" if he showed thus-and-such; after getting general assent from the panel, he proceeded to call out individual jurors' names: Were you on board? And you? Each, in turn, meekly assented. "The psychological research is very convincing that getting a promise does, in fact, work," an enthusiastic jury consultant told Adler. "[I]f you give them positions, they adopt them." In the famous Texaco/Pennzoil case, plaintiffs' attorney Joe Jamail, quizzing jurors, asked them, as a group, whether they would be willing to consider the language in a press release as *"powerful evidence"* of his clients' contentions. While they revolved this thought in their minds, Jamail asked them to raise their hands if they did *not* agree with him that it should be treated as powerful evidence. No one raised a hand. "I take it you would do that." Simply by taking the path of least resistance and doing nothing, jurors had given him a commitment.

Jury selection typically becomes a more unpleasant and intrusive process when lawyers succeed in wresting control of it from the judge. Many state courts allow lawyers to grill juror prospects directly, judges assuming, at most, a referee role. In New York, until recently, judges did not even have to be present during the grilling, with predictably horrendous consequences: Lawyers would browbeat captive and helpless juror-candidates for days at a time. By contrast, federal courts have more often (though trial lawyers have tried to change this) followed the sounder practice of having the judge ask the questions, with lawyers suggesting questions they would like to see asked.

The state of jury selection in state courts serves to symbolize one of the things foreign visitors tend to find so baffling about American trials, namely the extent to which we permit lawyers, rather than judges, to run them. Elsewhere, judges direct the inquiry, framing issues and ordering the assembling of witnesses and evidence; by contrast, as one commentator notes, "American judges generally act as passive umpires. . . . Lawyers produce, direct and dominate the trial process." Counsel for each side determines what evidence will be brought forward, by which witnesses, in what order, and which issues will emerge and with what kind of emphasis. If neither side's lawyers see fit to introduce a certain significant piece of evidence then it stays out of evidence, no matter how much light the judge or jurors think it might shed on the events in question.

Even in Great Britain, which shares with us a tradition of lawyer-driven procedure, the differences are crucial, as another commentator notes:

> The . . . British judge maintains strict courtroom control. While allowing considerable latitude in questioning, he will not tolerate hectoring of witnesses, strident rhetoric, misrepresentation of evidence or dilatory motions and objections. If testimony is confusing, he will intervene with questions. Procedural motions and questions of law are ruled on verbally after the law books are handed up to the judge. Above all, a British judge has full power to comment on the credibility of evidence and is required by law to sum up the case for the jury. If there is a serious discrepancy between the evidence and the verdict the entire record will be reviewed on appeal.[19]

The parade of evils that judges in other countries take pains to exclude can be seen on almost a routine basis in many

American courtrooms. Inflammatory language and inter-
ruptions; "endorsement" by lawyers of their clients' cases;
stagey eye-rolling when their opponents make points; badg-
ering of witnesses; appeals to sympathy or anger; parading
of blatantly rehearsed or coached testimony; comments that
mislead, distract, or confuse; opening arguments asserting
propositions there is no reasonable expectation of proving;
closing arguments that endeavor to slip across propositions
unsupported by what has come before; all are tolerated in
some, though far from all, American courtrooms. (Practices
differ enormously from one locality to the next and even
between different judges in the same locality.) The widely
deplored hijacking of the Simpson case, in which disruptive
tactics and grandstanding irrelevancies by the defense team
virtually seized control of the trial away from the less-than-
forceful Judge Lance Ito, was simply an extreme example
of the way lawyers in plenty of American courts are permitted to run things.[20]

The opening and closing arguments of trial, in which
lawyers speak directly to jurors, are particularly susceptible
to demagoguery. One attorney laments that the final argument stage "has increasingly turned into a quagmire of
personal character attacks, impermissible reference to non-
record evidence, and blatant pleas to jurors' sympathies and
prejudices."[21] Judges sometimes sit by while attorneys mis-
characterize what has been said before, compare opponents
to murderers or Nazis, insist on logical inferences that are
not, in fact, logically obligatory ("If the gloves don't fit, you
must acquit"), address jurors by name, and so forth; if a
private lawyer pulls out a Bible and starts quoting from it
in open court to explain why his opponent should lose, no

one from the American Civil Liberties Union (ACLU) will let out a peep. In the Simpson case, Cochran proceeded to spin for the jury lurid scenarios of a vast police frame-up effort against his client, far outrunning any actual evidence on hand of such a conspiracy. In *Romo*, plaintiff's counsel had railed against the "giant" and "wealthy" automaker, saying the case was about "corporate greed and arrogance . . . It's also about this. It's about Mrs. Romo's purse. . . . She didn't have furniture for crying out loud, and she's giving money to the church and she's putting it [in her purse] to provide for the education of her children." Damages? "You've got to say a number that gets on the front page of every newspaper in the country."[22]

Why do so many judges in America feel constrained *not* to take control of trials? One reason, notes Prof. David Bernstein of George Mason University's School of Law, is that the remedies available to them may seem inadequate to the task: Declaring a mistrial will usually seem like too drastic a reaction when a lawyer steps over the rhetorical line, yet merely instructing jurors to disregard any inflammatory bits is notoriously feeble. And on many matters—granting demands for sidebar conferences or more time to question witnesses—judges may accurately calculate that they face possible scrutiny from appeals courts if they take a hard line, but relatively little chance of such trouble if they let the lawyer have his way.[23]

There are ideological dimensions as well. A skilled advocate can easily muster arguments against civility, against dispassionateness, against judges' attempts to require constant relevance. Why insist on vicar's-tea-party *politesse* when letting lawyers express themselves in a blunt, vivid, or abrasive way might better force all sides to confront life-and-death issues? Why demand that lawyers conduct themselves with clinical dispassion in examining a witness when there are liars to be exposed on the one hand and victims who need to tell their stories on the other? Why cut off supposedly irrelevant lines of discussion when relevance is a matter of social context to begin with, and we don't know what the jury will choose to find relevant? For that matter, why cut off frequent mentions of, say, one party's in the case being rich and the other's being poor, or one side's being black and the other white, when those might be among the most important bits of social context of all? Some judges, as well as more than a few lawyers, find such arguments congenial.

Then again, getting the other side's evidence excluded can be as effective a path to victory as introducing prejudicial material of one's own. Such a pattern has turned up in quite a few "big" jury verdicts, starting with *Anderson v. GM*, where neither the drunk driver's role in causing the crash nor the car's overall safety record made it into testimony. After managing to get the guilt and imprisonment of Moreno (the drunk driver) excluded, plaintiffs then proceeded to inform the jury that Moreno's fault consisted of "five seconds of bad judgment," whereupon the jury allocated to him only 5 percent of the responsibility for the injuries.[24] Chrysler lost a $262 million verdict, mostly overturned later, over a crash in which little Sergio Jimenez II was thrown from a Dodge Caravan after the judge decided that jurors should not be told that the victim had not been wearing his seat belt or that his mother, driving the van, had run a red light.[25] Suzuki lost a $90 million verdict after the trial judge barred evidence that the driver in the crash had attended a wine tasting just before the accident. (The suit was filed by a passenger in the driver's car.) The company got that verdict thrown out, but even at a second trial, the company was still barred from obtaining medical records on the driver's blood-alcohol level.[26] In *Engle*, the Florida tobacco class action, Dade County judge Robert Kaye handed down numerous rulings favorable to the plaintiffs: admitting unorthodox expert testimony setting strikingly high valuations on the future economic prospects of the defendants; ruling that it was proper to place before the jury the companies' capacity to borrow funds to help meet a punitive-damage award; declaring that in calculating a basis for punitive damages jurors did not have to feel obliged to stop at a sum representing the tobacco companies' net worth; and barring the defendants from arguing that their earlier $246 billion settlement with the fifty states had punished them adequately.[27]

From much of the advice on jury handling found in the literature, one might conclude that practicing lawyers have no very high regard for jurors' acumen. Consultants advise that "logic plays a minimal role" in the courtroom and the real trick is to identify the jurors' "psychological anchors." A brochure from the San Diego Trial Lawyers Association has promoted a video entitled "Trying a Case to the Two Minute Mind; aka Trial by Sound Bite." It promises to explain how "to streamline each element of a trial based on the fact that most jurors are used to getting a complete story within a two-minute maximum segment on the evening news. This video demonstrates the effectiveness of visual aids, impact words and even colors, to influence the juror's perception and thought process in the least amount of time." A trial lawyer must—as prosecutor-turned-author Vincent Bugliosi has written—"put a bib on the jury and spoon-feed it."[28]

The question that naturally follows is how reliable the verdicts are that issue forth from this process. Stephen Adler, whose 1994 *The Jury* was among the last decade's more noteworthy journalistic explorations of the subject, said he began writing the book (while legal affairs editor of the *Wall Street Journal*) "under the influence of the usual myths and the conventional wisdom": juries were repositories of common sense, not easily manipulated, good at detecting liars, seldom got important matters wrong, and so forth. But when he took a close look at six real-life cases, he found a "dismaying" record of verdicts at variance with the facts and overly influenced by personable witnesses and lawyers. One numbingly complex antitrust suit lasted seven months and ended in an "illogical" verdict whose central concepts, jurors freely admitted, remained mysteries to them. Another case resulted in a large damage award whose amount was flagrantly unconnected to the legal rules that are supposed to govern such calculations. ("We were flying by the seat of our pants," one juror said: ". . . we had no clue.") He saw juries "missing key points," "failing to see through the cheapest appeals to sympathy or hate," and much swayed by tears, even on the cheeks of lawyers. He remained a supporter of the institution, but a much chastened one.[29]

Nor are such stories uncommon in other "big" cases, as witness the highly unconventional jury deliberations in

Romo brought to light by later juror interviews. Among the topics the jurors had discussed was a CBS *60 Minutes II* segment that had been aired weeks before the verdict and been seen by more than one juror, which attacked Ford over alleged safety problems in older Mustangs (as opposed to Broncos). The show included material that the court had excluded from evidence as prejudicial to Ford. One juror told colleagues that former Ford president Lee Iacocca had appeared on TV in the CBS show, saying the firm would rather deal with lawsuits than fix safety defects—the problem with that recollection being that the program did not show Iacocca saying anything of the sort. There was much more. A juror had told her colleagues that if there was a chance to save lives, they did not need to follow the law, and that comments by the plaintiff's lawyer should themselves be regarded as evidence. She further informed them at great length, several jurors testified, about an "omen" that had come to her in the form of a gruesome dream revealing the evil cast of mind of the Ford people, in which a Bronco repeatedly rolled over and killed all the jurors' children, while the company's line-up of attorneys and witnesses—armed with guns, no less—"stood by taunting the jurors by chanting, 'Where's the proof, where's the proof?' "[30]

No modern story, of course, has done more to shake public confidence in trial outcomes than the ultrapublicized 1995 O. J. Simpson trial, in which, after a 133-day, $15 million trial, a Los Angeles jury took just three hours to acquit the former football star of the murders of his ex-wife, Nicole Brown Simpson, and her friend Ron Goldman. The Simpson trial, the defense team's Johnnie Cochran (with help from jury consultant Jo-Ellen Dimitrius, whom he prominently thanked in his victory speech) had managed to secure a jury that in no sense "looked like" Los Angeles, California, or America. Eight of the twelve jurors were black women, a group that makes up only 5 percent of L.A. County's population. In all, ten of the twelve were women; nine blacks; all were Democrats; only two had graduated from college; none regularly read a newspaper. Simpson's defense had scored a key victory in getting the trial held in downtown L.A. rather than on the West Side where the crime had actually occurred, and where the jury pool was generally of higher income and education.[31]

Even within the American legal profession, so given to closing ranks against criticism, few cared to defend the Simpson trial's conduct or outcome. Instead, it was said to have been the fluke result of a never-to-be-repeated confluence of money, celebrity, bungling by the judge and prosecutors, and sheer luck. It was "aberrant," "one of a kind," "in no way typical," and so forth. "The Simpson case is [such] an anomaly that we cannot generalize from it," said a California jury consultant. Actually, the Simpson acquittal stood in a long tradition: By the nineteenth century, prominent lawyers in the nation's turbulent cities were already making a name for themselves winning acquittals for obviously guilty malefactors to the cheers of the mob. Such cases contributed to put the jury system itself under a cloud, despite its venerable pedigree in Anglo-American law and as a bulwark of liberty in colonial times. "The jury system puts a ban upon intelligence and honesty, and a premium upon ignorance, stupidity, and perjury," Mark Twain famously complained. We "swear in juries composed of fools and rascals, because the system rigidly excludes honest men and men of brains."[32]

By the turn of the twentieth century, uneasiness over the competence and objectivity of the jury as an institution was already something of a tradition in itself. Many reformers during the Progressive and New Deal Eras distrusted juries for their lack of expertise, their unpredictability, their cumbersomeness (trials are significantly longer and more expensive when juries are made part of them), the lack of a written record explaining their decisions, and, of course, their susceptibility to demagoguery and sectional feeling. What did the most to undermine support for the jury during the twentieth century was the record of southern all-white juries, notoriously lawless and hostile to blacks' interests. It took many years after the fall of Jim Crow for southern juries to lose their reputation as instruments for white prejudice.[33]

Eventually, the expectation that jury outcomes would be racially tinged was to subside—for a while, at least. Yet neither race nor sectionalist sentiment ever actually went away as factors in lawyers' practical courtroom work. In many parts of the country it was—and still is—considered advantageous, especially if you are an out-of-town litigant, to make sure your case is argued by local counsel who can speak in the accents of the jury room. (Some peripatetic lawyers are not above adjusting their accents, as well as their clothing style, from one venue to the next.) After the stunning Texaco/Pennzoil verdict, it was noted that winning attorney Joe Jamail, addressing Texas jurors, had kept needling his opponents about their being from New York, where they did things differently. In places with predominantly minority jury pools, some law firms not only send minority partners to argue the cases, but also take care to cast minorities in supporting roles, such as expert witnesses.

By the 1990s, concern was on the upswing again about racially tinted verdicts after a series of high-profile police brutality cases and others like them, where such factors had loomed large, as well as reports that prosecutors were finding it hard to obtain convictions on some types of charges in some heavily black cities like Detroit. A law professor at George Washington University provoked an outcry when he suggested that it might be appropriate for black juries to decline to enforce the law in some prosecutions for non-violent crimes. With the Simpson case, the debate reached the front burner. Ironically, one of the most telling facts about the case was that neither the defendant himself, nor anyone else, had at first expected his being black to play much of a role in what was to come. ("I don't see race," he told a friend. "Race is not an issue. . . ." "To put it bluntly," Cochran later explained, "nobody thought of him as black.") But shrewdly perceiving their big chance for a diversionary issue, Simpson's lawyers eventually were to go to such unsubtle lengths as wearing garments of African kente cloth to court appearances. When the jury was set to make an on-site visit to the football player's home, Simpson's defense team went so far as to spend a day stripping the walls of their many pictures of white girlfriends, celebrities, and corporate sponsors and replacing them with pictures of Simpson's black relatives, hastily done up as color photocopies at a local Kinko's and framed. In a crowning touch, Simpson's lawyers framed and hung up, in a conspicuous location, one of the most famous images to come

out of the civil-rights era, Norman Rockwell's 1963 image
of a young black girl being escorted to school by federal
marshals.[34]

Though it's a topic that defendants in lawsuits are extremely reluctant to discuss, racial sentiment is looming as
a factor against them in more and more civil cases, with
help from some in the plaintiffs' bar. Environmental lawsuits, such as those arising from low-exposure tanker spills
or pollution in minority neighborhoods, have increasingly
scored record-breaking verdicts as lawyers play the "environmental racism" card, arguing that the company would
have taken better care of the neighborhood had it been
white. It would be difficult to imagine a mass tort that had
less of a connection to race than the *Engle* case in Florida,
since smokers are drawn from all ethnic groups. Yet having
obtained a heavily minority jury, plaintiffs' attorney Stanley
Rosenblatt proceeded to try the case for a racial payoff,
putting experts on the stand who depicted smoking as particularly lethal to blacks and hammering away at the tobacco companies for advertising in black magazines and
consciously pursuing black customers. (That black publishers, radio stations, and event promoters had avidly pursued
such "targeted marketing," and even sometimes complained
of racism when they weren't able to get enough of it, didn't
seem to enter the argument.)

It's curious. If you criticize a bad decision by a judge, no
one will accuse you of being an opponent of the judge system. If you criticize a bad decision by a jury, however, a
dozen lawyers will jump up to accuse you of being against

the jury system. But that's how it goes. Many defenders of America's present litigation arrangements see rhetorical mileage to be gained in recasting any debate about overly high, unpredictable, passion-driven, or arbitrary jury verdicts into a debate about whether you're for juries or agin'em. This allows them to portray critics of exorbitant awards as *thoughtless innovators* willing to tamper with a precious legal inheritance from the time of the Founders (though, in fact, the jury's nature and role has already changed quite drastically from what it was then); as *unpatriotic* and even *un-American*, since our system relies much more heavily on juries than other countries' (though the differences are much less stark than we are usually told, since European countries often empanel ordinary citizens as "lay judges" to participate in trials in a not unjurorlike way); and as *undemocratic* in temper, eager to criticize the one element of the judicial system where the common man can get his say and a broad cross section of the public makes its voice felt. ("The jury is more truly representative of the public than it ever has been before in history," enthuses Valerie Hans of the University of Delaware.)[35] It is even said that critics of awards like *Anderson* and *Engle* are wasting their time, since some surveys have found that most juries decide cases the same way judges would do if it were up to them—though very few trial lawyers conduct their practices as if they believe that proposition.

Although the litigation lobby likes to carry on as if the jury is in imminent danger of abolition, there is virtually no organized or even disorganized sentiment in this country in favor of such a drastic step (which in any event would face the insurmountable hurdle of having to repeal the constitutional provision that prescribes the use of juries in common-law trials). The consensus that juries are here to stay, however, should not imply that it is impossible to hold a public debate about how best to structure their role. A legal system needs multiple lines of defense against miscarriages of justice, and historically the jury has had few rivals as a way of protecting defendants from overweening official power. But like any other part of government, a jury can pose a danger to liberty when it begins wielding government power in an affirmative way, as when it extends legal liability into new areas or inflicts arbitrary damage awards. A mechanism that works extremely well as a brake may lead to disaster when pressed into service as an accelerator.

One of the areas where juries are widely seen as having the worst difficulties is in the credible and consistent computation of damages. Given that, one reform worth considering would be to keep with the jury the decision of whether defendants are to be held liable, but reserve to the judge the calculation of remedies—just as in most criminal trials the jury resolves the defendant's guilt but the judge alone then decides on sentencing.[36] Even better, perhaps, would be a rule by which judge and jury would separately arrive at damage numbers, and then the verdict would issue at whichever of the two numbers was lower, following the idea that a two-signature check should issue only in the amount for which both parties are willing to feel responsible.

Another set of reforms worth careful consideration would endeavor to give juries more power, rather than less, by rousing them from their artificial passivity. At present juries are subject to numerous constraints that almost seem designed to leave them vulnerable to the forensic skills of those who practice before (and on) them. Usually, for example, they are forbidden to take notes, even while everyone else in the courtroom is scribbling away; nor are they usually supposed to ask or suggest questions, a method well calculated to stifle any intellectual initiative they might show. The legal instructions on how jurors are to resolve the case are commonly withheld until the last moment, a mode of proceeding one judge has compared with asking jurors to watch a ball game and decide who won without letting them know the rules till play is over. When the guidelines finally do arrive, the judge or his clerk has frequently cast them in legal jargon aimed at withstanding appellate review, which to lay listeners might as well be Serbo-Croatian. Courts in Arizona and elsewhere have recently experimented with relaxing some of these constraints by letting juries take notes and allowing them to pose questions to the judge. Much of the legal establishment has greeted these experiments quite tepidly; many who style themselves as defenders of the jury system may, in fact, be most comfortable with the institution when it serves as a sort of Queen Bee, all-powerful in theory but immobilized and force-fed in practice.

The Simpson aftermath led to renewed public calls for judges to take a firmer hand in managing trials, keep questioning on track, curb bullying of witnesses by lawyers, and so forth, which would be all to the good if it happened. It also led to long-overdue calls for reforming the jury-selection system, including the abolition or curtailment of peremptory challenges and narrowing of the grounds of for-cause challenges. Great Britain, which like most English-speaking countries retains juries for criminal though not most civil cases, never embraced most of the baroque extremes of American jury selection, and in recent years has streamlined the process even further so that empanelment of a jury is commonly accomplished within a couple of hours at most with little direct influence from lawyers. Long-overdue reforms have also been made in the state of New York, where the changes, initiated by the state's chief justice Judith Kaye, brought the Empire State more into line with the practice around the rest of the country by increasing, for example, judges' supervision of the juror-selection process and curtailing peremptories, thus greatly reducing the time jurors and others must spend cooling their heels on benches during empanelment. Who's unhappy? The state's bar association, of course; it opposed reform in the first place, complained afterward that its members feel "increasingly constrained by time limits and other restrictions,"[37] and conducted a survey "suggest[ing] that many lawyers feel that new practices are cramping their style." (Yes, indeed—that was the idea.)

Why does the litigation lobby fight such reforms? Why does it carry on at such length about the jury as a representative institution, and then do its best during selection to make it as unrepresentative as it knows how? Why does it endlessly compare the jury box to the ballot box, and then turn away from it people it suspects of planning to vote the "wrong" way? These varied positions are not united by any common theme of somehow maximizing the power juries get to exert. On closer inspection, they can be seen to share only one common theme: They all arrange matters so as to maximize the power trial lawyers themselves get to exert. Should we be surprised?

9

The Lawsuit Lobby

Were you to go looking for the nation's sharpest legal talents to spearhead an assault on a target as formidable as the tobacco industry, it might seem unlikely that Hugh Rodham's resumé would wind up anywhere near the top of your stack. The Florida attorney had spent much of his career as an assistant public defender, and his background was notably lacking in mass tort or product-liability experience. But when the so-called Castano Group of trial lawyers hired him, it could not but be aware that Rodham brought with him a different qualification: Through his sister, First Lady Hillary Rodham Clinton, he was the brother-in-law of Pres. Bill Clinton. The Castano lawyers were vying with the Dickie Scruggs/Mike Moore constellation of lawyers for the recognized lead role in the fight against the industry, and one Castano chieftain, mindful of Scruggs's family relationship with then–Senate Majority Leader Trent Lott (R-Miss.), had reportedly vowed that he was not going to let himself get "out-brother-in-lawed."

Rodham proceeded to use the occasion of a Thanksgiving dinner at the White House to approach the president directly on the tobacco matter, upon which Clinton assigned his trusted right-hand man Bruce Lindsey to the task of using White House clout to bring settlement talks to a successful conclusion. Although Rodham attended some of the marathon negotiating sessions that preceded a settlement of the suits, he can hardly be said to have played a commanding role in them: According to the *Washington Post*, he spent "the last hours of the talks in a corner reading" a paperback thriller. Later, toward the end of Clinton's presidency, it was revealed that the chief executive had been prevailed upon to cut a videotape—a canned commercial, really—on behalf of the Castano lawyers' request in arbitration for fees that could reach $3.4 billion. "The way I understand it, they pushed him into a bedroom during a fund-raiser, gave him a script, and shot the tape," said a local official who had been involved in the president's visit.[1]

A commercial endorsement by a sitting president was something virtually unprecedented in the annals of American government—no one could remember any previous president even floating a trial balloon for such an idea. And although it would have been bad enough form for a chief executive to have endorsed, say, his brother-in-law's company's brand of chewing gum, this was a lot worse: Chewing gum is a matter of private taste, but overseeing the impartial enforcement of the laws is part of a president's job description. But there seemed no end to the favors the Clinton administration had been willing to do for the tobacco bar. The Justice Department had launched a splashily announced criminal investigation of the tobacco industry that went nowhere but generated considerable publicity to the lawyers' advantage. And the Clinton White House, overruling career Justice Department staffers, ordered that a federal medical-cost-recoupment suit be filed against the tobacco industry, a step for which the Castano Group and the Scruggs team had both been lobbying for years. Later, when Rodham turned up assisting a group of the Castano lawyers in their suits against the gun industry, he seemed to think it was his legal acumen that had kept him in such strong demand: "It was totally unforeseen, when we joined," he told *Time*, "that there would be any connection with politics."

For twenty years, there has been talk of action in Washington to reform the excesses of the liability system and rein in the power of trial lawyers. And over those twenty years, little if any reform of any real significance has made it to enactment at the federal level. Product-liability reform, though passing the House of Representatives, has stalled in the Senate. Controls on tobacco fees went down to narrow defeat. Shareholder-suit reform, after an enormous battle, passed over a veto from President Clinton, but accomplished only marginal alterations to that much-criticized sector of litigation. There have also been a series of isolated reforms, mostly consisting of minor tinkering to resolve some crisis affecting a narrowly defined, sympathetic constituency such as community volunteers, makers of light aircraft, or suppliers of childhood vaccines—situations where the consequences of open-ended liability had proved to be so damaging that trial lawyers were almost better off yielding a bit of ground than continuing to face an angry public. For the most part, however, the litigation lobby rightly boasts of its record, year in and year out, under Republicans and Democrats alike, of turning back any threats to its prosperity. *Fortune*, which publishes periodic rankings of lobby clout, has ranked trial lawyers among the top half dozen most powerful lobbies in Washington, ahead of the AFL-CIO, the Chamber of Commerce, government employees, the bankers, the doctors, the real estate community, organized teachers, and the entertainment industry.

At the state level, the record of litigation reform is only a little more encouraging. In most big states, trial lawyers have either blocked the enactment of reforms or have managed to get reform-minded statutes struck down by lawyer-friendly courts after their enactment. Before curbs on litigation can reach the floor in a state legislature, they commonly must run a gauntlet of judiciary committees on which trial lawyers and their allies are heavily represented. In California, for example, it was state senator Bill Lockyer, longtime guardian of trial lawyer interests and himself in plaintiffs' practice, who chaired the judiciary committee of the upper house in Sacramento for many years before going on to win the state's attorney generalship in a well-funded campaign. In New York, any proposed curbs on litigation must get past such committed opponents as Assembly Judiciary Committee chair Helene Weinstein, of counsel to her family's personal-injury firm; assembly speaker Sheldon Silver, whose law firm rents office space from one of the city's most prominent tort firms; and, over in the state senate, committee chair James Lack, who unlike most of his Republican colleagues maintains close relations with the trial bar, as do GOP lawmakers in New Jersey and some other northeastern states.

In Maryland, one opponent describes the power of attorney Peter Angelos, who owns the Baltimore Orioles as well as dominating asbestos and tobacco litigation in the state, as "absolutely magical" and "amazing" the *Washington Post* reported that Angelos is often considered the most powerful private citizen in the state. Annapolis lawmakers have long made it an annual habit to pass "Angelos bills," which he sometimes drafts personally, the effect of which is variously to retroactively increase the level of damages he can obtain in pending cases, expand the range of defendants he is entitled to sue, or overturn some court decision that has gone against him. Angelos sports a roster of ten registered lobbyists, and a number of highly placed members of the state legislature happen to earn their daily livings as lawyers at his firm. His allies, however, deny that they are engaged in private interest legislation when they pass Angelos's bills, given that their patron counts as a pillar of the Maryland economy in his own right, like the bay crabbery. "Peter Angelos in and of himself is a major economic interest in the state," explains House Majority Leader John Hurson.[2]

The insider role of lawyers in political life goes back almost as far as politics itself. It is they who are trained in the skill of knowing how to draft, analyze, and interpret legal enactments, which is why rulers who try to govern without the help of talented lawyers are a menace to friends and foes alike, loading the books with clumsily written and easily abused decrees. By the nature of their work, lawyers pick up skills of persuasive argument and public advocacy; and if they often appear before juries they can develop skills of old-fashioned oratory seldom matched these days outside the pulpit. Active from the start in American government, attorneys have in recent years held more than half of all cabinet posts, governorships, and U.S. Senate seats, along with a large share of seats in the House of Representatives, often upwards of 40 percent of its membership. When they run for office, successful trial lawyers also gain an edge from laws that favor candidates wealthy enough to finance their own campaigns (and then get by on low lawmakers' salaries).

The most common role for lawyers in electoral politics is not as candidates themselves, but as influences in the background. Now as ever, most American politics develops out of local politics, with much of that being courthouse politics. Law practices also make a good base from which to offer in-kind political donations, ranging from phone banks and meeting space to legal services themselves. The attorney who renders legal services to party regulars and the influential quickly tends to become an insider himself, especially if the service is provided free or at concessionary rates (in some localities lawyers can even provide free legal services to the clerks and judges of courts they practice in, a surefire gratitude-builder). Furthermore, every stage today of the campaign process itself has come to be enmeshed in a web of law and regulation—from ballot access to party administration to ad-buying to (above all) fund-raising—making lawyers' assistance vital in avoiding illegality and identifying what it is still advantageous and legal to do. So the political world broadly defined—party organizations, clubs, machines, private lobbying groups and associations, even political journalism—grows ever more dependent on its lawyer participants.

What accounts for the disproportionate influence of plaintiffs' trial lawyers, who constitute only a smallish fraction of all lawyers? One reason is the contingency fee, which, in effect, makes them part owners of the volume of claims moving through the system and gives them a far sharper and more personal interest in courtroom trends than, say, divorce or real estate lawyers are likely to have. Indeed, the financial livelihood of lawyers who sue for a living depends more or less entirely on access to governmental processes, which may be why they tend to take their lobbying so much more seriously than do, say, dentists or department store executives. They can also focus their interest with great intensity on a relatively short agenda to pursue with politicians, while farmers, doctors, and manufacturers find their interests affected by a lengthier and more diffuse list of issues. And the pursuit of litigation is in many ways the perfect preparation for involvement in a hotly contested political campaign: It's a zero—if not negative—sum game in which inflicting cost and credibility damage on an opponent is often more advantageous than trying to win a halo for oneself. A lawyer who practices commercial transactions or trusts and estates law may know little of the art of generating negative publicity for adversaries; a seasoned plaintiffs' lawyer assuredly knows all about it.

Nor are trial lawyers reluctant to contribute their services in somewhat less visible capacities, such as state or county party chairman, finance chairman, campaign chairman, and party treasurer. In many states—a recent sampling would include South Carolina, Iowa, Tennessee, and Nebraska—the chairman of the state Democratic Party is also a prominent local plaintiffs' lawyer. The treasurer of the Democratic Party in Rhode Island is the senior Ness Motley local partner, John J. McConnell Jr. In Illinois, Philip Corboy finds time away from his many commitments as one of Chicago's most successful tort lawyers to serve as general counsel of the Illinois Democratic Party. Sen. Joseph Lieberman of Connecticut, who unlike many of his fellow Democrats has had many quarrels with the organized plaintiffs' bar, has said: "This is a remarkable story of a small group of people who are deeply invested in the status quo who have worked the system very effectively and have had a disproportionate effect."[3]

Their best-known asset in doing so, of course, is money. Leading trial lawyers as a group are highly liquid, with relatively little of their wealth tied up in big payrolls or fixed assets such as real estate. And they are known for recycling a remarkable share of their wealth into political donations (the word "tithing" comes up often). When Ness Motley settled on the state of Rhode Island as its base for expanding into the Northeast, the firm soon established itself as the state's largest political contributor, shelling out $540,950 in the 2000 election. Florida's Jim Wilkes, who sues nursing homes, told the *Orlando Sentinel* that he "probably gave at least $1 million of his own money to campaigns in the last election. 'If you took the national and state money that my firm has contributed to campaigns, I could have probably retired on the money.' "[4]

The trial bar's massive volume of donations is only part of the story. Equally important are the ways in which they give it. Most big business political action committees (PACs)—less than aggressive by inclination, scared of regulatory retaliation, and, above all, prizing "access" to elected officials—either give to both sides or at least avoid challenges to incumbents. Not so with trial lawyer political giving, whose guiding motto was once spelled out by former ATLA president Leonard Ring: "You help your friends and kill your enemies." Like other savvy givers, trial lawyers often pull out their checkbooks at strategic times likely to provoke gratitude, such as at the very beginning of a campaign, or afterward when debts need to be repaid. Conveniently for them, most of their giving is couched as donations from individuals, which is more loosely regulated and less scrutinized by the press than PAC giving; their favored politicians can thus make a big deal out of rejecting PAC donations to their campaigns without having to turn away the nourishing flow of lawyer cash.[5]

When trial lawyers do employ PACs, they have been known to employ them in ways that make it hard to track their generosity accurately. In such states as Texas and Alabama, they have shuffled funds among multiple PACs with innocuous or meaningless names: Spouses, minor children, office receptionists, and other employees all have turned up as surprisingly generous donors. "Any contribution that you make . . . of $99 dollars or less will not be publicly reported," confided a "Dear Fellow Attorney" mailing from the California trial lawyers' group seeking donations to fight ballot initiatives that would have curbed litigation.[6] The *Los Angeles Times* said the nonreportability of under-$100 donations, though a fact well known to political pros, was "almost never one on which they base written fund-raising appeals," while the state chapter of Common Cause called it "unbelievable": "These are attorneys appealing to attorneys to violate the spirit of the law."

When it comes to one major branch of electoral office, the state judiciary, there is no disguising the lawyers' dominant role. Visitors from other countries are often surprised to learn that non-federal judges in most American states must run for election. They are downright astounded to learn that in such campaigns the judges are expected to, and do, accept money from lawyers who practice before them (and may also allow such lawyers to manage and organize their campaigns). "There are exactly two types of people who contribute to judicial candidates," observes Yale law professor John Langbein, "mothers, and those who have an interest in the outcome of litigation."[7]

Though even trial lawyers find it hard to defend this arrangement in principle, they sometimes try to put the best face on it by saying that their contributions to judges merely recognize jurists' competence, hard work, and equable judicial temperament, rather than serving as any sort of quid pro quo for favorable treatment. That makes it even harder to understand why it would be that—in at least one big city, according to Judge Michael Keasler—"attorneys can subscribe to an information service that lists the amounts and sources of campaign contributions to individual judges."[8] In 2000, *Texas Lawyer* reported that plaintiffs' lawyers were forming PACs in Dallas and Fort Worth to "target" judges for defeat. "Organizers from both cities say PAC money could put as much as $100,000 into a single race to defeat an incumbent. But hopefully they won't have to, they say. 'It's like forming a union,' says Chuck Noteboom, president of the Tarrant County Trial Lawyers Association. 'You may never strike, but you may have the threat of a strike.' "[9] The same year in Michigan, they failed in an effort to knock off three sitting Supreme Court justices, despite pledges by plaintiffs' firms of up to $500,000 each to the campaign and an ad campaign against the justices that the *Detroit News* assailed as "truly vicious."[10]

In October 2000, perhaps stung by widespread reporting of the huge volume of trial lawyer political donations, ATLA published on its Web site an article claiming that its members were, in fact, "being outspent by a factor of at least 10-to-1" in federal political giving by its combined adversaries.[11] For example, lawyers and lobbyists as a group had given "only" (ATLA's word) $75 million to federal parties and candidates at that point in the campaign, much of which did not come from plaintiffs' lawyers, whereas (for example) the "Communications/Electronics industry" had given $72 million, the "Health industry" had given $49 million, the "Agribusiness sector" had contributed $34 million, and the "Construction industry" had given $30 million. The obvious spin is that lawyers' spending is at most reactive and inadequate to keep pace with its opponents.

ATLA's logic on this matter is revealing. It reaches its 10-to-1 comparison by the simple expedient of counting just about every other donor in the country, with the possible exception of labor unions, as an adversary whose donation is linked as clearly to opposition to litigation issues as those of ATLA members are linked in support of them. Thus, if a Hollywood producer contributes to someone's campaign, even if it's the same politician the trial lawyers are backing, it counts toward the total of "Communications/Entertainment Industry" donations; every psychiatrist or birth control clinic operator gets counted as "Health Industry"; every farmer in "Agribusiness"; and so forth. Yet it should be clear enough that a donation from a wheat farmer worried about the future of price supports and export subsidy programs in no way serves as a counterweight to the trial lawyers' agenda. By such a yardstick, the only way lawyers would ever not wind up being "outspent" is if they managed to bestow a majority of all political donations all by themselves, which they don't (yet, anyway).

ATLA's Web site statement further asserts that of political donations in the "lawyers and lobbyists" category, "a mere fraction" come from plaintiff trial lawyers. It doesn't say how high a fraction, but it does go on to make the following interesting claim: "The category of lawyers and lobbyists includes a greater proportion of corporate lawyers who are contributing in favor of tort 'reform' as opposed to plaintiffs lawyers who are contributing to candidates who support the protection of America's civil justice system."

Can this be true? As ATLA must have been aware, the political giving of lawyers as a group tilts very heavily in favor of Democratic as against Republican candidates. Over the past decade, the ratio at the federal level has fluctuated between 68–31 and 75–25 Democratic, with the 2000-cycle figure coming in at 69–30. And, in fact, donation figures indicate that the biggest "corporate" (transactional and defense) law firms tended to split their donations more or less evenly between the two parties (members of these firms, it should also be noted, give far smaller amounts per lawyer than do the plaintiffs' firms). Meanwhile, the figures for large plaintiffs' firms indicate that their contributions are overwhelmingly Democratic.

The role of trial lawyer support in the national Democratic Party has been a widely covered story and is not denied by Democratic officials themselves. "The trial lawyers are a terrifically important Democratic constituency," executive director Jim Jordan of the Democratic Senatorial Campaign Committee (DSCC) has explained. "[T]hey can do more than just write checks ... [they] are comfortable in using populist rhetoric." The connection became embarrassingly obvious with the "call sheet" affair, in which a slip of paper left over from the 1996 campaign became public four years later: "I know [you] will give $100K when the president vetoes tort reform, but we really need it now," read one of a list of scripted talking points prepared by a staffer for a scheduled telephone call Vice President Al Gore was to have with Walter Umphrey, the Beaumont, Texas, asbestos/ tobacco attorney. (When the memo came to light, both the lawyer and the Democrats strenuously denied that any unlawful quid pro quo of money for a veto had taken place.)[12]

On Capitol Hill, the lineup of reliable trial lawyer allies has included in the Senate former trial lawyer and longtime Commerce Committee chair Ernest Hollings (D-S.C.), tobacco fee defender Dick Durbin (D-Ill.), plaintiff's lawyer spouse Barbara Boxer (D-Calif.), former Alabama senator

Howell Heflin (D-Ala.), and many others. On the House side, then-minority leader Rep. Richard Gephardt (D-Mo.) has made few bones about his allegiances, appearing before ATLA's 1996 annual convention where he (as the *Boston Globe* reported) "derided corporate 'whining' over frivolous lawsuits."[13] Rep. Patrick Kennedy (D-R.I.), chair of the Democratic Congressional Campaign Committee (DCCC), in an appearance on CNBC's *Hardball* said those who criticize the American litigation system should "go someplace else and live."[14]

When the Republicans captured control of Congress in 1994, it soon became apparent that the trial bar had long and assiduously been cultivating contacts on the GOP side of the aisle as well. The next year, as part of the famed "Contract with America" episode, the House of Representatives passed a series of significant measures aimed at reforming litigation, but the GOP-run Senate did not deign even to hold hearings on most of the proposals. The Senate has likewise balked at anything more than the skimpiest versions of product-liability reform or tobacco fee limitation. When matters came to a vote, the trial lawyers always seemed to peel away enough Republican votes to win, the crucial margin obtained from such major recipients of trial lawyer money as Richard Shelby of Alabama, Fred Thompson of Tennessee, and former senators Bob Packwood of Oregon and Alfonse D'Amato of New York.

Indeed, many of the Republicans, like their Democratic counterparts, turned out to have personal or family connections to the trial lawyer trade. Maine's senator William Cohen, for example, not only served as an officer of his state's trial lawyers association but actually worked for

ATLA in the 1960s. Sen. Alan Simpson had a similar story to tell: "I was one of the officers and founders of the Wyoming Trial Lawyers Association," he told the *Washington Times.* "That allegiance runs deep."[15] To be sure, then–majority leader Trent Lott (R-Miss.), given his in-law relation to Dickie Scruggs, recused himself from votes on tobacco fee limits, and has been counted in support of most other litigation curbs. Perennial GOP defector Arlen Specter (R-Penn.) is yet another with a family stake in the matter: His son Shanin is among the state's best-known plaintiffs' lawyers, whose major wins at trial for his firm Kline & Specter include a $158 million verdict against the Ford Motor Company.[16]

The trial bar's most valuable asset of all in public debate, of course, has long been its ally Ralph Nader, one of the few public figures who can obtain news coverage just by showing up somewhere, and who, since his emergence in public life nearly forty years ago, has reliably been on hand to hold press conferences and tape commercials for whatever the trial lawyer cause of the moment may happen to be. "We are what supports Nader," prominent Florida trial lawyer Fred Levin told *Forbes* years ago. "We all belong to his group. We contribute to him, and he fundraises through us." "I can get on the phone and raise $100,000 for Nader in one day," said California's Herb Hafif. "We support him overtly, covertly, in every way possible," said Pat Maloney of San Antonio. "I would think we give him a huge percentage of what he raises. What monied groups could he turn to other than trial lawyers?"[17]

The plaintiffs' bar has long arranged for its desired messages to come from groups other than itself. The press release beating up on tort reform advocates will bear the name of some group like Texans for Public Justice (TPJ), Public Citizen, or the Center for Justice and Democracy (CJD). Indeed, the trial bar was pioneering techniques of "Astroturf," or the simulation of grassroots support, long before most interest groups got into the act. The grand-sounding Alliance for Consumer Rights (ACR), for example, turns out to operate from the offices of the New York State Trial Lawyers Association. In his book on a Connecticut medical malpractice lawsuit, *Damages*, author Barry Werth notes that prominent trial lawyer Michael Koskoff, along with a partner, "provided [Mary] Gay with a platform by recruiting her to head the Victims' Rights Association," whose agenda included doubling the number of judges and courtrooms so as to make it easier for lawsuits to get to trial. The group "exist[ed] largely on paper" and, in fact, was created by the state trial lawyers group. "Gay was a 'figurehead,' she says, Koskoff having assured her there was no real work or responsibility involved." ATLA has an entire nonprofit arm, the Civil Justice Foundation (CJF), whose quiet function is to dispense grants to consumer advocacy groups.[18]

Even more modest and retiring about its mission is ATLA's Roscoe Pound Institute, which funnels money to law professors and other academics who conduct research that it finds agreeable. The most widely cited research arguing that the awarding of punitive damages in our system is rational and not excessive, which originated in a Pound Institute grant, has been cited hundreds of times in opposition to punitive damage reform.[19] Recently, as more and more trial lawyers have arranged to have endowed chairs, programs, conference series, or whole law schools named after them, an ever-growing set of job prospects have opened up for academics willing to assure each other that all talk of excessive litigation is a "myth" with no real basis, folktales spread by sore losers in the courtroom process.

Nothing if not flexible, the trial bar maintains a presence on the more conservative side of the political spectrum as well. In Texas, when a conservative voter trend began making the GOP nomination increasingly tantamount to election in judicial races, trial lawyers began dropping serious money into GOP primaries. A new crop of candidates was soon observed running for judgeships as Republicans, sometimes over the objections of party leaders, many with résumés rich in recent Democratic connections.[20] In the 1998 California elections, a Conservative Attorneys for Civil Justice PAC sprang up to inject $200,000 into GOP primaries on behalf of a slate of right-wing "family values" candidates, though it did poorly.[21] Even more adventurous alliances were struck by trial lawyer Dick Harpootlian, Democratic state party chair in South Carolina, as part of his successful effort to turn back Republican governor David Beasley's 1998 reelection bid. Beasley had tried to search for the middle of the road on the polarizing issue of what to do about the state's historic display of the Confederate flag. Soon an obscure right-wing group sprang up to attack him in rural white areas ("Keep the Flag, Dump Beasley") for being insufficiently enthusiastic about displays of the old Dixie symbol. After the election it came out that Harpootlian had quietly slipped a few thousand dollars to the pro-

Confederate group, even as the state Democratic Party he chaired was raising money from national donors by portraying itself as engaged in an embattled crusade to get the Rebel flag taken down.[22]

Some of the plaintiffs' bars' most valuable allies are found among other lawyers, including its sometimes rather nominal adversaries, the defense and transactional bar. The American Bar Association (ABA), for example, whose membership consists mostly of defense and transactional lawyers, has for many years tenaciously opposed most measures that would curb litigation. So little internal opposition arose to this stance that in the mid-1990s a resolution opposing Republican plans for lawsuit reform was passed on the ABA floor by acclamation. When voter initiatives have been placed on the ballot in California and elsewhere to curtail litigation, both transactional and defense lawyers have been conspicuously absent from lists of financial and organizational supporters. "We in the defense bar have earned a living defending these cases," explained a senior partner at Weil, Gotshal & Manges. "Were they to dry up, we would lose another source of income. I don't mean to be crass about it, but that is a fact of life."[23]

Sometimes the relevant facts of life are even more blatant. When California legal reformers placed a series of initiatives on the ballot that would have curbed car crash cases and other categories of litigation, defense attorneys were sent mass solicitations to contribute money against the measures—that is to say, against the interests of their own clients—with the warning that "defense business will dry up" if the measures pass. "Dear Fellow Attorney," began one such letter. "On March 26, 1996, your future as a lawyer will be at stake! . . . No one will be handling automobile cases if this passes!" Twenty-two officials of the Association of Southern California Defense Counsel (ASCDC) signed a letter soliciting funds against the initiative. "Getting up close and personal," another appeal explained, "even if you do not do auto work, this initiative promises to have a significant impact on your practice. Passage of Proposition 200 will trigger a mass exodus of capable auto claims counsel into other areas of work. . . . The ASCDC has asked its members to contribute $1,000 per defense lawyer." *National Journal* columnist Stuart Taylor Jr. marveled at the letters' "blatant appeal to the mutual self-interest of lawyers in perpetuating the profits they reap by litigating against one another at their clients' expense."[24]

Either from conviction or from a sense of loyalty to their clients, of course, many individual defense lawyers do support measures to reduce litigation, even knowing that such measures might cut into their own volume of business. But individual lawyers of this stripe seem to exert little sway within the defense bar's major professional organization, the 22,000-member Defense Research Institute (DRI). DRI regularly, if quietly, sends officials to legislative hearings to testify against proposed curbs on litigation, right alongside the witnesses sent by its supposed opposite number, ATLA. A lawyer/commentator in DRI's magazine *For the Defense* notes that the organization has "always taken the position" that "the basic principles of the liability reparation system are sound." Indeed, the casual reader perusing DRI's literature might sometimes find it easy to confuse DRI's point

of view with ATLA's. Thus one DRI publication dismisses
the notion that the present-day "civil justice system is either
flawed or over-used. It is simply utilized for the purpose it
was designed."[25]

Even transactional lawyers, who do not have such a direct stake in keeping up the volume of litigation, may find
themselves prospering indirectly from it, since when clients
are frightened by a high incidence of courtroom trouble
they tend to avail themselves of more preventive legal services—negotiations to head off disputes, more effort spent
crafting warning labels and employee handbooks, compli-
ance training for managers, and so forth. Mostly, however,
the transactional lawyers just sit out the fights, while powerful panels that help guide the development of litigation
procedure are made up in what the participants appear to
consider a perfectly fair manner—equal numbers of participants from the plaintiff's and defense trial bar. As a member of one such panel on procedural revision, federal
appeals judge (and Yale law professor) Ralph Winter says
he saw defense firms put up "ferocious and often unprin-
cipled" resistance to proposals that would lessen the expense of cases for their clients by reducing the burdens of
pretrial discovery.[26] Winter concluded that the process il-
lustrates the way the practicing bar "presses its self-interest"
in "maximizing the demand for legal services." Nor does
he expect the situation to change any time soon, given that
law firms are "the principal source of information to clients
as to how reforms will affect them."

———

Meanwhile, the adversaries of the litigation lobby are both divided and easily intimidated. Trial lawyers typically perceive a threat to one of their number as a threat to the whole fraternity. Their targets, on the other hand, show no such solidarity. The doctors won't go out of their way to help the product manufacturers, who have nothing good to say about the insurers, who won't lift a finger for the gun makers, who are not about to spare any sympathy for the pharmaceutical companies, and so forth. No matter how clear it is that the precedents forged in lawsuits against the defendants of the moment will later be used against others, virtually all these groups comply with the First Law of Risk-Averse Public Affairs: Never speak out on behalf of anyone who's less popular at the moment than you are.

Besides, the trial bar takes names and has long memories. If you are the chief sponsor of a major bill adverse to ATLA's interests, you had better have a safe seat back home or you are likely to end up like ex-senator Robert Kasten (R-Wisc.), who once sponsored product-liability reform bills, or ex-senator Slade Gorton (R-Wash.), who led the fight for curbs on tobacco lawyers' fees. "I just came from a discussion on product-liability reform," said former senator Tim Wirth (D-Colo.) in 1992. "The room was filled with trial lawyers—and with fear of them."[27] Other groups, political dabblers by comparison, lack staying power, but you know the trial bar is going to be a major player in your state's politics ten or twenty years down the road.

After legal reformers placed a series of antilitigation initiatives on the California ballot, trial lawyers did not just content themselves with defeating the measures through huge ad buys and PR campaigns; they bankrolled a new and distinct genre of ballot measure that came to be known as the "revenge initiative." Liability insurers, for example, were among the first groups to tangle publicly with the lawyers, backing an early California initiative that went down to defeat in the 1980s. Trial lawyers soon struck back with the famous Proposition 103, a venture in something-for-nothing demagogy that decreed massive cuts in the price of insurance without reducing the cost of providing it. Eventually the courts struck down many of the proposition's most confiscatory provisions as unconstitutional, but by that time it had inflicted massive losses on insurance providers in the nation's largest state, and many of the companies, nursing their wounds, have stayed well away from a direct confrontation with the trial bar ever since.[28]

The same lesson was taught to a group of high-tech executives angered at shareholder class actions who backed another unsuccessful set of initiatives in 1996. Trial lawyers struck back with a so's-your-mom initiative, whose harshly punitive provisions would, for example, have put tech executives' homes at risk by forbidding their companies from reimbursing judgments against them in shareholder litigation. Terrified Silicon Valley managements shelled out $40 million to make sure the measure lost, and since that point have appeared to give up on challenging the political dominance of the state's trial lawyers. The two well-known tech entrepreneurs who personally backed the 1996 initiatives, Al Shugart (Seagate disk drives) and Thomas Proulx (Intuit financial software), were both given personal reason to be sorry they got involved. Enemies of the initiative put up a Web site attacking Proulx, which included not only a picture of his expensive house, but also, threateningly, its street address. The *Wall Street Journal* also reported in its news columns that opponents "hired a private detective to seek damaging information about him, apparently to no avail." Decades earlier a similar gumshoe operation against Ralph Nader had touched off an enormous outcry and secured the consumerist a permanent public reputation, but this time around no one seemed to care much, least of all Nader. Proulx quit politics in disgust. Meanwhile, lawyer-bought ads defending securities class-action suits showed a picture of notorious Lincoln Savings & Loan figure Charles Keating, whose face then "morphed" into that of Al Shugart, the initiative backer: "Protect yourself from the next Charles Keating," the voice track blared. A court ruled that the implication that Shugart was himself the "next Charles Keating" was clear enough that he could ask a jury for punitive damages, upon which the state trial lawyers' group, which had been refusing to apologize, abruptly changed its tune and settled the case. By that point, of course, the initiative had long since gone down to defeat.[29]

The shenanigans got even more extreme in the same year (1996) over in Alabama, where control of the state supreme court was at issue. A trial lawyer–backed incumbent faced a challenge from Republican Harold See, a law professor who had moved to the state some years before. Eleven days before the election, a political committee was quietly formed, filing a campaign disclosure document that listed only one donation, of $500, from one individual. By state law, donations that came after that point would not have to be disclosed until after the election. The campaign fund called itself the "Coalition for Family Values."

Then the radio blitz hit. "There are some things," a voice darkly intimated, that "Harold See hasn't told you." The anonymous new "coalition," it seemed, had laid their hands on papers from the professor's twenty-year-old divorce and proceeded in their ad to regale listeners with what the *Washington Post* described as "tawdry" details. (The same details figured in a whispering campaign in many of the state's fundamentalist Christian churches.) After the divorce, the radio ad continued, See had "fled Illinois for Alabama." Fortunately for See, his ex-wife was willing to issue a public statement defending him from the charges, and he won anyway. Disclosures filed after the election revealed the source of funding for the last-minute effort: $449,000 from a PAC affiliated with the Alabama Trial Lawyers Association.[30]

Even worse was to come. In Alabama, as in many southern states, the post of lieutenant governor is extremely powerful and includes a large say in how the legislature is organized. Just before the 1998 election, a woman stepped forward with sensational charges against Republican lieutenant governor candidate Steve Windom, who was up against a trial lawyer–backed opponent: Years earlier, she said, Windom had beaten and raped her. "Blast-faxed" to media around the state, the story was picked up more or less instantaneously. Later it turned out that an official of the state trial lawyers association had paid to have three hundred copies of the woman's videotaped accusations run off and distributed to press outlets around the state. The complainant, a former prostitute and heroin addict, soon recanted her story and began telling authorities she had been encouraged to make the charges and had even been given money. Windom, like See, managed to win the race anyway, once again because the story had fallen apart faster than anyone could have anticipated. "The evidence clearly showed that there was a great deal of involvement at every stage" in the affair by the trial lawyers, Windom said later. "It would have been impossible to disprove the charges in time for the election if it were not for a whistleblower—a trial lawyer who gave us the plot, chapter and verse."[31]

Despite trial lawyers' skill in achieving their own version of the much-lamented legislative "gridlock," most of the fifty state legislatures have, since the 1980s, enacted at least some measure of tort reform. In a still underreported story, however, the lawyers have proceeded to bring their skills to bear to get the state court systems to throw out most of the reforms as inconsistent, not with the federal constitution, but with their state constitutions. The supreme courts of Ohio and Illinois, for example, unceremoniously tossed two of the nation's most significant sets of legal reforms in the wastebasket. By 2001, an actual majority of state court systems had done likewise with reform enactments in their states. A special task force of ATLA attorneys had worked for years to devise and coordinate legal strategy, concentrating on state constitutional challenges because those decisions cannot be appealed to the federal courts, since the prevailing view in federal law is that state courts are free to interpret their own constitutions as unreasonably as they like.

Once again, the lawyers were winning their victories by getting courts to override the decisions of elected legislatures. When the Ohio high court in 1999 by a 4-3 margin, tossed out the legislature's comprehensive legal reform package, an editorial in the *Columbus Dispatch* called the decision "an act of arrogance and an affront to the doctrine of separation of powers." In their contributions to the elected justices up to that date, the trial bar had shown their usual exquisite sense of friend/foe identification, giving the four prevailing majority justices $1,528,054 in the previous seven years, while allotting just $70,704 to the three justices destined to dissent. In addition to wiping the existing reform statute from the books, the Ohio court also made clear that it would tolerate no similar enactments in the future: That is, it decreed that tort law should remain exclusively a judicial province, although the drafters of the Ohio Constitution would no doubt have been astonished at the proposition that lawmakers have no business trying to determine what the future state of the law should be. The point, however, was not to institute any consistent constitutional theory, but just to reach a particular result: Trial lawyers win, and their tort-reform adversaries lose.[32]

In its use of the state courts to slam the door—permanently, or so it intends—against any attempt to roll back its power, the trial bar has achieved its ultimate act of contempt for democracy. Lawyers themselves, of course, will still be free to do their utmost to persuade the courts to change the state of the law drastically at any time and on any issue—guns, tobacco, managed care—no matter what the views of the duly elected lawmaking branch of government might be. And once the judiciary seizes the reins, on the Ohio theory, there will be nothing the legislature can do, no enactment it can pass, by which it can reclaim the power to state what the law should be. Judicial elections are something the trial lawyers feel capable of handling: In the year 2000, they successfully defended their majority on the Ohio court, and if they have their way, no other sorts of elections at the state level will have to matter again.

More than one observer nominated the 2000 political season as the Year of the Trial Lawyer. The trial bar spent huge amounts of money trying to defeat Republican presidential candidate George W. Bush, who as governor of Texas had made a name in battling for liability reform and had fought high tobacco fees in particular. "It would be very, very horrifying to trial lawyers if Bush were elected," said attorney John Coale.[33] "There is some serious tobacco money being spread around." After the uncannily close vote, the hard-fought Florida recount—in which the fate of the presidency came to depend on which side had the better legal advice—was a fitting cap. Meanwhile, the U.S. Senate had a new star in North Carolina's trial lawyer/senator John Edwards. Elected in 1998, Edwards had delighted national Democrats by sinking an estimated $10 million from his personal fortune into his first campaign to knock off a Republican incumbent. Such was the impression Edwards made as a public and TV personality that, despite his newcomer status, candidate Gore came very close to picking him as his vice presidential running mate. Before long Edwards was canvassing New Hampshire as a prospective candidate in 2004 for the top job himself—the first plaintiffs' lawyer president, were he to win.

Actually, it is open to much doubt whether a career in litigation is really a winning background for an aspirant to the nation's highest office. Trial lawyers, who tend to accumulate enemies as they go, are prone to develop combative or abrasive personas. They have done rather poorly over the years in races for governors' seats in California, Michigan, Iowa, and other states; success in an executive post like a governorship demands the ability to unite a wide array of practical players over the long haul. They have enjoyed far more success in running for attorney generalships and U.S. Senate seats, the two great power bases in American politics that allow their occupants to stay more or less indefinitely in crusade or attack mode.

But with the new, explicit alliance between private trial lawyers and government actors such as state attorneys general and mayors, it isn't really necessary for trial lawyers to get themselves elected to anything. Their fortunes can, to an unprecedented extent, be founded directly on their real or perceived clout with political actors. Consider, for example, the details that emerged when the team of lawyers who had represented the state of Michigan in the tobacco litigation put in their request for fees in arbitration. The arbitration panel's press release announcing its award, as it happened, recounted some of the reasoning and testimony that underlay its decision. It said that the successful lawyers had followed—and were entitled to be compensated for—an "acknowledged three-prong strategy" of which only one prong consisted of work on strictly legal matters. The other two "prongs" consisted of political and public relations work. According to the panel, Mississippi attorney general

Michael Moore, referring to Richard Scruggs, had testified as follows:

> [Senate Majority Leader Trent Lott (R-Miss.) is] Dickey's brother-in-law. You don't think that this had anything to do with it? . . . Our team had the Senate Majority Leader as a brother-in-law of the lead lawyer, and it had an impact on this. And every AG and every other person recognized the power of that. Again, political one-third, PR one-third, and legal one-third.

And here is then–Michigan attorney general Frank Kelley:

> What was necessary to this case was not [Scruggs's] legal ability but his imagination in developing the media situation and the political situation. . . . when I was called down to the Rose Garden at the White House and I was seated next to C. Everett Koop and Mike Moore in the front row and the President of the United States came out to announce the FDA regulation on tobacco, as I entered the Rose Garden, who came out of the office from conference with the President but Mr. Scruggs. And I knew at that time that I had hired the right operative.

For a public official to have the gall to go before a public panel and boast openly of how one of his colleagues had used his status as brother-in-law of one of the nation's leading politicians for purposes of influence peddling and self-advancement would have provoked outrage even in the age of the Credit Mobilier and Teapot Dome scandals. For him to demand that his colleague be richly compensated precisely *because* of his cleverness in playing on such political connections is something imaginable only in an era where a power elite has abandoned all sense of shame.[34]

Litigators on Horseback

"It is a maxim among these lawyers," wrote Jonathan Swift in a passage of *Gulliver's Travels* satirizing English law, "that whatever has been done before, may legally be done again: and therefore they take special care to record all the decisions formerly made against common justice, and the general reason of mankind." Mass tort litigation, for its part, is fueled in large part by the pushing forward of practical precedent: Once lawyers succeed in breaking through against one defendant industry, they typically find themselves with the means and momentum to besiege new targets.

The success of the breast-implant campaign, for example, was full of implications for future defendants. It showed with great clarity how: (1) sheer volume of client recruitment and suit filing, combined with vigorous media efforts, could force even large defendants to cry uncle and agree to pay billions; (2) it wouldn't necessarily be fatal to such a campaign that the factual allegations behind it were invalid, since the courts were ill equipped to distinguish genuine from spurious causation; and (3) even if the basis of the scare were eventually refuted, organizers would still face no serious downside: no obligation to return their winnings, no levying by courts of sanctions or costs, no investigations by outraged lawmakers, no real cost even in reputation. And it did not take long, as those lessons sank in, for the basic pattern to be repeated in mass litigation against other medical and pharmaceutical products.

Throughout the 1970s and 1980s strange new precedents were reported from the rapidly expanding field of product-liability law. As old principles of "assumption of risk" eroded, for example, more courts agreed to let complainants sue over what had once been considered the obvious and notorious hazards of life's activities, from the shattered knees of the downhill ski slope to the scalding effects of hot coffee. When suits over cigarettes and guns began to be pushed seriously, they often provoked what was viewed at the time as a scathing *reductio ad absurdum:* why, next you'll propose suing the makers of soft drinks and potato chips! But sure enough, within a few years exactly such suits were being proposed by presumably serious law professors.

It was the same way with the decay of one of the most important old restraints on litigation, the idea of statutes of limitation. Lawyers exerted considerable creativity, arguing that the maker of a threshing machine or elevator sold in the 1920s, and still in operation, should be hauled into court and made to pay for a user's current injury. Even to the companies defending these suits, these seemed like freak occurrences, and it hardly made front-page news when courts began ignoring the old time limits and allowing such suits. But once the idea got well abroad that it was fair game to start mining history for grievances, it turned out that there were a great deal of grievances to be mined indeed. Whole sectors of litigation were soon premised on Coolidge Era sales of asbestos, tobacco, and lead paint; and it was a natural jump to the idea of suing for reparations for Jim Crow, for slavery itself, and perhaps for earlier indignities still, such as the dispossession of original American Indian tribes.

No litigation in memory cast as broad a shadow of likely future precedent as the state tobacco litigation. It was more boldly and baldly retroactive than almost anything that had come before, demanding as it did that the tobacco companies be punished for actions taken in years past which were plainly lawful under the legalities of that day. (In the event anyone missed the point, there were the bills authored by trial lawyers and steered to enactment in Florida and elsewhere that explicitly changed the rules of liability in order to help the states win their cases in progress.) The recoupment theories advanced in the Medicaid suits not only broke with all past ideas on the subject but had obvious application to many other industries, even if the attorneys general strenuously denied that they intended to apply them in such a way. The use of strong-arm litigation methods to change the way tobacco was sold was explicitly defended, in terms pregnant with implications for the future, as if anything superior to the use of conventional legislation through the democratic process. And, of course, the audacious "privatization" of public law enforcement, handing over its powers to contingency fee lawyers, set a precedent for many a future scheme in which private parties might commandeer public legal authority for their own advantage.

It's not as if the tobacco escapade escaped broad censure across the political spectrum. On the conservative side, *Wall Street Journal* editorialists compared the tobacco bar to the robber barons of the nineteenth century. Prominent liberal Robert Reich, the former Secretary of Labor, assailed the new suits as "blatant end-runs around the democratic process. . . . the answer is to make democracy work better, not give up on it." Centrist *Washington Post* columnist Robert Samuelson, meanwhile, lamented that "we now have government by and for the lawyers," who had "hijacked the public policy process for private enrichment" in a "daring, inventive and brazen" campaign. Newspapers around the country assailed the huge fee awards in a heartfelt if futile manner.[1]

And yet after the complaints had been aired a bit, the issue somehow just dropped from sight. Congress showed scant interest in pursuing the matter, and the cigarette companies themselves were definitely not encouraging public scrutiny of the settlements' details. The backroom settlements themselves had been presented to the public and the states as a fait accompli, subject to no reconsideration and no amendment, so there seemed to be little point in debate. The national chattering class, while no doubt sincere in feeling that something had gone badly wrong, found it easy to move on to other matters. Besides, too many members of the political stratum had too much to lose by any very close inquiry into what had happened. Too many officeholders, from both political parties, had participated in the deals; too many academics, nonprofits, and miscellaneous activists had found niches for themselves in the antitobacco machine; besides which, hadn't the new approach gotten results in curbing tobacco?

But it is not so easy to evade the issues raised by the new model of regulation through litigation. The more embarrassing details of the tobacco episode might soon be swept out of sight, but the same basic techniques and methods were sure to raise their heads again and again as lawyers pursued their quest for the next tobacco. And given that no one had managed to restrain the lawyers' ambition last time around, it was going to be all the harder for anyone to stand up to them at a point at which they were going to be billions of dollars richer and commensurately more influential.

What, if anything, has been learned from the tobacco round, and what is being done to prevent its abuses from being repeated? In both cases the answer would seem to be: not much.

True, there have been some halting efforts in state legislatures to head off a few of the most noxious practices. Against ferocious resistance from the litigation lobby, for example, a number of states have passed laws requiring that future selection of outside private lawyers to represent a state be carried on through competitive bidding or be approved in advance by the state's governor; requiring lawyers to submit expenses and time sheets over the course of a case; and so forth. In addition, about half the states have been moved by widespread gun-owner outrage to pass laws specifically restraining cities within their boundaries from pursuing recoupment lawsuits against gun makers. These measures are certainly better than nothing at all, but they fall far short of what the occasion demands, which should begin with a declaration, in accord with longstanding principles of legal ethics, that lawyers representing public entities have no business getting paid on a contingency basis at all.

In the U.S. Congress, despite occasional lip service paid to the cause of litigation reform, the trial bar has been more than capable of fending off any serious threat to its interests. Take asbestos, for example, which has held a place on the federal lawmaking agenda for more than a decade, given the heavily interstate character of asbestos litigation, the serious burden it has placed on the caseload of the federal courts, the original responsibility of the federal government for a large share of asbestos exposure, and the ever-escalating tendency of asbestos liabilities to be resolved at last in the federal bankruptcy courts. Remarkably, all nine members of the currently constituted U.S. Supreme Court, notwithstanding the wide ideological gulfs that separate such figures as David Souter, Sandra O'Connor, and Antonin Scalia, have, on various occasions, expressed support for some form of legislated system of alternative compensation that would end the asbestos litigation lottery and mandate rapid payments to those claimants who can objectively be shown to be suffering serious injury. But such reform has gone nowhere over the decade, thanks to the trial bar's clout in Washington.[2]

Virtually the only group of officials that has tried in any very systematic way to curb litigation abuses is the federal bench. In recent years federal judges have generally discouraged the treatment of personal-injury cases on a class-action basis, have made repeated efforts to curb excessive fees in class actions, and have tended toward skepticism when the pretense is put forward in settlements that a class lawyer's fee paid "separately" by defendants (as in the tobacco case) is somehow immune to challenge by class members. As the Seventh Circuit's influential Judge Richard Posner put it in a 1995 decision, courts should not lightly choose to impose class treatment of suits on defendants and thus subject them to the "undue and unnecessary risk of a monumental industry-busting error." Even more notably, the U.S. Supreme Court has declared that federal trial judges should endeavor to exclude unreliable scientific testimony ("junk science"), a key step in preventing lawyers from using the federal courts as a springboard for repeats of the silicone-implant episode.[3]

Unfortunately, many of these reformist trends have little discernible influence on the fifty state court systems, which not only are independent of the federal courts but handle a much greater volume of business overall. While the federal courts have taken some important steps to armor themselves against litigation abuses, the net effect is to ensure that clever plaintiffs' lawyers simply transfer their filing of suits to the wide-open state courts in the Jackpot Belt and elsewhere.

It would seem that only the U.S. Congress can rein in the outrages of the Jackpot Belt by exercising its constitutional authority (and perhaps responsibility) to supervise or provide a substitute for state courts' handling of interstate litigation. It should start by fixing the loopholes in federal jurisdiction so as to ensure that class actions claiming to represent large national classes will land in federal, not state court. Cases where the amount in controversy is lower, as well as cases with no interstate contacts, can conveniently remain in state courts, which will leave those courts continuing to handle the great bulk of litigation, including the vast majority of fender benders and other routine liability cases. By refusing to supervise the state courts' handling of national causes, we ensure that a few judges, courts, and juries—carefully selected by lawyers as part of their forum-shopping efforts—go on imposing their sentiments on the entire nation.

At the root of America's litigation problem is a simple issue of power: We first give lawyers far more power than other countries do and then provide less supervision of the way they use that power. Our distinctively liberal civil procedure puts a distinctively wide array of weapons in the hands of our litigators: the power to start a suit on scanty evidence, to demand extensive pretrial "discovery," to file a large variety of motions, and to introduce a wide range of issues, and so on. Each of these weapons can inflict serious cost on an opponent. And then, crucially, by not following most of the rest of the world in the "loser pays" principle, we give lawyers virtual carte blanche to wield these powers without fear that they or their clients will be held accountable when costs are imposed on an opponent in a poor cause. In short, we assure lawyers that they won't have to worry about compensating the people *they* injure.

This would be less objectionable were lawyers' use of their powers closely supervised by some credible authority whose duties included protecting the interests of nonlawyers and the general public. Historically, judges and professional guilds of legal practitioners have served as the two most important of such authorities, acting to sanction or even disbar abusers. But the disciplinary toothlessness of U.S. state bar associations has long since become a joke, even aside from the difficulty in expecting association lawyers to restrain other lawyers from engaging in litigious excesses that may contribute to their own steady employment. Bar associations these days even risk potential antitrust liability if they attempt to regulate some kinds of self-seeking activity by member lawyers. Realistically, there is no reason to expect the legal fraternity to clean its house any time soon and much reason to expect it not to.

And judges? Both at trial and during pretrial phases, our civil procedure is designed to empower lawyers to pursue their aims with minimal interference from judges. Beyond that, most cases settle rather than go to trial, and judges typically have relatively narrow scope to ride herd on the way a settled case has been prosecuted. Sanctions for wrongful litigation, it is true, can constitute one of the most effective oversight methods available to judges; but in the early 1990s, Congress quietly bowed to pressure from the bar by gutting the main federal sanctions provision. As for the state judiciary, as we have seen, large sectors of it have in practice long been tamed, if not outright captured, by the lawyers who practice before it. To make matters worse, by engaging in forum-shopping lawyers can select their own "regulators" by filing suit in whatever convenient county in Alabama or Mississippi is offering a legal blue-plate special this week. The simple fact is that there is no genuine watchdog agency at any level to stand guard over the litigation industry. And the need for such an agency— competent, authoritative, and independent of the lawyers it regulates—would make a good subject for a public campaign one of these days.

Among the things such an agency could do is simply begin to gather information. How much money each year flows through trial lawyers' offices? How much of it goes to them, and how much to clients? Which firms make the most money? Is the overall industry growing by 2 percent a year or by 20 percent? We know next to nothing reliable about these matters, and, of course, these gaps in our knowledge are by design rather than inadvertence: Even as lawyers make a living by compelling disclosures from others, so they are adept at concealing their own doings from inspection. In other sectors of the economy, even rather small enterprises routinely face record-keeping and reporting obligations, while such agencies as the U.S. Department of Commerce (DOC), the Internal Revenue Service (IRS), and the Bureau of Labor Statistics (BLS) assemble the resulting data into statistical pictures of industry activity. Yet it seems to be regarded somehow as overly intrusive to require billion-dollar law practices to file reports on the quantities of money that flow through their coffers.

It seems fair to assume that this dearth of disclosure is directly connected with the widespread feeling of those in the mass tort business that they enjoy a right to do their business behind closed doors. Reporters, interested citizens, and even members of represented classes are rigorously excluded from the meetings at which the trial bar dreams up novel causes of action, maps out client recruitment and media campaigns, negotiates settlements with defendants, and wheedles fees from friendly arbitrators. After a class action is settled, it is routine for lawyers to claim that it is none of the reporters' business—or even the business of class members—how settlement funds wind up being disbursed or how fees are divided among lawyers. The habit of concealing key details from public scrutiny prepared the way for the abuses of the tobacco affair, in which money flows were repeatedly designed to leave as little paper trail as possible, and lawyers again and again were observed springing up to claim enormously lucrative shares in fees even though it had never been a matter of public record that they were participating in the action at all.[4]

Some of these manifestations of secrecy would be more understandable were the litigation industry merely a private endeavor whose doings were of no wider public significance. And indeed, it is common for trial lawyers to claim for their doings the same presumption of privacy and freedom of action that we might accord to, say, a privately owned family business. Why should they be expected to disclose the percentage extent of their fee participation in a lawsuit, for example, when that is a matter for private agreement between themselves and their client?

Observe how the litigation lobby skillfully switches back and forth between presenting itself as "public" and as "private," the more deftly to obtain for itself the privileges of both kinds of status and the responsibilities of neither. Obviously, litigators pursue a line of business that is based on the exertion of a form of government power: the right to drag possibly innocent opponents into compulsory legal process. The most indulgent way of interpreting this as a form of private enterprise would be to compare litigators with certain kinds of regulated private enterprises that depend on rights-of-way obtained by eminent domain, such as railroads and electric utilities. And yet the intrusions of the litigation "utility" are not a one-time cost but rather never-ending; it is as if a nightmare electric company had the right to send work crews at any time into the offices and workshops of its customers, and then charge them a handsome fee in exchange for agreeing to leave.

The litigation industry does resemble various other sorts of business—yet in virtually every case it faces less regulation than those ordinary businesses face. It is a consumer service business, somewhat resembling the funeral business in the way it deals with many first-time customers who seldom buy its services and are under the sort of stress that keeps them from shopping carefully. Funeral operators have long since come under consumer-protection rules requiring them to apprise clients fully of their options, give them an informative accounting of work done, and allow them to buy some services but not others if they wish. Trial lawyers generally come under no such consumer-protection rules. Or again: The mass tort business is, in part, a financial business, handling huge sums of money that it holds in trust for unsophisticated beneficiaries, much as do banks and Wall Street firms. Yet no authority oversees the probity and soundness of lawyers' handling of these clients' interests, despite much evidence that abuses are not rare. Or yet again: Ordinary businesspeople can face civil and even criminal liability under antitrust laws if they collude with competitors to divide markets and customers among themselves, but many mass tort firms have been left free to collude with their competitors in just such a way.

In short, the litigation business is the sort of business that by all rights you would expect to come under tight public regulation. Yet it somehow has managed to escape such regulation almost entirely. And with the rise of tobacco-style litigation, mass tort lawyers have added yet another privilege to their already long list: the privilege of doing business with the government without activating the red tape entanglements that commonly afflict government contractors. It is hard to believe most states would sign contracts for private companies to carry out, say, the laying of concrete for state highways with as few fiscal controls as they hired private lawyers to pursue billion-dollar tobacco claims in exchange for a share of the swag. At the federal level and often the state level as well, businesses that get classified as government contractors must submit to a wide and onerous range of laws and regulators over and above those that apply to other businesses. These include "whistle-blower" laws that forbid them from retaliating if one of their employees steps forward to report questionable goings-on in their offices, and "citizen suit" provisions that allow anyone at all to initiate litigation accusing them of overcharging their government client and then collect a bounty based on the size of any resulting verdict or settlement. If there were justice in the world, lawyers holding themselves out as representing the government would be the first to volunteer to accept oversight provisions of this sort. Why shouldn't those who help administer and enforce burdensome laws live by them themselves?

The self-serving ploys by which trial lawyers simultaneously present themselves as tribunes of the overall public interest, and as private actors who need answer only to themselves and their clients, were bad enough. But the whole pretense should have come crashing to the floor when the trial bar decided to become, in Wendell Gauthier's phrase, a Fourth Branch of government.

You can't deny the audacity of the premise. Until the lawyers galloped onto the scene, it would have been natural to take the view that this nation, like other nations, was afflicted with a number of longstanding social problems that admitted to no quick or easy solutions. There was the question of how to handle vices that are injurious to health but are widely pursued nonetheless because they are found pleasurable. There was the problem of health-care financing, which policy makers had been addressing with first one set of reforms and then another over years, trying to escape the alternating dangers of ruinous cost escalation and restrictions on the availability of useful therapy. There was the passionately divisive matter of gun control, which often seemed to evoke a kind of displaced class warfare between well-off antigun suburbanites and the sorts of rural conservatives and midwestern factory workers who were thought to typify the progun camp. There was by far the most intractable problem in the nation's history, that of race relations. Who could imagine a quick and generally satisfying solution to any of these conundrums?

But that was before we called 1-800-LAWSUIT. Once we spoke with the operators standing by there, we would

realize that the problems were not actually so tragic or in-
soluble after all; we just needed to apply to them the modus
operandi of personal-injury law, with its demands for punitive damages, creative jury selection, and battles of the
hired expert witnesses. We would sue our health plan providers until we achieved an exactly optimal mix of cost con-
tainment and availability of therapy. We would sue the gun
makers until the point at which the supply of guns exactly
corresponded with the number of responsible persons who
wanted and deserved to own guns, neither more nor less.
We would sue businesses and institutions whose history
could be traced back to eras of rampant racism, and the
resulting damage awards would do much to apply balm to
old wounds and work toward making race less relevant in
American life.

We were entitled to call the lawsuit hotline—or its owners, perhaps, were entitled to call us first—because the older
idea of working out differences through legislative give-
and-take had failed: It had fallen victim to "gridlock" and
"special interest paralysis." How did we know this? Well,
Congress had failed to enact a new federal law restricting
managed-care practices—the same practices that it had set
out to encourage a few years earlier—even though a public
outcry had been in progress for a year or two on the subject.
The same Congress had failed to enact tighter controls on
guns and tobacco even though many prestigious newspapers
had editorialized in favor of its doing so. And it had certainly failed to solve the race problem.

Actually, despite the "stalemate" and "gridlock" charges
that were so freely tossed around, most of the causes embraced by the lawyers had been making steady if incremen-

tal progress in the legislative process for years. Congress had enacted major new antigun legislation within relatively recent memory; managed-care companies were liberalizing their coverage rules in response to public discontent, one reason being that such discontent was being heard by employers, who make the decision whether to retain the companies as operators of their health plans. Legislatures around the country had for years been hiking tobacco taxes and enacting antismoking measures; as Martha Derthick notes, "per capita consumption of cigarettes had plummeted during the three decades in which legislatures had dominated public policymaking, going from 4,287 in 1966 in 1966 to 2,493 in 1994." The myth that the target industries were somehow too powerful to be challenged in any ordinary or direct way was just that—a myth.[5]

Even more absurd is the notion that the lawyers had any sort of superior pipeline to the state of the public will; if anything, most of their schemes evidently stood in opposition to that will. When polled, after all, solid majorities of the American public have been counted in opposition to the idea of making cigarette and gun manufacturers pay for the costs occasioned by their products; in the gun case, for example, the margin was a lopsided 67 to 28 percent. In May 1998, at more or less the peak of the agitation against tobacco companies, a *National Journal*/NBC poll found only 38 percent of the public agreeing that government was doing too little to regulate tobacco—a proposition being hammered away at in the press more or less daily—while 31 percent thought it was already doing the right amount, and 28 percent thought it was doing too *much*. When Gallup asked 1,063 adults their opinion of a Florida jury's $145 billion punitive verdict against tobacco companies, 59 percent disapproved, 37 percent approved, and 4 percent had no opinion. Asked in another poll who was predominantly to blame for smokers' illnesses, 59 percent said it was "mostly" or "completely" smokers themselves and 26 percent said it was tobacco companies (20 percent "mostly," 6 percent "completely"), with another 14 percent blaming the two equally. It is true that steep hikes in the tobacco excise tax scored relatively well with the public in polls, but the states' attorneys general and their defenders have trouble taking any solace from that result since they are committed to the position that their settlement did *not* amount to a tax increase.

Results at the ballot box tell much the same story. Although at the height of the antitobacco agitation some Democratic strategists hoped the tobacco issue would help their candidates, political observers agree that it did not do so, and it soon fell from sight. As for the much-touted gun issue, it actually backfired badly on the Democrats, costing them key support in such swing states as Missouri, West Virginia, and Michigan in the year-2000 presidential election. As the debacle unfolded for the national party, many of its leading figures began darting for cover, led by presidential candidate Al Gore, who a short time earlier had been counted a strong antigun voice but now startled his audience by announcing that he believed homeowners have a right to keep guns for self-defense, a position many of his supporters had associated with "gun nuts." By 2002, gun-control groups were once again in the Democratic doghouse and suffering their worst disarray in years.

So in retrospect, it is apparent that neither the antitobacco nor the antigun crusades had any special access to the state of Main Street sentiment. It was not by happenstance that Scruggs and Moore in Mississippi took care to avoid a jury trial on the state's tobacco-Medicaid case (polling had indicated that they would lose it) and that they advised fellow attorneys general to follow their example by avoiding juries. Where both the antitobacco and the antigun crusades were strongest was in the appeal they held for elite opinion—the kind of opinion that dominates the prestige media, bar associations, and law schools. The advocates turned to the courts precisely because they did not have a very high expectation of winning a purely democratic fight.[6]

None of which would have even remotely surprised the framers of the American Constitution. While Madison, Hamilton, and the rest might not have recognized "partisan gridlock" as a phrase, they were keenly aware of the phenomenon itself and tended to regard it as being often a wholesome and necessary thing. Long experience had shown that it was possible for advocates to set up a momentary clamor for some measure whose evident importance or popularity would recede if it were looked at again after time had elapsed. With that in mind, the framers won the praise of judicious political theorists of all later generations by consciously erecting an obstacle course to the making of hasty new law. They began by vesting all legislative powers—the word "all" is theirs—in an elected Congress. They required that laws be approved by two chambers, and designed those chambers so that they would be in frequent disagreement with each other: of two different sizes, elected on different timetables, and from different geographical constituencies. New legislative enactments were also, of course, subject to a president's veto. The checks and balances were well engineered to fend off the twin (and closely related) dangers of rule by the mob and rule by a man on horseback.

The great boast of the Fourth Branch, as it rides in to break up partisan gridlock, is that it gets quick and decisive results. It would hardly be a surprise to learn that trial lawyers operate more nimbly and resourcefully than do the officials who administer conventional government regulatory agencies. After all, the lawyers labor under virtually none of the constraints with which we hedge in the freedom of action of public officials. To begin with, they typically need not worry about facing the voters and being replaced in the next election; nor are they subject to confirmation by a Senate or other legislative body; nor need they compete with each other for preferment in Civil Service exams. Even if they are making fortunes through their government "service" (fortunes that genuine government officials would never be allowed to make), the lawyers need not waste energy complying with the myriad disclosure rules that we apply to much of federal officialdom, such as regular financial disclosures, outside income limits, blind trust requirements, conflict of interest rules, "sunshine" and open-records laws, and so forth. Unlike government agencies that want to launch major regulatory initiatives, trial lawyers need not preannounce their intention to do so, invite public notice and comment, or risk having their actions held up in court because they have not complied with the prerequisites of the Administrative Procedures Act. They need not submit to interrogation by nosy inspectors from the General Accounting Office or appear regularly before legislative committees to account for the handling of their job duties. Most government officials find themselves constrained by one of the most celebrated and powerful of all checks and balances, the "power of the purse" by which the British tamed their kings: Lawmakers can cut off some or all of an agency's funding if, say, its enforcement efforts grow too zealous and stir a public outcry. Trial lawyers arrange for their activities to be self-funding, which means they often dodge this kind of legislative check even when they ostensibly represent governments.

Given their freedom from the many legal constraints to which actual government officials are subject, it would be no surprise if trial lawyers held an edge as to their ability to cut through bickering and indecisiveness and just "get things done." But that is merely to beg the question: If just getting things done is the main priority, why then do we go to such lengths to constrain the powers held by "real" government officials? The answer, of course, is that we do not for a moment trust these officials to wield the intimidating powers of government office without imposing on them a high degree of transparency and predictability, because we know how likely it is that the power would otherwise soon be abused. And yet somehow we allow the Fourth Branch to seize the historic powers of government while escaping the long-evolved constraints on the abuse of that power.

———

The complaints against representative legislatures haven't really changed much since the time of the French Empire, the English Civil War, or, for that matter, the ancient Greeks. From early on, parliaments and houses of Congress have been criticized as all talk and no action, as being the lackeys of special interests, as reflecting the backward opinion of provincial backwaters, as allowing obstructionist minorities to hold up needed measures. What is called for, or so the enemies of parliamentary democracy always argued, are strong leaders not entangled by obligations to the capital's power brokers; leaders who can act decisively on behalf of the overall public interest rather than temporize and compromise. Such were the arguments long made on behalf of kings, generalissimos, lord protectors, and emperors. Such are the arguments now made on behalf of letting the litigator on horseback ride in to bring us the changes in law that our superiors know in their wisdom are needed.

But it is equally possible that the public will prove in the end superior in wisdom to its would-be rulers. In its very first outings, the new Fourth Branch has already shown itself an arbitrary and untrustworthy plutocracy, unelected and unaccountable, with no special insight into the nature of the public interest. While we lecture Latin America and the former Soviet Union on the need for "transparency" in public affairs, we find ourselves disposing of billions in public revenues and large swaths of public authority through backroom deals that would bring a blush to the cheeks of a tinpot caudillo.[7]

The new rule of lawyers brings us many evils, but perhaps the greatest is the way it robs the American people of the right to find its own future and pursue its own destiny. No doubt democratic processes often fall short of perfection; they have not to date managed to eliminate the age-old temptation posed by enjoyable forms of human vice, or make the finest medicine readily affordable, or set our racial enmities behind us, or cause the eagle and dove to cuddle in one nest on the role of gun ownership in self-defense. But however uncertain the results of democracy, however slow and clumsy its procedures, we can feel quite sure that it is a better course than agreeing to turn over our rights of self-government to a new class of unaccountable lawyers.

Year upon year, we do nothing to govern our elite litigators, and the result at length is that they have decided to govern us. Fortunately, there is time to stop them.

NOTES

Many of this book's themes have been explored by the author in his periodical writings, especially in his columns in the magazine *Reason*, such as "Puff, the Magic Settlement: The Joy of Enormous Tobacco Fees" (January 2000); "Big guns" (October 1999); and "Thanks for the Memories: How Lawyers Get the Testimony They Want," on asbestos litigation (June 1998). Also see "Plaintiff's Lawyers Take Aim at Democracy" on the Smith & Wesson settlement, *Wall Street Journal*, March 21, 2000; Engle, "The Florida Tobacco Jurors: Anything but Typical," *Wall Street Journal*, July 12, 1999; "It Didn't Start with Dateline NBC," *National Review* (June 21, 1993); the Manhattan Institute's civil justice memo series, various dates; and "Better Living Through Litigation?" *The Public Interest* (Spring 1991). All these articles delve into more detail on particular controversies than it has been possible to do in this book.

Introduction: Better Living Through Litigation
1. Beverly C. Moore Jr. and Fred Harris, "Class Actions: Let the People In," in *Verdicts on Lawyers* eds. Ralph Nader and Mark Green. (New York: Crowell, 1976).
2. See Walter K. Olson, *The Litigation Explosion* (New York: Truman Talley Books/E. P. Dutton, 1991), chap. 15.
3. Monroe Freedman, "Access to the Legal System: The Professional Responsibility to Chase Ambulances," in *Lawyers' Ethics in an Adversary System*, ed. Monroe Freedman (Indianapolis: Bobbs-Merrill, 1975), cited in *The Litigation Explosion*, pp. 31, 353.

4. See Peter Huber, *Liability* (New York: Basic Books, 1998).

5. *Escola v. Coca-Cola Bottling Co.* 150 P.2d 436 (1944).

6. See *The Litigation Explosion*, p. 57 and chaps. 3, 12.

7. Andrew Blum, "Billions for Asbestos Bar?" *National Law Journal* (January 16, 1995).

8. Daniel LeDuc, "Angelos, Md. Feud over Tobacco Fee," *Washington Post*, October 15, 1999, quoting state senate president Thomas V. (Mike) Miller Jr. On the evils of retroactive legislation generally, see Daniel E. Troy, *Retroactive Legislation* (Washington, D.C.: AEI Press, 1998); Walter K. Olson, "Retro Style: Redefining Yesterday's Green Light as Red," *Reason* (August/September, 1997).

9. Rob Walker, "Evil Inc.," *New York Times Magazine*, August 6, 2000.

10. Philip J. Hilts, *Smokescreen: The Truth Behind the Tobacco Industry Cover-Up* (Reading. Mass.: Addison-Wesley, 1996), pp. 216–17, cited in Jacob Sullum, *For Your Own Good* (New York: Free Press, 1998), p. 9.

11. Robert Draper, "A Heavyweight in State Politics," *Texas Monthly* (September 1996), profiling and quoting Dan Morales.

12. James Bennett, "Anti-Smoker Presses Shea Billboard Battle," *New York Times*. April 26, 1993, quoting Joseph Cherner, cited in Sullum, *For Your Own Good*. p. 5.

13. David Goetz, "Brown-Forman Concedes Alcohol Could Be Target of Legal Assault," *Louisville Courier-Journal*, September 16, 1997, quoting attorney Richard Gurfein. Certainly worth pursuing: John Berlau, "Will Other Vices Be Targeted?" *Investor's Business Daily*, February 12, 1998, quoting George Hacker of the Center for Science in the Public Interest; "Family Values, Killer Industries," Public Citizen (December 23, 1998); "Killer Industries Fund Congressional Champions of " 'Family Values,' " press release, December 28, 1998, both at Public Citizen Web site.

Chapter 1: The Joy of Tobacco Fees

1. Martha A. Derthick, *Up in Smoke: From Legislation to Litigation in Tobacco Politics* (Washington, D.C.: CQ Press, 2001), p. 106.

2. Michael Orey, *Assuming the Risk: The Mavericks, the Lawyers and the Whistle-Blowers Who Beat Big Tobacco* (Boston: Little, Brown, 1999), p. 263.

3. Orey, p. 239.

4. Orey, p. 241–42.

5. See *The Litigation Explosion*, pp. 46–47.

6. Charles Mahtesian, "Governing—1998 Public Officials of the Year: Tobacco's Nemesis," *Governing* (1998).

7. "In nearly all civilized countries," noted the *Encyclopedia Britannica* in 1910 under "Tobacco," "the cultivation of tobacco and its manufacture are conducted under state supervision and form an important source of public revenue." The main differences were between countries where tobacco was sold by direct public monopoly, and those which accomplished the same aim by applying heavy excise taxes to private commerce in the commodity.

8. Willard G. Manning et al., "The Taxes of Sin: Do Smokers and Drinkers Pay Their Way?" *Journal of the American Medical Association* (March 17, 1989), Rand corporation researchers; Jane G. Gravelle and Dennis Zimmerman, "Cigarette Taxes to Fund Health Care Reform: An Economic Analysis," Congressional Research Service, 1994; Jan J. Barendregt et al., "The Health Care Costs of Smok-

ing." *New England Journal of Medicine* (October 9, 1997). Also see Sullum, *For Your Own Good*, pp. 128–34, 299.

9. See Michael DeBow, "The State Tobacco Litigation and the Separation of Powers in State Governments: Repairing the Damage," *Seton Hall Law Review* 31 (2001), pp. 563, 571–72: "The states sought to define their recoupment claim as excluding any offset in favor of the tobacco companies for either state revenues generated by taxes on cigarettes, or state Medicaid savings on, *inter alia*, nursing home expenditures as a result of the higher mortality rate of smokers. Economic research shows definitively that the value of either of these two items, if recognized, would zero-out the states' claims." The analysis in the text is indebted to DeBow's article and to two other important critiques of the tobacco settlement: Margaret A. Little, "A Most Dangerous Indiscretion: The Legal, Economic, and Political Legacy of the Governments' Tobacco Litigation," *Connecticut Law Review* 33 (2001), p. 1143; and Thomas C. O'Brien, Constitutional and Antitrust Violations of the Multistate Tobacco Settlement, *Cato Policy Analysis*, no. 371 (May 18, 2000).

10. *United States v. Standard Oil Co. of California*, 332 US 301 (1947); *City of Flagstaff v. Atchison, Topeka & Santa Fe*, 719 F.2d 322, 323 (9th Cir. 1983); *District of Columbia v. Air Florida, Inc.*, 750 F.2d 1077, 1079, 1086 (D.C. Cir. 1984). See DeBow, "Repairing the Damage," pp. 572–74. On the novelty and inadequacy of the states' theories, see DeBow, p. 569: "Viewed as of the time the suits were filed, the tobacco suits had no support in either case law or statutory law"; p. 571: commentators "virtually unanimous" as to novelty; and p. 572: "In short, the states' recoupment theories of recovery were utterly without precedent in American law. In fact, the case against the states' claims can be stated even more strongly. The states' recoupment concept had been rejected in principle by one U.S. Supreme Court decision, and more recently by two different U.S. circuit courts of appeal."

11. See Sec. 402a, Comment I, "Unreasonably dangerous."

12. W. Kip Viscusi, *Smoking: Making the Risky Decision* (New York: Oxford, 1992), pp. 61–78. See Sullum, *For Your Own Good*. p. 66.

13. Sullum, *For Your Own Good*, p. 104: "no consistent relationship."

14. "Tobacco Fee Arbitration Panel Announces Michigan Decision," PR newswire release, Tobacco Fee Arbitration Panel, September 7, 2001.

15. Dave McKinney, "Law Firms Decry Cut in Tobacco Fees," *Chicago Sun-Times*, October 12, 1999.

16. "Tobacco Fee Arbitration Panel Announces Iowa Decision," PR newswire, December 29, 1999.

17. Glen Justice, "Critics Protest Monumental Legal Fees in Pennsylvania Tobacco Case," *Philadelphia Inquirer*, October 4, 1999.

18. Lucy Morgan, "Lawyers Say They Had to Hire Chiles' Friends," *St. Petersburg Times*, March 25, 1998.

19. "All Aboard the Gravy Train" and "Busting the Fee Bonanza," September 17, 2000 and *St. Louis Post-Dispatch* editorials, December 18, 2000.

20. *Topeka Capital-Journal* coverage, including Roger Myers, "Fees Likely to Exceed Cap," January 22, 1999; "State Will Be Rewarded for Early Entry to Suit," March 12, 1999; Jim McLean, "Battle Between Stovall, Critic a Draw," March 13, 1999; Trevor Armbrister, "Trial Lawyers on Trial," *Reader's Digest* (January 2000).

21. Sheila R. Cherry, "Litigation Lotto," *Insight* (March 11, 2000).

22. Thomas Scheffey, "Jedi Blumenthal," *Connecticut Law Tribune*, December 1, 1999, quoting Richard Blumenthal; Thomas Scheffey, "Winning the $65 Million Gamble," *Connecticut Law Tribune*, December 8, 1999; "After the Lion's Share," February 5, 2000, quoting David Golub.

23. Tim O'Brien, "A $350M Boardwalk Bonanza," *New Jersey Law Journal* (September 27, 1999).

24. Michael Perlstein, "Tobacco Attorneys' Huge Fees Questioned," New Orleans *Times-Picayune*, May 17, 2000, quoting Richard Ieyoub.

25. Carolyn Lochhead, "The Growing Power of Trial Lawyers," *Weekly Standard*, September 23, 1996, quoting Mississippi assistant attorney general Trey Bobinger, cited at Derthick, *Up in Smoke*, p. 107.

26. Editorial column by Ohio attorney general Betty D. Montgomery, December 4, 1998, online at Montgomery's Web site, http://www.ag.state.oh.us/civilrts/columns/settlement.htm, visited November 10, 2001.

27. Betsy Z. Russell, "Tobacco Money Gets Closer to Idaho," Spokane *Spokesman-Review* (October 24, 1999), quoting Idaho official Brett DeLange.

28. "Still a Health Threat," *New York Times*, November 24, 1998.

29. Saundra Torry, "Huge Fees for Anti-Tobacco Lawyers," *Washington Post*, December 12, 1998, quoting John Coale.

30. "Multi-Billion Dollar Lawyers' Windfall in Tobacco Cases," CNN.com, December 12, 1998, quoting Robert Kerrigan.

31. "Regulation by Litigation: The New Wave of Government-Sponsored Litigation," Manhattan Institute Center for Legal Policy conference proceedings, June 22, 1999, remarks of Richard Scruggs; according to Martha Derthick, *Up in Smoke*, p. 185, many of the state fee settlements paid by the industry have remained entirely secret. For an overall fee estimate of $13 billion, see Thomas Edsall, "Lawyers Get Tobacco Fees Early," *Washington Post*, February 14, 2001.

32. *Milwaukee Journal Sentinel* coverage, July 13, 1999, and other dates; Ashland *Daily Press*, April 8, 1999.

33. Sheila R. Cherry, "Litigation Lotto," *Insight* (March 11, 2000), quoting state senator Troy Fraser.

34. Tim O'Brien, "A $350M Boardwalk Bonanza," *New Jersey Law Journal* (September 27, 1999).

35. "Temps Did Most Work in Tobacco Case," AP, June 29, 2000.

36. Carlos Sanchez, "Costs Claimed by Lawyers in Tobacco Case Include $300 for Coffee Service, $952 for Lunch," Fort Worth *Star-Telegram*, February 21, 1998.

37. Susan Borreson, "Making Pennzoil Look Paltry," *Texas Lawyer* (January 26, 1998), and Sanchez, above.

38. Glen Justice, "In Tobacco Suit, Grumblings Over Legal Fees," *Philadelphia Inquirer*, October 4, 2000.

39. Clay Robison, "Cornyn Moves in On Anti-Tobacco Lawyers," *Houston Chronicle*, April 27, 2000; Brenda Sapino Jeffreys, "As Tobacco Lawyers Return Money, Questions Return," *Texas Lawyer* (June 9, 2000); Miriam Rozen, "Smoke-Filled Room," *Dallas Observer*, September 17, 1998. Further information can be found at Overlawyered.com, September 1–3, 2000.

40. See references in fn 39.

41. Jon Burstein, "Lawyer Wants $34 Million for Working 118 Hours on Florida's Case Against Tobacco Companies," Fort Lauderdale *Sun-Sentinel*, July 14, 2000

(Alan Dershowitz); Bob Van Voris, "Tobacco Road Not Gold for All," *National Law Journal* (December 28, 1998–January 4, 1999), (Richard Daynard).

42. David Rice, "Wicker Aide Calls for the Disclosure of Attorney's Fee," *Winston-Salem Journal*, April 25, 2000.

43. *Regulation by Litigation*, p. 24, remarks of Mike Wallace and Richard Scruggs.

44. Orey, *Assuming the Risk*, p. 265.

45. Scott Shane, "Lawyers' Tobacco Suit Fees Divisive," *Baltimore Sun*, December 24, 2000.

46. Janet Elliott, *Texas Lawyer* (March 27, 2000); "Tough Questions: Taking the High Road," *National Jurist* (October 2000) quoting Frank Newton.

47. Matt Fleischer, "And to the Victors Go the Spoils. Right? Not always," *National Law Journal* (April 17, 2000).

48. Pamela Coyle, "Lawyers Reap Big Money from Big Tobacco," New Orleans *Times-Picayune*, February 6, 2000.

49. Bill Ainsworth, "Lungren Now a Paid Advocate for His Former Foes," *San Diego Union-Tribune*. March 14, 2001.

50. Lawrence W. Schonbrun, "Class Actions: The New Ethical Frontier," *Manhattan Institute Civil Justice Memo* 30 (November 1996).

51. "Regulation by Litigation," comments of Eliot Spitzer.

52. "Regulation by Litigation," comments of John Langbein.

53. "Tobacco and Torts" (editorial), *St. Petersburg Times*, December 19, 1998 ("almost disgusting"); "Lawyers' Tobacco-Suit Fees Invite Revolt," *USA TODAY* May 22, 2000; "All Aboard the Gravy Train" (editorial), *St. Louis Post-Dispatch*, September 17, 2000; "Busting the Fee Bonanza" (editorial), *St. Louis Post-Dispatch*, December 18, 2000; "Wizard of Oz 'Justice' " (editorial), *Capital Times*, September 30, 1999.

54. Having long excoriated opponents of the tobacco litigation, the newspaper's editorialists finally acknowledged in an editorial in early 1998 ("Billion-Dollar Legal Fees," *New York Times*, February 11, 1998) that at least in theory plaintiffs' lawyers might be set to receive excessively high fees, raising the specter of an undesirable public "backlash" against the effort as a whole. Over the next several years, as arbitrators announced their series of astounding fee awards for lawyers representing New York and many other states, the paper did not see fit to devote any further editorials to the subject of lawyers' tobacco fees.

55. The research for this book, for example, at one point encountered a hurdle when the author discovered that the site that had previously hosted a full copy of the text of the MSA had taken it down, and that results from a major search engine found no other copies of the document online. Some weeks later it reappeared, hosted at a different site.

56. Derthick, *Up in Smoke*, pp. ix, 175–76.

57. Master Settlement Agreement ss. IX(d)(2)(B), (E), and (F).

58. Jonathan Gruber and Jonathan Zinman in "Youth Smoking in the U.S.: Evidence and Implications" (Cambridge, Mass.: *National Bureau of Economic Research Working Paper* 7780, July 2000).

59. Dwight R. Lee, "Will Government's Crusade Against Tobacco Work?" (Washington University in St. Louis: *Center for the Study of American Business Contemporary Issues Series* 86, July 1997), pp. 11–12.

60. Mike Males, "The Culture War Against Kids," Alternet.org, May 22, 2001. "[i]n the four years after Joe's advent, every survey showed teenage smoking declined—down 19 percent among high schoolers from 1988 to 1992, twice as

fast as the drop among adults. Further, the biggest decline came among the youngest group (12–13).")

Chapter 2: Serial Litigation

1. "Puff Daddies," *George* (June 1999).
2. Susan Borreson, "Beaumont's Million-Dollar Men," *Texas Lawyer* (March 15, 1999).
3. Adam Cohen, "Are Lawyers Running America?" *Time* (July 17, 2000), quoting Frederic Levin, who said he was "giving much of it to charity."
4. Barry Meier, "Fund-Raiser May Be Achilles' Heel for Gore," *New York Times*, June 4, 2000, profile of Frederick Baron.
5. Daniel LeDuc and Michael E. Ruane, "Orioles Owner Masters Political Clout," profile of Peter Angelos, *Washington Post*, March 28, 1999. See Molly Rath, *Baltimore City Paper*, August 16, 2000; "A Lawyer's Chutzpah" (editorial), *Wall Street Journal*, March 14, 1996.
6. David Shepardson, "Filers of Gun Lawsuits Plan More White House Talks," *Detroit News*, January 20, 2000, quoting chief judge Michael Sapala.
7. Mary Flood, "The Royal Treatment," *Houston Chronicle*, May 12, 2001.
8. Elaine McArdle, "Trial Lawyers, AGs Creating a New Branch of Government?" *Lawyers Weekly USA* (July 12, 1999). Other trial lawyers grew "heated" and "vehement" when the examples of liquor and fast food came up, recalls one observer: Michael DeBow, "The States vs. the Tobacco Industry: Smoke and Assorted Mirrors," *Heartland Institute* (June 4, 1997).
9. Douglas McCollam, "Long Shot," *American Lawyer* (June 1999). We've started a war: Peter J. Boyer, "Big Guns," *The New Yorker* (May 17, 1999), quoting John Coale.
10. Eric Siegel, Scott Shane, and Sean Somerville, "Lead Could Be Target of Next Major Suit," *Baltimore Sun*, April 7, 1999.
11. Mark Curriden, "Tobacco Fees Give Plaintiffs' Lawyers New Muscle," *Dallas Morning News*, October 31, 1999, quoting Ron Motley.
12. Peter S. Goodman, "Angelos Suits Allege Cellular-Phone Danger," WashTech.com/*Washington Post*, April 19, 2001; "More Dumb Lawsuits" (editorial), *Washington Post*, April 23, 2001. See National Cancer Institute, "No Association Found Between Cellular Phone Use and Risk of Brain Tumors," press release, December 21, 2000.
13. Douglas McLeod, "Suits by Public Entities Expected to Increase," *Business Insurance* (October 18, 1999). In a letter to another attorney general, Rhode Island Sheldon Whitehouse proposed "going after" glove makers.
14. Chris Williams, "Cornyn Defends Involvement with Conservative Group," AP (datelined Austin, Texas), March 30, 2000, quoting Jane Brady.
15. James K. Glassman, "Sorry State of Affairs: Politicians Regulating by Litigation," *Houston Chronicle*, February 25, 2001.
16. Charles Condon press release, September 13, 2000; David Shuster, "South Carolina AG Threatens Suit Against Entertainment Industry," *Fox News*, September 15, 2000.
17. David Segal, "Drawing a Bead on HMOs," *Washington Post*, December 14, 1999, quoting Richard Blumenthal.
18. Jacqueline Soteropoulos, "City Solicitor Banks on Lawsuits," *Philadelphia Inquirer*, September 26, 2000, quoting Philadelphia city solicitor Kenneth I. Trujillo.

19. Michael D. Goldhaber, "Class Action Blues, New Orleans Style," *National Law Journal* (June 28, 1999), quoting Russ Herman. See also Patrick E. Tyler, "Tobacco-Busting Lawyers on New Gold-Dusted Trails," *New York Times*, March 10, 1999.

20. "Actions Without Class" (editorial), *Washington Post*, December 2, 1999, criticizing tactic of "peddling their suit around Wall Street in a deliberate attempt to depress the companies' stock value and thereby pressure them to settle. This isn't law. It's an extortion racket."

21. David Shepardson, "Filers of Gun Lawsuits Plan More White House Talks," *Detroit News*, January 20, 2000, quoting Brian Siebel of Brady/CPHV; Eric Siegel, Scott Shane, and Sean Somerville, "Lead Could Be Target of Next Major Suit," *Baltimore Sun*, April 7, 1999, quoting Thomas Graves, National Paint & Coatings Association; "Jaws 2000: Deutsche Banc Alex. Brown's Gary Frazier Releases Groundbreaking Report on the Legal Issues Facing the HMO Industry," PR Newswire, April 25, 2000, analyst Gary Frazier on managed health care; Dave Shiflett, "Gambling and Its Discontents," *American Spectator* (March 1999), quoting National Coalition Against Legalized Gambling's Tom Grey; David Segal, "New Legal Guns Train on Microsoft," *Washington Post*, November 12, 1999; Scott Baldauf, "Lone Star Lawsuit Takes On Oil Giants," *Christian Science Monitor*, April 27, 1998, quoting Danielle Brian; "Toxic Mold a Growing Legal Issue," *UPI/ENN*, October 6, 2000, quoting Alexander Robinson.

22. "Beyond Tobacco—Cigarette Litigation's Offspring: Assessing Tort Issues Related to Guns, Alcohol, and Other Social Villains in Light of the Tobacco Wars," held in Los Angeles, March 6, 1999.

23. David Segal, "After Tobacco Success, Lawyers Pick Gun Fight; Same Tactics Aimed at Firearms Industry" *Washington Post*, January 5, 1999, quoting John Coale.

24. "I Have No Clients," *Forbes* (October 11, 1993), quoting William Lerach.

25. Amy Stevens, "The Mouthpieces: Class-Action Lawyers Brawl over Big Fees in Milli Vanilli Fraud," *Wall Street Journal*, October 24, 1991.

26. David Segal, "In Race to Sue Microsoft, Some Trip," *Washington Post*, December 21, 1999.

27. William Glaberson, "Dispute over Ads Draws Wide Scrutiny After Award," *New York Times*, July 22, 2001.

28. Mark Ballard, "Junk Fax Ban Taken Seriously," *National Law Journal*, May 17, 1999, quoting Steven Zager of Brobeck, Phleger & Harrison.

29. Joe Stephens, "Coupons Create Cash for Lawyers," *Washington Post*, November 14, 1999.

30. Dan Neel, *Info World* (November 8, 1999), quoting Jennifer Winch.

31. Joseph Menn, "Toshiba OKs Settlement of $1 Billion over Laptops," *Los Angeles Times*, October 30, 1999; see Walter Olson, "Gold Bugs: Class Action Lawyers Discover Silicon Valley," *Reason* (February 2000).

32. Janet Cooper Alexander, "An Introduction to Class Action Procedure in the United States," paper presented at Duke University and University of Geneva conference, "Debates over Group Litigation in Comparative Perspective," held at Geneva, Switzerland, July 21–22, 2000, fn. 10.

33. Brian Wolfman, Alan B. Morrison, and Richard Bennett, attorneys for class members Angela Williams et al., brief dated January 5, 1998, visited July 14, 2002, at http://www.citizen.org/litigation/briefs/Tobacco/articles.cfm?ID=779.

34. Prepared statement concerning H.R. 1283, The Fairness in Asbestos Com-

pensation Act, by Professor Christopher Edley Jr., Harvard Law School, at House Judiciary Committee hearing July 1, 1999.

35. Douglas McCollam, "Long Shot," *The American Lawyer* (June 1999), discussing views of Wendell Gauthier.

36. Adam Cohen, "Are Lawyers Running America?" *Time* (July 17, 2000), quoting Richard Scruggs.

37. Douglas Jehl, "Fearing a Bush Presidency, Groups Plan Pollution Suits," *New York Times*, December 7, 2000, quoting Michael Papantonio.

38. Peter Boyer, "Big Guns," *The New Yorker* (May 17, 1999).

39. Patrick E. Tyler, "Tobacco-Busting Lawyers on New Gold-Dusted Trails," *New York Times*, March 10, 1999, quoting John Coale.

40. "Election 2000: The Florida Vote," CNN Live Event, November 29, 2000, comments of Richard Scruggs (transcript available on NEXIS).

41. James Dao, "Gun Maker Agrees to Curbs in Exchange for Ending Suits," *New York Times*, March 18, 2000.

42. Edward Walsh and David A. Vise, "U.S., Gunmaker Strike a Deal," *Washington Post*, March 18, 2000, quoting Clinton official.

43. Elaine McArdle, "Trial Lawyers, AGs Creating a New Branch of Government?" *Lawyers Weekly USA* (July 12, 1999), quoting Michael Papantonio.

44. James Dao, "Gun Maker Agrees to Curbs in Exchange for Ending Suits," *New York Times*, March 18, 2000.

45. Paul Barrett, "Americans Turn to Lawyers to Cure Nation's Social Ills," *Wall Street Journal*, January 4, 2000.

Chapter 3: Gunning for Democracy

1. "Gun Makers Lobby Lawmakers to Outlaw Lawsuits," AP/*Salt Lake Tribune*, February, 5, 1999.

2. *Broward Daily Business Review* (July 1, 1999), quoting Miami's Albert Maloof.

3. "Statement by Attorney General Spitzer on New York City Gun Lawsuit," press release from office of Attorney General Spitzer, June 19, 2000.

4. David Shepardson and Cameron McWhirter, "Wayne County, Detroit Sue Gun Makers, Dealers," *Detroit News*, April 27, 1999, quoting Max Bandy.

5. Paul Barrett, "Gun-Industry Leader Backs Clinton Bid for Pact," *Wall Street Journal*, December 9, 1999.

6. Hans H. Chen, "Colt's Handgun Plan Heats Up Debate," APBNews.com, October 11, 1999, quoting John Coale.

7. Paul M. Barrett, "Gun Retailers Form Group to Push Views," *Wall Street Journal*, January 6, 2000.

8. Elaine McArdle, "Trial Lawyers, AGs Creating a New Branch of Government?" *Lawyers Weekly USA* (July 12, 1999), quoting Daniel Abel.

9. Ellen Goodman, "Victims Saying Ready, Aim, Sue," *Birmingham News*, February 27, 1999, quoting Laurence Tribe, quoted in Michael DeBow, "Restraining State Attorneys General, Curbing Government Lawsuit Abuse." *Cato Institute Policy Analysis* 437 (May 10, 2002).

10. Paul M. Barrett, "Evolution of a Cause: Why the Gun Debate Has Finally Taken Off," *Wall Street Journal*, October 21, 1999, quoting Elisa Barnes.

11. Peter Boyer, "Big Guns," *The New Yorker*, May 17, 1999.

12. Art Levine, "Taking Aim at the Weapon Makers: a One-Man Campaign for Smarter Firearms," *U.S. News & World Report* (December 6, 1999) profiling Stephen Teret.

13. See Jill Smolowe, "The N.R.A.: Go Ahead, Make Our Day," *Time* (May 29, 1995); Evelyn Theiss, "Clinton Blames Losses on NRA," Cleveland *Plain Dealer*, January 14, 1995. The background check provision was later found unconstitutional by the Supreme Court in *Printz v. United States*, 521 U.S. 98 (1997).

14. David Kopel, "Strongarm Suits," *Liberty* (February 2000).

15. "New Orleans First City to Sue Gun Manufacturers," Center to Prevent Handgun Violence/Handgun Control Press Release, October 30, 1998, quoting center's Dennis Henigan.

16. Douglas McCollam, "Long Shot," *American Lawyer* (June 1999).

17. Andrew Jay McClurg, "The Tortious Marketing of Handguns: Strict Liability Is Dead, Long Live Negligence," *Seton Hall Legislative Journal* 19, p. 777 and no. 178 (1995).

18. Private communication to author from Eugene Volokh, professor of law, University of California, Los Angeles, December 2001.

19. Paul M. Barrett, "Evolution of a Cause: Why the Gun Debate Has Finally Taken Off," *Wall Street Journal*, October 21, 1999, quoting Alex Penelas.

20. Paul Barrett, *Wall Street Journal*, April 23, 1999.

21. Daniel LeDuc, "Dumbing Down Smart Guns: Md. Senate to Vote on a Weakened Version of Bill," *Washington Post*, March 23, 2000. See David Kopel, Strongarm Suits, *Liberty* (February 2000). On the question of gun locks, it should be noted that one reason we can equip aspirin bottles with safety caps is that no one needs to gulp down aspirin in an emergency; drugs for which every second may count in administration, such as those found in asthma inhalers, epinephrine injectors and snake antivenin kits, dispense with the puzzle packaging. Locks aside, the much-demanded "child-proofing" of guns turned out to mean things like raising the resistance of triggers to the point where the strength in a young finger would no longer be enough to squeeze off a shot. Such a change not only would render guns unusable for many disabled and elderly adults, but also make guns significantly less controllable for ordinary users, increasing the rate of accidents in their hands. As for "smart guns," only one company, Smith & Wesson, had gotten even to prototype stage on such a project, and its Captain Marvel-esque details (tailored to police use) would suit the needs of relatively few other legitimate users: To fire the gun the user would have to be wearing a special wristband that emitted a coded radio signal picked up by a microchip in the gun's handle. There were also concerns about the reliability of any product based, as smart gun designs would have to be, on advanced personal-recognition micro-technologies. Even familiar products like video players, desktop computers and supermarket bar-code scanners, which never need to be taken out of doors or stored amid extremes of dust, humidity, or temperature, frequently suffer jams and malfunctions. Jumping into unproven gun technologies is itself a good way to invite ruinous product-liability claims.

22. "New Orleans First City to Sue Gun Manufacturers: Center to Prevent Handgun Violence Co-Counsel in Landmark Lawsuit," Brady Campaign press release, October 30, 1998, quoting Morial.

23. Jake Tapper, "City clickers," *Salon* (July 13, 1999); *Detroit Free Press*, August 25, 1999; *Boston Globe*, August 17, 1999.

24. Peter Boyer, "Big Guns," *The New Yorker* (May 17, 1999).

25. David Kopel, "Abusive Lawsuits Against the Second Amendment," *Independence Institute* (January 24, 2000). See David Kopel, "Strongarm Suits," *Liberty* (February 2000).

26. Lt. Gen. William M. Keys USMC (ret.), chief executive officer of the New Colt's Holding Company, prepared remarks before the Senate Judiciary Committee, November 2, 1999.

27. Peter Boyer, "Big Guns," *New Yorker* (May 17, 1999).

28. Sharon Walsh, "Gun Industry Views Pact as Threat to Its Unity," *Washington Post*, March 18, 2000, quoting John Coale.

29. Fox Butterfield, "Relying on Bush, Gun Makers End Talks," *New York Times*, May 4, 2000, quoting unnamed head of California handgun company.

30. Paul M. Barrett, "Some Small California Gun Firms File Under Bankruptcy Code as Cities Sue," *Wall Street Journal*, September 13, 1999, quoting David Hagen, lawyer for Sundance Industries.

31. Adam Eventov, "Mira Loma, Calif.-Based Gun Maker Bites the Dust as Legal Showdown Looms," *The Business Press* (Ontario, Calif.) (September 6, 1999), quoting Luis Tolley of Handgun Control, Inc.; David B. Ottaway, "Legal Assault on Firms Is Armed by Foundations," *Washington Post*, May 19, 1999, quoting Nancy Mahon.

32. Sharon Walsh, "Insurers Are Bailing Out on Gun Industry," *Washington Post*, November 26, 1999, quoting Robert Hartwig.

33. Paul Barrett, "Swiss Gun Maker SIG Plans to Sell U.S. Unit," *Wall Street Journal*, January 19, 2000.

34. Gary Kleck, "The Misfire That Wounded Colt's Manufacturing," *New York Times*, October 23, 1999; Matt Bai, "Unmaking a Gunmaker," *Newsweek* (April 17, 2000); Paul M. Barrett, "Evolution of a Cause: Why the Gun Debate Has Finally Taken Off," *Wall Street Journal*, October 21, 1999.

35. Paul M. Barrett, " 'Smart' Guns Trigger a Debate," *Wall Street Journal*, January 27, 2000 (quoting John Rigas, a partner in the company's controlling owner, the New York investment group Zilkha & Co.

36. Paul Barrett, "Swiss Gun Maker SIG Plans to Sell U.S. Unit," *Wall Street Journal*, January 19, 2000.

37. "Gun lawsuits effective" (editorial), *Atlanta Journal-Constitution*, Oct. 12, 1999.

38. "Gun Makers Lobby Lawmakers to Outlaw Lawsuits," AP/*Salt Lake Tribune*, February 5, 1999, quoting Bob Baker.

39. Sharon Walsh, "Insurers Are Bailing Out on Gun Industry," *Washington Post*, November 26, 1999, quoting Tom Deeb.

40. Edward Walsh and David A. Vise, "U.S., Gunmaker Strike a Deal," *Washington Post*, March 18, 2000, quoting Andrew Cuomo.

41. Andrew W. Singer, "The Perils of Doing the Right Thing," *Across the Board* (October 2000), quoting Edward Shultz; Yale law professor Peter Schuck was quoted as "doubt[ing] [that Smith & Wesson] would have lost a court case": Barry Meier, "Bringing Lawsuits to Do What Congress Won't," *New York Times*, March 26, 2000. See also Jeff Donn, "Maker of the .44 Magnum Turns to Golf Putters and Teddy Bears," AP/Minneapolis *Star Tribune*, April 14, 2001.

42. Richard Simon and Eric Lichtblau, "Police Feel Pressure to Choose the 'Code,' " *Los Angeles Times*, April 9, 2000, quoting Capt. Garry Leonard of L.A. County Sheriff's Department; Vanessa O'Connell, "Plan to Pressure Gun Makers Hits Some Snags," *Wall Street Journal*, April 11, 2000. See David Kopel, "Smith & Wesson's Faustian Bargain," *National Review Online* (March 20, 2000), and "Smart Cops Saying 'No,' " April 19, 2000.

43. Stuart Taylor Jr., "Guns and Tobacco: Government by Litigation," *National Journal* (March 25, 2000), quoting Andrew Cuomo.

44. Mark Sherman, "Governments' Pledge Pressures Gun Makers," *Atlanta Journal-Constitution*, March 23, 2000, quoting Eliot Spitzer. According to a *Wall Street Journal* news report, one faction of private lawyers "argued against an early settlement" in strategy sessions, one reason being that "[p]rolonged litigation and larger legal costs . . . would increase the financial pressure on the industry to accept new curbs": Paul M. Barrett, "Gun Makers, Municipal Representatives Ready to Meet on Settlement of Lawsuits," *Wall Street Journal*, September 24, 1999.

45. Paul M. Barrett, "Smith & Wesson Rivals Face Antitrust Probe," *Wall Street Journal*, March 30, 2000; see also Peter Slevin and Sharon Walsh, "Conn. Subpoenas Firms in Gun Antitrust Probe," *Washington Post*, March 31, 2000.

46. "Washington in Brief: Some Cities Holding Back on Gun Deal," *Washington Post*, March 25, 2000, quoting Josh Horwitz of the Educational Fund to End Handgun Violence.

Chapter 4: Stacked: The Breast-Implant Affair

1. "Breast Implants on Trial," *Frontline*, February 27, 1996.

2. Kathy McNamara-Meis, " 'It Seemed We Had It All Wrong," *Forbes Media Critic*, Winter See also Trevor Armbrister, "Trial Lawyers on Trial," *Reader's Digest* (January 2000), criticizing Chung show.

3. See generally Huber, *Galileo's Revenge* (New York: Basic Books, 1991).

4. William D. Morain, "Silicone Implants: Health Hazard, or Gold Mine for Trial Lawyers?" *San Diego Union-Tribune*, February 2, 1992; Fawn Vrazo, "Lawyers Seek Bonanza from Breast Implant Suits," Journal of Commerce, March 23, 1992; Joseph Nocera, "Fatal Litigation," *Fortune* (October 16, 1995); William D. Morain, "Silicone Implants: Health Hazard, or Gold Mine for Trial Lawyers?" *San Diego Union-Tribune*, February 2, 1992.

5. Daniel Murphy, "Fast Track for Trial Lawyers?" *Investors' Business Daily*, (May; letters to editor, *Wall Street Journal*, September 12, 1997, from Sharon Smith Holston, Dep. Comm. for External Affairs, FDA, and October 1, 1997, from Richard A. Samp, Chief Counsel, Washington Legal Foundation. For leak on bone screws see Max Boot, "A Screwy Way to Treat Companies," *Wall Street Journal*, July 16, 1996. On the bone-screw litigation generally, an excellent account is L. Stuart Ditzen, "The Bone Screw Files," *Inquirer* magazine *(Philadelphia Inquirer)*, August 27, 2000. We were in touch: Peter Boyer, "Big Guns," *The New Yorker* (May 17, 1999), quoting John Coale.

6. Peter Brimelow and Leslie Spencer, "Just call me 'Doc,' " *Forbes* (November 22, 1993).

7. Federal News Service, January 2, 1992 (available on Nexis).

8. See Rena Selya, "Error Pressure," Knight Ridder/*Arizona Republic*, December 7, 1995. For a sample of *Wall Street Journal* news coverage favorable to plaintiffs' contentions, see, e.g., Thomas M. Burton, "Breast-Implant Study Is Fresh Fuel for Debate," February 4, 1993 (balance of experts cited tilts toward view that implants cause serious disease).

9. See Nocera, "Fatal Litigation" (estimating that O'Quinn grossed overall around $100 million in implant settlements); Mimi Swartz, "Silicone City," *Texas Monthly*; Max Boot, "King John's Guide to Breast-Implant Riches," *Wall Street Journal*, June 19, 1996; Max Boot, *Out of Order* (New York: Basic Books, 1998), chap. 7.

10. See Gary Taubes, "Silicone in the System," *Discover*, (December 1995).

11. Marcia Angell, *Science on Trial: The Clash of Medical Evidence and the Law in the Breast Implant Case* (New York: Norton, 1996), pp. 147–51. The author reviewed *Science on Trial* in *National Review*, November 11, 1996.

12. David Perlman; "Breast Implant Studies Find No Health Risks," *San Francisco Chronicle*, October 25, 1995, quoting Sidney Wolfe.

13. Gina Kolata, "Legal System and Science Come to Differing Conclusions on Silicone," *New York Times*, May 16, 1995, and "A Case of Justice, or a Total Travesty?" *New York Times*, June 13, 1995. See also *Los Angeles Times* editorial "Why Judges Must Fight Bad Science," June 28, 1995.

14. "Junk Science Redux" (editorial), *Wall Street Journal*, November 22, 1996 (Fenton Communications signed "to a multimillion-dollar contract" to represent plaintiffs).

15. Gina Kolata, "Legal System and Science Come to Differing Conclusions on Silicone," *New York Times*, May 16, 1995; Angell, *Science on Trial*, pp. 145–46.

16. Ibid., p. 81.

17. Nader, http://www.nader.org/releases/63099.html, *Multinational Monitor* (May 1995).

18. Charles Ornstein, "Norplant Company Agrees to Settle Suits," *Dallas Morning News*, August 26, 1999; Leslie Laurence, "Your Perfect Birth Control . . . Blocked?", *Glamour* (September 1999); Marc Arkin, "Products Liability and the Threat to Contraception," *Manhattan Institute Civil Justice Memo* 36 (February 1999).

19. Barnaby J. Feder, "Implant Industry Is Facing Cutback by Top Suppliers," *New York Times*, April 25, 1994; Daniel J. Murphy, "FDA Agenda: A Cosmetic Killing?" *Investor's Business Daily*, November 22, 1994. Dow Corning withdrawal as biomaterials supplier, quote from "Liability Concerns Threaten Medical Implant Research," *Science* (November 4, 1994). On implants generally, see Michael Fumento, "A Confederacy of Boobs," *Reason* (October 1995).

20. Atul Gawande, "A Queasy Feeling: Why Can't We Cure Nausea?" *The New Yorker* (July 5, 1999) and Huber, *Galileo's Revenge*, chap. 7.

21. Gina Kolata, "Panel Confirms No Major Illness Tied to Breast Implants," *New York Times*, June 21, 1999, quoting David Bernstein. In March 2000, serving to bounce the rubble, the *New England Journal of Medicine* published a combined analysis by University of North Carolina researchers of twenty earlier studies which concluded that "the elimination of implants would not be likely to reduce the incidence of connective-tissue diseases."

Chapter 5: Trial Lawyer TV

1. Robert J. Samuelson, "Who Elected the Lawyers?" *Washington Post*, July 2, 1997.

2. Peter Boyer, "Big Guns," *The New Yorker* (May 17, 1999).

3. Tad Friend, "Dead Air," *The New Yorker* (May 7, 2001).

4. Christopher A. Sawyer, "Burned by the Media," *Automotive Industries* (September 1993).

5. Bill Zwecker, "The 'Inside' Story," *Chicago Sun-Times*, November 24, 1996.

6. Howard Rosenberg, "A Tabloid Pattern of Behavior at NBC," *Los Angeles Times*, February 15, 1993.

7. William A. Henry III, "Where NBC Went Wrong," *Time* (February 22, 1993).

8. "Waiting to Explode": the show aired November 17, 1992.

9. Elizabeth Kolbert, "NBC Settles Truck Crash Lawsuit, Saying Test Was 'Inappropriate,' " *New York Times*, February 10, 1993.

10. Walter Olson, "It Didn't Start With *Dateline NBC*," *National Review* (June 21, 1993).

11. Steven Brill, "Ending the Double Standard," *The American Lawyer* (April 1993).

12. Jayne O'Donnell, "To Serve or to Litigate?" *AutoWeek* (November 9, 1992). On Ditlow's involvements with trial lawyers, see also Max Boot, "Guardian of the Lawyers' Honey Pot," *Wall Street Journal*, September 19, 1996.

13. Open letter to Ditlow from NHTSA staff (1989): copy in possession of author.

14. Jane Hall, "NBC Criticized for Rigging Crash," *Los Angeles Times*, February 11, 1993.

15. See Olson, "It Didn't Start with *Dateline NBC*."

16. See Huber, *Galileo's Revenge*, chap. 4; Christopher A. Sawyer, "Burned by the Media," *Automotive Industries* (September 1993).

17. See Olson, "It Didn't Start with *Dateline NBC*."

18. Ibid.

19. Ibid. It is worth noting that real-world statistics on cars' cumulative safety record in actual highway use make many of the safety scares of the past look dubious indeed, to the point that even the affair of the "exploding" Ford Pinto—universally hailed as the acme of product-liability success—has begun to look a lot like hype. In a summer 1991 *Rutgers Law Review* article the late UCLA law professor Gary Schwartz demolished "the myth of the Pinto case." Actual deaths in Pinto fires have come in at a known twenty-seven, not the expected thousand or more. More startling, Schwartz shows that widely received ideas about the fabled "smoking gun" memo are false. The actual memo did not pertain to Pintos, or even Ford products, but to American cars in general; it dealt with rollovers, not rear-end collisions; it did not contemplate the matter of tort liability at all, let alone accept it as cheaper than a design change; it assigned a value to human life because federal regulators, for whose eyes it was meant, themselves employed that concept in their deliberations; and the value it used was one that they, the regulators, had set forth in documents. In retrospect, Schwartz writes, the Pinto's safety record appears to have been very typical of its time and class. The dread Pinto gets rear-ended every day, but Pinto fires killed an average of 4.5 people a year in the car's heyday. Ford, like GM, lost a $100 million verdict, although not much of that survived appeal. See Gary T. Schwartz, "The Myth of the Ford Pinto Case," Rutgers Law Review 43 (1991), p. 1013.

20. Ibid.

21. *The Quill* (November 1994). Pauley's speech drew much of its content from (and gave suitable credit to) "It Didn't Start with *Dateline NBC*."

22. From the Safety Forum's Web site.

23. D. M. Osborne, *Brill's* (October 1998). The *20/20* show on Chrysler minivan latches was "Open to Danger" (October 27, 1995).

24. Harry Stoffer, "NHTSA: No Sudden-Acceleration Probe," *Automotive News* (May 15, 2000). The report was issued April 6, 2000, under File DP00-004.

25. "Vehicles That Take Off on Their Own?" *NBC News/MSNBC* (February 10, 1999). See "Appeals Court Rules in Favor of Ford in Cruise Control Suit," AP/ *Auto.com* (June 21, 1999).

Chapter 6: Asbestos Memories

1. Paul Brodeur, *Outrageous Misconduct: The Asbestos Industry on Trial* (New York: Pantheon, 1985). Brodeur's book won the ATLA Special Literary–Public Service Award in 1985. For a critique, see Peter Huber, *New Republic* (February 3, 1986).

2. On the effective retroactivity of asbestos law, a leading liability scholar has written that "at the time that Manville and other corporations sold asbestos, right up to the 1960s, they were subject to no discernible risk of tort liability." See Richard A. Epstein, "Manville: The Bankruptcy of Product Liability Law," *Regulation* (September/October 1982).

3. Liberty and Victory Ships: Lester Brickman, "The Asbestos Litigation Crisis: Is There a Need for an Administrative Alternative?" *Cardozo Law Review* 13 (1992), p. 1819, 1884. The discussion of U.S. Navy responsibility in the text relies on Professor Brickman's account, and this chapter is more generally indebted to his writings, which also include "The Asbestos Claims Management Act of 1991: A Proposal to the United States Congress," *Cardozo Law Review* 13 (1992), p. 1981 and "On the Relevance of the Admissibility of Scientific Evidence: Tort System Outcomes Are Principally Determined by Lawyers' Rates of Return," *Cardozo Law Review* 15 (1994), p. 1755. On shipbuilding, see also *The Handbook of Texas Online: Shipbuilding* by Robert H. Peebles (University of Texas Web site).

4. Memo Comdr. C. S. Stephenson, U.S. Navy, to Admiral McIntire, March 11, 1941, quoted in Brickman, "Crisis."

5. In re Eastern and Southern Dists. Asbestos Litigation, 772 F. Supp. 1380 (EDNY and SDNY 1991) (Weinstein, J.). Cited in Brickman, "Crisis," at p. 1885. Navy took initiative to develop, turned down reformulation offer: Statement of Samuel J. Heyman, Chairman, Chief Executive Officer and President, GAF Corp., Prepared for the Subcommittee on Administrative Oversight and the Courts of the Senate Committee on the Judiciary, October 5, 1999, on S.758, the Fairness in Asbestos Compensation Act of 1999.

6. Karen Dillon, "Only $1.5 Million a Year," *The American Lawyer* (October 1989), quoting Ness Motley attorney Ann Kimmel Ritter.

7. Brickman, "Crisis," pp. 1821, 1845.

8. Monte Burke, "An Affair to Remember," *Forbes* (June 11, 2001). The Pennsylvania legislature proceeded to pass a statute limiting lawsuits against the company: see Shannon P. Duffy, "Pennsylvania Court Upholds Law Limiting Asbestos Liability," *The Legal Intelligencer* (June 13, 2002).

9. In re Hawaii Federal Asbestos Cases, 734 F. Supp. 1563 (D. Haw. 1990). Cited in Brickman, "Crisis," p. 1826. See also, e.g., Richard Doll and Julian Peto, "Asbestos: Effects on Health of Exposure to Asbestos" 2 (1985): "The benign conditions of the pleura that are produced by asbestos are seldom of any lasting importance . . ." quoted in Prepared Statement Concerning H.R. 1283, The Fairness in Asbestos Compensation Act, by Professor Christopher Edley, Jr., Harvard Law School, at House Judiciary Committee hearing July 1, 1999 ("Edley Statement").

10. Karen Dillon, "Only $1.5 Million a Year," *The American Lawyer* (October 1989), quoting Ness Motley attorney Terry Richardson. "Inactive docket programs," which defer consideration of the claims of the unimpaired while also preventing them from being time-barred, would be one way of addressing the legal needs of workers who fear that they will fall sick in future from past asbestos exposure: see Mark A. Behrens and Monica G. Parham, "Stewardship for the

Sick: Preserving Assets for Asbestos Victims Through Inactive Docket Programs," *Texas Tech Law Review* 33 (2001), p. 1.

11. Brickman, "Crisis," p. 1857. The summary of the outcome in the Beaumont, Texas, case (*Cimino*) follows that of Stuart Taylor Jr. in "Why Congress Should Fix the Asbestos Litigation Mess," *National Journal* (July 10, 1999). Ninety percent of one defendant's claims now paid to persons without serious ill effects: Paul M. Sherer, "Federal-Mogul Gets New Credit Lines, Plans to Fight Against Asbestos Litigation," *Wall Street Journal*, January 4, 2001, quoting Federal-Mogul executive. "Vast majority" of another defendant's claimants not ill: "Background Information on Asbestos," USG Corporation Web site. http://www.usg.com/special/asbestosbkgrnd.asp, visited July 19, 2002.

12. Brickman, "Crisis," pp. 1830–31. According to Suzanne L. Oliver and Leslie Spencer, "Who Will the Monster Devour Next?" *Forbes* (February 18, 1991), a 1989 study published in the *American Journal of Industrial Medicine* found that refinery workers have a lower incidence of cancer than the general population.

13. See, e.g., Oliver and Spencer, "Who Will the Monster Devour Next?" (finding by 1991 "16,000 suits against A. P. Green Industries for refractory products that usually contained just 1% asbestos. . . . Foster Wheeler, too, is a defendant in 14,000 asbestos-related suits claiming injury from cements and block insulation that contained just 3% asbestos").

14. Susan Warren, "Asbestos Suits target Makers of Wine, Cars, Soups, Soaps," *Wall Street Journal*, April 12, 2000, quoting James Early.

15. Christopher E. Grell Web site, visited Jan. 21, 2001.

16. Brickman, "Proposal," p. 1894, at fn. 5, quoting In re Eastern & Southern Districts Asbestos Litigation, 772 F. Supp. 1380, 1398 (EDNY & SDNY, 1991). Before Manville's bankruptcy its share of product use was estimated as high as 80 percent in Brooklyn Navy Yard cases, afterward falling below 20 percent.

17. Patrick Williams, Christine Biederman, Thomas Korosec, Julie Lyons, "Toxic Justice," *Dallas Observer* (August 12, 1998); Julie Lyons, "The Control Freak," *Dallas Observer* (August 12, 1998); Thomas Korosec, "Bench Press," *Dallas Observer* (March 9, 1998); Alison Frankel, "Traitor to His Class," Baron profile, *American Lawyer* (January 6, 2000), sidebar, "Hey, No Coaching." See generally Walter Olson, "Thanks For the Memories: How Lawyers Get the Testimony They Want," *Reason* (June 1998). In its exposé, the *Dallas Observer* interviewed former Baron & Budd employees who "say that the information and techniques contained in the memo are widely used, even taught to employees" and that the memo was not an aberration. "Paralegals say—and neither Baron nor Budd denies—that workers are selectively shown pictures of asbestos products they should identify." Former B&B paralegal Cheryl Kuntze says that in meetings with clients she gave "pretty strong encouragement" to recall products from "every manufacturer that we needed to get ID for," and that identification of products from bankruptcy manufacturers was sometimes discouraged. Kuntze says when she went to her supervisor and expressed disquiet about practices. " 'I was basically told to be quiet or leave. . . .' She says she then went to her immediate supervisor, who she recalls also told her to 'fill it in, make up stuff.' A former lawyer with the firm says the firm's lawsuit process was designed to exaggerate the fear of cancer in many clients who had little increased risk of cancer, because a scared client is an effective witness. She found this incredibly cruel. 'I would tell my clients after the deposition that they have a higher likelihood of being hit by a bus than being killed by asbestosis,' she recalls. They would hug

her and say thanks." Principals and supervisors at the law firm deny some of the charges in the *Observer* article, contend that others are accurate but consistent with adherence to ethical legal practice, and say they have no memory or knowledge of yet others. ("Toxic Justice," *Dallas Observer*, August 13, 1998).
18. Barry Meier, "Fund-Raiser May Be Achilles' Heel for Gore," *New York Times*, June 4, 2000.
19. James S. Kakalik et al., "Variation in Asbestos Litigation Compensation and Expenses," *Rand* (1984), cited in Edley statement. Prof. Edley adds that the "figure [has] been cited as authoritative in numerous court opinions."

Chapter 7: The Jackpot Belt
1. "The Sahara of the Bozart," in H. L. Mencken, in *Prejudices: Second Series* (New York: Knopf (1920)), reprinted in *A Mencken Chrestomathy* (New York: Knopf, 1978).
2. Sandra Barbier, "Family Awarded $1 Billion in Lawsuit," New Orleans *Times-Picayune*, May 23, 2001; Brett Martel, "Exxon Mobil to Appeal $1 Billion Fine," *Reuters/New York Times*, May 23, 2001. British firms: "Brits Discover North Carolina," *Wall Street Journal*, August 25, 1997. The Meineke verdict was later reversed and remanded by a federal appeals court.
3. Walter Olson, "A Small Canadian Firm Meets the American Tort Monster," *Wall Street Journal*, February 14, 1996; Michael Krauss, "NAFTA Meets the American Torts Crisis: The Loewen Case," *George Mason Law Review* 9 (2000), p. 69; D. Geoffrey Cowper, Q.C., "The American Experience: A Canadian Litigator Looks at the American System," in *Law & Markets: Is Canada Inheriting America's Litigious Legacy?* eds. John Robson and Owen Lippert, (Vancouver, B.C.: Fraser Institute, 1997); Renée Lettow Lerner, "International Pressure to Harmonize: The U.S. Civil Justice System in an Era of Global Trade," *Brigham Young University Law Review* 229 (2001); see also Jonathan Haar, "The Burial," *The New Yorker* (November 1, 1999).
4. Tim Burt and Robert Rice, "Weighted Against Outsiders," *Financial Times*, February 14, 1997 ("Some investment bankers claim these legal hazards have become a powerful deterrent to smaller companies contemplating U.S. expansion.") See also "The people v. America Inc.," *The Economist* (March 22, 2001).
5. David P. Hamilton and Robert A. Guth, "Toshiba Explains Accord as Other PC Firms Study Suits," *Wall Street Journal*, January 4, 2000.
6. Michael M. Bowden, "$581 Million for a Satellite Dish Scam," *Lawyers Weekly USA*, roundup of year's top verdicts, http://www.lawyersweekly.com/00top-ten4.cfm, visited July 17, 2002.
7. "Lender Hit with $71M Verdict," Jackson *Clarion-Ledger*, June 14, 2001.
8. Jerry Mitchell, "Out-of-State Cases, In-State Headaches," Jackson *Clarion-Ledger*, June 17, 2001.
9. *BMW of North America, Inc. v. Gore*, 517 US 559 (1996).
10. Dale Russakoff, "Legal War Conquers State's Politics," *Washington Post*, December 1, 1996.
11. "Bronx Juries: All Things to All People," AP/*Newsday* (December 18, 1999).
12. Mark Ballard, "Mississippi Becomes a Mecca for Tort Suits," *National Law Journal* (April 30, 2001). Jerry Mitchell, "Hitting the Jackpot in Mississippi Courtrooms: $1.2B Drug Lawsuit Opens in Jefferson," Jackson *Clarion-Ledger*, June 18, 2001.

13. Mark Ballard, "Biggest Little Court in Texas," *National Law Journal* (August 30, 1999).

14. Walter Olson, "Some of the Very Bad Reasons Our Legal System Is Well-Known," *Houston Post*, February 20, 1993.

15. Derthick, *Up in Smoke*, pp. 76–77.

16. Orey, *Assuming the Risk*, p. 282 (one-pager with no explanation on refusal to dismiss); p. 347 (eight lines on denying economic balance defense).

17. Prepared Statement of John H. Beisner, O'Melveny & Myers LLP, before the Subcommittee on Courts and Intellectual Property of the Committee on the Judiciary, U.S. House of Representatives, Hearing on H.R. 3789, "The Class Action Jurisdiction Act of 1998," June 18, 1998 (hereinafter "Beisner statement,") citing Susan Koniak.

18. "Jonathan Ringel, "Farmers' Suit Plants Questions on Class Actions," *The Recorder* (San Francisco) (June 18, 1999).

19. Mark Ballard, "Biggest Little Court in Texas," *National Law Journal*, (August, 30, 1999).

20. Joseph Nocera, "Fatal Litigation," *Fortune* (October 16, 1995).

21. Peter Brimelow and Leslie Spencer, "The Plaintiff Attorneys' Great Honey Rush," *Forbes* (October 16, 1989).

22. Daniel J. Murphy, "When State Judges Are Elected," *Investor's Business Daily*, November 7, 1994.

23. Roger Parloff, "Is This Any Way to Run a Court?", *American Lawyer* (May 1997). Details on Barbour County: Dale Russakoff, "Legal War Conquers State's Politics," *Washington Post*, December 1, 1996; see also Max Boot, *Out of Order* (New York: Basic Books, 1998), chap. 7. Alabama judge took donations though not on ballot: Leslie Spencer, "America's Third Political Party?" *Forbes* (October 24, 1994).

24. Richard Neely, *The Product Liability Mess* (New York: Free Press, 1989). See also Neely's opinion in *Blankenship v. General Motors*, 406 S.E.2d 781 (1991), announcing intention to follow proplaintiff product-liability rules since the benefits of doing so fall within the state and the costs mostly outside it. Study on judicial elections: Eric Helland (Claremont McKenna College) and Alex Tabarrok (Independent Institute): "Exporting Tort Awards," *Regulation* 23, no. 2; "The Effect of Electoral Institutions on Tort Awards," *Berkeley Olin Program in Law & Economics, Working Paper Series* 53 (April 2, 2002). For the story of how the state courts wriggled out of old rules which used to restrain them from projecting their power across state lines, see *The Litigation Explosion*, chaps. 4 and 9.

25. John Fund, "Invasion of the Party Snatchers," *MS/NBC* (May 2, 2000).

26. See Mark Ballard, "Mississippi Becomes a Mecca for Tort Suits," *National Law Journal* (April 30, 2001). Many of the forty-one lawyers in the firm of Alabama's Jere Beasley had recently taken the Mississippi bar exam.

27. Beisner statement, citing study by Dr. John B. Hendricks.

28. Hearings on S. 353, The Class Action Fairness Act of 1999, before the Subcommittee on Administrative Oversight and the Courts of the Senate Committee on the Judiciary, May 4, 1999, statement of Stephen G. Morrison, board chair of Lawyers for Civil Justice.

29. Beisner statement.

Chapter 8: The Art of the Runaway Jury

1. David Boldt, "We All End Up Paying for a Litigious Society," *Baltimore Sun*, November 24, 1999, reprinted from *Philadelphia Inquirer.*
2. Frederic Biddle, "GM Verdict Cut $3.8 Billion in Suit over Explosion," *Wall Street Journal*, August 27, 1999.
3. "Casino Justice," *Washington Post* (editorial), July 13, 1999.
4. Christa Zevitas, "$295 Million for Three Children Orphaned in Ford Bronco Crash," *Lawyers Weekly USA*, roundup of year's top verdicts, http://www.lawyersweekly.com/00topten6.cfm, visited July 19, 2002 *(Romo v. Ford Motor Co.).*
5. Tom Vanden Brook, "Jury Orders Philip Morris to pay $3B to Smoker," *USA Today* (June 20, 2001) *(Boeken v. Philip Morris Inc.)*
6. See roundups at *Overlawyered.com* (July 19–20 and 24–25, 2000). The New Zealand comparison is taken from Jacob Sullum, "The $145 Billion Message," *Creators' Syndicate* column (July 19, 2000).
7. *Daytona Beach News-Journal* trial coverage and Jim Oliphant, "Many Called, Few Chosen," Miami *Daily Business Review*, October 5, 1998.
8. Shepard's/McGraw Hill advertisement cited at Stephen J. Adler, *The Jury: Trial and Error in the American Courtroom* (New York: Times Books, 1994), pp. 53, 252. On jury selection generally, see Neil J. Kressel and Dorit F. Kressel, *Stack and Sway: The New Science of Jury Consulting* (Boulder Colo.: Westview, 2002).
9. Robert A. Wenke, *The Art of Selecting a Jury* (Springfield, Ill.: Charles C. Thomas, 1989).
10. Jeffrey Abramson, *We the Jury: The Jury System and the Ideal of Democracy* (New York: Basic Books, 1994), pp. 147, 282, citing Wenke, p. 78. The author reviewed the Adler and Abramson books in Walter Olson, "Juries on Trial," *Reason* (February 1995).
11. Race: *Batson v. Kentucky*, 476 US 79 (1986) and sex: *JEB v. Alabama* ex rel. TB, 511 US 127 (1994).
12. Abramson, *We the Jury*, p. 131.
13. Laura Mansnerus, "I Think, Therefore I Am Not a Juror," *New York Times*, April 5, 1997.
14. Mansnerus, "I Think, Therefore I Am Not a Juror."
15. Catherine Wilson, "Jury Selection Thorny in Fla. Tobacco Lawsuit," *USA Today* (July 7, 1998).
16. Adler, *The Jury*, p. 99.
17. Adler, *The Jury*, p. 105, quoting Donald E. Vinson, *Jury Trials: The Psychology of Winning Strategy* (Charlottesville, Va.: Michie, 1986), p. 138.
18. Adler, *The Jury*, pp. 104–255; see also Orey, *Assuming the Risk*, pp. 84–85.
19. Charles Maechling Jr., "The Crisis of American Criminal Justice," *(Cosmos Journal* 1996), quoting Judge Marvin Frankel.
20. "Famous Trials: O. J. Simpson," at University of Missouri, Kansas City law school Web site.
21. Bradley R. Johnson, "Closing Argument: Boom to the Skilled, Bust to the Overzealous," *Florida Bar Journal* (May 1995), p. 12, quoted in David Bernstein, "The Abuse of Opening Statements and Closing Arguments in Civil Litigation," *Manhattan Institute Civil Justice Memo* 38 (August 1999).
22. Christine Hanley, "Ford Alleges Jury Tainting, Asks Judge to Throw Out $295 Million Damages Award," AP, September 10, 1999.
23. Bernstein, "The Abuse of Opening Statements." According to Bernstein, PBS *Frontline* asked two of the jurors in *Laas v. Dow Corning Corp.*, a major plaintiff

breast-implant win, "how the jury reached its verdict. The transcript of the episode reveals that the jurors ignored the most significant piece of scientific evidence that existed at the time of the trial, and illicitly shifted the burden of proof to the defendants to disprove causation."

24. "The Litigation Lottery" (editorial), *Investors Business Daily*, August 26, 1999; "GM Appeal," *City News Service*, December 6, 2000.

25. Eric Freedman, "$259 Million Award Tossed in DCX Minivan Latch Case," *Automotive News* (December 24, 2001); David Hechler, "Defense Win of the Month: Reversing $250 Million in Punitives," *National Law Journal* (November 19, 2001). See also letter to the editor, *Wall Street Journal* December 19, 1997, from Chrysler's A. C. Liebler.

26. *Rodriguez v. Suzuki Motor Corp.*, 936 SW.2d 104 (Mo. 1996); "Second Jury Sees Same Suzuki Defect as Did First," *National Law Journal* (November 24, 1997).

27. Milo Geyelin, "Judge Won't Allow Tobacco Industry to Cite Settlements," *Wall Street Journal*, May 18, 2000; "Jury Can Hear About Tobacco Industry's Borrowing Power, Judge Rules," *FindLaw*, May 31, 2000; "Economist estimates tobacco industry worth $157 billion," AP/*FindLaw*, June 6, 2000; Gordon Fairclough, "Judge in Smoking-Illness Suit Tells Jury Not to View Settlements as Punishment," *Wall Street Journal*, June 14, 2000.

28. "Trying a Case to the Two Minute Mind; aka Trial by Sound Bite" by Craig McClellan, Esq., was worth one hour in continuing legal education credits. See *Overlawyered.com* (June 29, 2000). Vincent Bugliosi, *Outrage: The Five Reasons Why O. J. Simpson Got Away with Murder* (New York; Norton, 1996). See Walter Olson, "Taking Aim at the Trial of the Century" (review of Bugliosi, *Outrage*, and H. Richard Uviller, *Virtual Justice*, New Haven: Yale University Press, 1996), *Wall Street Journal*, July 24, 1996.

29. *The Jury*, pp. xii–xv.

30. AP dispatch, September 17, 1999, and Ford Motor Company motion to set aside punitive damages. In July 2002, an appeals panel reinstated the punitive verdict, accepting the plaintiffs' contention that Ford had not shown that the irregularities in juror conduct tainted the final outcome. Ford was expected to pursue further appeal.

31. Kenneth Jost, "The Jury System," *CQ Researcher*, November 10, 1995, quoting California jury consultant Lois Heaney: "The Simpson case is [such] an anomaly that we cannot generalize from it."

32. Mark Twain, *Roughing It* (Hartford Ct.: American Publishing Co., 1891) chap. 48.

33. Jerome Frank: *Courts on Trial* (Princeton, N.J.: Princeton University Press, 1949), chaps. 8 and 9.

34. Paul Butler, "Racially Based Jury Nullification: Black Power in the Criminal Justice System," *Yale Law Journal* 105 (1995), pp. 677–725. Jeffrey Rosen, "The Bloods and the Crits," *The New Republic* (December 9, 1996); Christopher Caldwell, "Johnnie Cochran's Secret," *Commentary* (March 1997).

35. Kenneth Jost, "The Jury System," *CQ Researcher* (November 10, 1995).

36. David Bernstein, "Legal Reform: Learning from the Commonwealth," *Manhattan Institute Civil Justice Memo* 25 (May 1996).

37. John Caher, "NYS Bar Favors More Voir Dire Leeway," *New York Law Journal* (April 12, 2000).

Chapter 9: The Lawsuit Lobby

1. Saundra Torry and John Schwartz, "Tobacco Agreement Needed Nudge from White House," *Washington Post*, June 23, 1997; Matt Labash, "Lawyers, Guns, and Money," *Weekly Standard* (February 1, 1999) Viveca Novak and Jay Branegan, "Are Hillary's Brothers Driving Off Course?", *Time* (November 1, 1999); Barry Meier, "Rodham and Group Seeking Legal Fees Uses Clinton Testimonial," *New York Times*, March 8, 2001.

2. Molly Rath, "The Last Tycoon," *Baltimore City Paper*, August 16, 2000; Daniel LeDuc and Michael E. Ruane, "Orioles Owner Masters Political Clout," *Washington Post*, March 28, 1999.

3. *Dallas Morning News*, March 28, 1996, quoting Joseph Lieberman. See Walter Olson, "Not All Liberals Love Lawsuits," *Opinion Journal* (August 14, 2000).

4. Michael Freedman, "Turning Lead into Gold," *Forbes* (May 14, 2001); Mark Hollis, "Nursing Homes, Lawyers Plan Fight in Capital," *Orlando Sentinel*, March 6, 2001, quoting Jim Wilkes.

5. Richard B. Schmitt, "Trial Lawyers Glide Past Critics with Aid of Potent Trade Group," *Wall Street Journal*, February 17, 1994, quoting Leonard Ring. Prominent California politician Willie Brown has referred to trial lawyers as "anchor tenants" of the Democratic Party: Tom Hayden, "No One Brings Clean Hands to This Affair; On Workers' Compensation, It's Wilson's Bullying Versus the Democrats' Obligation to the Party's 'Anchor Tenants,' " *Los Angeles Times*, October 7, 1992.

6. Dan Morain, "Lawyers' Campaign for Funds Draws Fire," *Los Angeles Times*, December 1, 1995. See Leslie Spencer, "America's Third Political Party?" *Forbes* (October 24, 1994).

7. "Regulation by Litigation."

8. Michael E. Keasler, "The Ethics of Electing Judges," *Long Term View* (Massachusetts School of Law), Summer 1997, p. 124.

9. John Council, "Trial Lawyers Get Political with PACs; Plaintiffs Counsel Hope Group Effort Influences Judicial Races," *Texas Lawyer* (May 15, 2000), quoting Chuck Noteboom.

10. See *Detroit News* editorials, November 1 and November 6, 2000.

11. "The Political Influence of Corporate America," atla.org Web site, posted October 3, 2000.

12. Don Van Natta Jr. with Richard A. Oppel Jr., "Memo Linking Political Donation and Veto Spurs Federal Inquiry," *New York Times*, September 14, 2000; Susan Schmidt, "1995 Documents Appear to Link Lawyer's Contribution to Veto," *Washington Post*, September 14, 2000.

13. Maria Shan, "For Trial Lawyers Gathered in Hub, the Suit's the Thing," *Boston Globe*, August 1, 1996.

14. *CNBC* "Hardball," October 10, 2000.

15. Frank J. Murray, "3 Republicans Let Senate Kill Curb on Lawyers," *Washington Times*, September 14, 1992.

16. Specter's son Shanin: Kline & Specter site, www.klinespecter.com.

17. Peter Brimelow and Leslie Spencer, "The Plaintiff Attorneys' Great Honey Rush," *Forbes* (October 16, 1989), quoting Frederic Levin, Herb Hafif, and Pat Maloney; Peter Brimelow and Leslie Spencer, "Ralph Nader, Inc.," *Forbes* (September 17, 1990). See also Jayne O'Donnell, "To Serve or to Litigate?" *Autoweek* (November 9, 1992); Levin "says he contributes to "all the consumer groups that Nader is involved in. Ralph Nader acts as a spokesperson for trial lawyers and

their groups," says Levin. "His groups are most effective at presenting evidence for use by the tort system." "Ralph Nader, Pro and Con," *Forbes* (October 29, 1990), includes RN's response; Leslie Spencer, "America's Third Political Party?" *Forbes* (October 24, 1994); Andrew Tobias, "Ralph Nader Is a Big Fat Idiot," *Worth* (October 1996); "Nader Praises Trial Lawyers, Defends His Opposition to Tort Reform Initiatives on March 26 Ballot," *Metropolitan News-Enterprise*, March 7, 1996, ("Michael Johnson, executive director of the Alliance to Revitalize California, the primary sponsor of the measures, said earlier this month that when he at one time worked for the Nader-founded group Public Citizen, virtually every dollar raised . . . came from trial lawyers.")

18. Barry Werth, *Damages: One Family's Legal Struggles in the World of Medicine* (New York: Simon & Schuster, 1998), p. 41. The Civil Justice Foundation underwrites seventy-five consumer groups: Richard B. Schmitt, "Trial Lawyers Glide Past Critics with Aid of Potent Trade Group," *Wall Street Journal*, February 17, 1994.

19. "Remarks by Prof. [Michael] Rustad Accepting Endowed Chair," luncheon held at Suffolk University Law School, December 8, 2000, Suffolk University Law School Web site (crediting Roscoe Pound Foundation fellowship with "the beginning of my life as a torts scholar" writing "in defense of tort law"). For an example of reliance on Rustad's work, see Ralph Nader and Wesley Smith, *No Contest: Corporate Lawyers and the Perversion of Justice in America* (New York: Random House, 1996), pp. 280–81. See also Andrew Blum, "Debate Still Rages on Torts," *National Law Journal* (November 16, 1992), reporting that an ATLA "Academic Liaison Committee" convened with "about 20 academics from across the country." Among law schools with chairs endowed by practicing trial lawyers are DePaul University College of Law (Robert A. Clifford "Chair of Tort Law and Social Policy").

20. Bruce Hight, "Justices Favor Business, Say GOP Rivals," *Austin American-Statesman*, March 6, 2000; Pete Slover, "State Judge Hopefuls Flock to GOP," *Dallas Morning News*, March 10, 2000; John Williams, "Republicans Want Distance from PAC," *Houston Chronicle*, March 7, 2002.

21. Steve Scott, "Republican Trial Lawyers Make Primary Splash," *Capitol Journal* (June 1, 1998) (trial lawyers, advised by GOP political consultant Wayne Johnson, expected to invest more than $200,000 in Republican California primaries); Tony Quinn, "Trial Lawyers Hook Up with Conservatives," *Sacramento Bee*, June 14, 1998.

22. See Peter Wallsten, "Lawsuit Limits a Campaign Issue," *St. Petersburg Times*, August 22, 1998; "Addie Greene Wins Fourth Term with 73.4% of Vote," *Palm Beach Post*, September 2, 1998 ("The lawyers, using a front group called the Coalition for Family Safety, spent $21,373 on mailings and telephone 'push polls' in the last two weeks to urge voters to oust [conservative two-term Republican Bill] Andrews," who won anyway); James Roland, "Bitner Reclaims Seat for Last Time," *Sarasota Herald-Tribune*, September 2, 1998 (state senator David Bitner survives similar attack), Jim Pinkerton, "Clueless on Campaign Reform," *Cincinnati Enquirer*, March 30, 2000. See also Marc Lacey, "Clinton Enters Confederate Flag Debate," *New York Times*, March 30, 2000.

23. Amy Stevens, "Lawyers and Clients: Corporate Clients, Some Lawyers Differ on Litigation Reform," *Wall Street Journal*, March 17, 1995.

24. Stuart Taylor Jr., "Closing Argument: Self-Interest vs. Tort Reform," *The Recorder* (San Francisco), Jan. 31, 1996.

25. Michael H. Gladstone, statement on behalf of DRI, House Commerce Committee hearing, May 20, 1998. See also, e.g., Richard L. Griffith, "The American Jury System on Trial," *For the Defense* (July 1998); "Plaintiff's and Defense Lawyers Join to Oppose 'Auto Choice' Bill," *Liability Week* (June 14, 1999).

26. Hon. Ralph K. Winter, "Achieving Meaningful Civil Justice Reform: Is the Defense Bar a Problem?" in The Federalist Society, Litigation Practice Group *Litigation* 1, no. 2 (Spring 1997).

27. Stanley W. Cloud and Nancy Traver Washington, *Time* (Jun. 8, 1992).

28. Scott Harrington and Walter Olson, "Canute's Revenge: Prop 103 and Its Aftermath," *Manhattan Institute Civil Justice Memo Series* 13 (February 1989).

29. G. Pascal Zachary and Jill Abramson, "Silicon Volley," *Wall Street Journal*, March 11, 1996; "Tort Ad Dirt," *Sacramento Bee*, March 1, 1996; Ed Mendel, "Tort-Reform Fight Is Backed with Personal Bad Blood," *San Diego Union-Tribune*, March 13, 1996; Scott Graham, "Libel Suit Against Trial Lawyers Will Go Forward," *The Recorder* (San Francisco) (May 22, 1997); Jennifer Oldham, "Attorneys' Group Apologizes to Seagate Exec," *Los Angeles Times*, July 24, 1997.

30. Dale Russakoff, "Legal War Conquers State's Politics," *Washington Post*, December 1, 1996.

31. The case received extensive coverage in the Alabama press between late 1998 and 2000, including John M. Sandlin, "Ivey Sues Windom, Indictment Reported in Mobile," *Daily Mountain Eagle* (Jasper, Alabama), August 17, 1999; AP/*Washington Post*, August 19, 1999; Garry Mitchell, "Ex-prostitute's Bombshell Ignites Political Dirty Tricks Trial," AP, June 16, 2000. Arianna Huffington, "Happy Ending No Savior in Political Horror Story," *Chicago Sun-Times*, September 1, 1999, quoting Steve Windom.

32. "Role Reversal: High Court Again Tries Hand at Lawmaking" (editorial), *Columbus Dispatch*, August 18, 1999. On trial lawyers' use of state courts to dispose of democratically enacted liability reform statutes, see Victor E. Schwartz and Leah Lorber, "Judicial Nullification of Civil Justice Reform Violates the Fundamental Federal Constitutional Principle of Separation of Powers: How to Restore the Right Balance," *Rutgers Law Review* 32 (Summer 2001), p. 4.

33. Leslie Wayne, "Trial Lawyers Pour Money into Democrats' Chests," *New York Times*, March 23, 2000.

34. September 7, 2001 PR Newswire release, Tobacco Fee Arbitration Panel, "Tobacco Fee Arbitration Panel Announces Michigan Decision."

Chapter 10: Litigators on Horseback

1. Robert B. Reich, "Smoking, Guns," *The American Prospect* (January 17, 2000); Robert Samuelson, "Who Elected the Lawyers?" *Washington Post*, July 2, 1997.

2. See, e.g., *Amchem Products, Inc. v. Windsor*, 117 S. Ct. 2231, 2252 (1997). (Ginsburg, J.: legislated compensation "would provide the most secure, fair, and efficient means of compensating victims of asbestos exposure"); *Ortiz v. Fibreboard Corp.*, 527 US 815, 821 (1999), Souter, J.: asbestos litigation an "elephantine mass" which "defies customary judicial administration and calls for national legislation" (see Stuart Taylor, Jr. "Why Congress Should Fix the Asbestos Litigation Mess," *National Journal*, July 10, 1999).

3. Paul Elias, "$2 Million Fee Reduction Stands in Securities Case," *The Recorder*, October 20, 1999 (9th Circuit, Occidental Petroleum, Weiss & Yourman); Matter of Rhone-Poulenc Rorer, Inc., 51 F.3d 1293 (7th Cir. 1995); *Daubert v. Merrell Dow Pharmaceuticals*, 509 US 579 (1993).

4. Prof. Lester Brickman has commented regarding asbestos litigation that "Most fee information in this area is more highly classified than even national security documents." Andrew Blum, "Billions for Asbestos Bar?" *National Law Journal* (January 16, 1995). See Walter Olson, "Taming the Litigators: Why Not More Disclosure?" *Manhattan Institute Civil Justice Memo Series* 24 (February 1996).

5. Derthick, *Up in Smoke*, p. 24.

6. See, among other similar results, August 30, 1999 *Washington Post* poll, results at *WashingtonPost.com* (public opposes gun manufacturer liability by 70 to 25 percent margin and by a margin of 59 to 38 percent opposes holding tobacco companies legally responsible for the ill health of smokers); *National Journal* (May 16, 1998), (*National Journal*/NBC poll on whether government was doing too much or too little to regulate tobacco); "Cigarette Makers Absolved: Six in 10 Reject Liability for Tobacco Companies," *ABCNews.com*, November 3, 1999 (ABCNEWS poll: by 60 to 34 percent margin public don't think tobacco companies should have to pay damages for smoking-related illnesses); Carol Rosenberg, *Miami Herald*, July 19, 2000 (Gallup: public disapproved of Florida's Engle verdict 59 to 37 percent margin and blamed smokers themselves, rather than tobacco companies, for smokers' health problems by an even wider 59 to 26 percent margin). See generally Derthick, *Up in Smoke*, pp. 131–35.

7. See Renée Lettow Lerner, "International Pressure to Harmonize: The U.S. Civil Justice System in an Era of Global Trade," *BYU Law Review* 229 (2001) at fn 2–4 and accompanying text.

FOR FURTHER READING

Further information on virtually all the controversies explored in this book can be found at the author's Web site Overlawyered.com. On the breast-implant litigation, an authoritative but readable source is Marcia Angell, *Science on Trial* (New York: Norton, 1996), while the classic journalistic treatment of the affair is Joseph Nocera, "Fatal Litigation," *Fortune* (October 16, 1995). Those seeking more detail on the state-tobacco litigation should seek out political scientist Martha A. Derthick's cogent *Up in Smoke: From Legislation to Litigation in Tobacco Politics* (Washington, D.C.: CQ Press, 2001). Jacob Sullum explores the antitobacco crusade more generally in *For Your Own Good* (New York: Free Press, 1998). The various writings of David Kopel and Eugene Volokh will be of use to anyone developing a critique of the gun litigation, while Michael I. Krauss has published a useful short monograph on the guns-tobacco theme titled "Fire and Smoke: Government Lawsuits and the Rule of Law," (Oakland, Calif.: Independent Institute 2000). The lay reader will find much of what is written on asbestos law forbiddingly technical, but the press has published a few ringing popular indictments such as Roger Parloff's and Jr.'s "The $200 Billion Miscarriage of Justice," *Fortune* (March 4, 2002) and Stuart Taylor Jr.'s "Why Congress Should Fix the Asbestos Litigation Mess," *National*

Journal (July 10, 1999). Finally, the mass tort boom is itself a sequel to the more general boom in litigation of recent decades that has followed America's dramatic liberalization of the right to sue, on which see the author's book *The Litigation Explosion* (New York: Truman Talley Books/E. P. Dutton, 1991).

ACKNOWLEDGMENTS

As with my earlier books, the Manhattan Institute provided patient and uninterfering support for which I am deeply grateful. The themes of many of the book's chapters were pursued in earlier form in a variety of magazine and newspaper articles over the past decade, and I am particularly indebted to *Reason* and its editors Virginia Postrel and Nick Gillespie, *The Public Interest, National Review*, and the *Wall Street Journal*. All errors are my responsibility, of course. My family was an inspiration.

INDEX